THE MESSERSCHMITT 210/410 STORY

THE MESSERSCHMITT 210 / 410 STORY

JAN FORSGREN

FONTHILL

Fonthill Media Language Policy

Fonthill Media publishes in the international English language market. One language edition is published worldwide. As there are minor differences in spelling and presentation, especially with regard to American English and British English, a policy is necessary to define which form of English to use. The Fonthill Policy is to use the form of English native to the author. Jan Forsgren was born and educated in Umeå, Sweden; therefore, British English has been adopted in this publication.

Fonthill Media Limited
Fonthill Media LLC
www.fonthillmedia.com
office@fonthillmedia.com

First published in the United Kingdom and the United States of America 2019

British Library Cataloguing in Publication Data:
A catalogue record for this book is available from the British Library

ISBN 978-1-78155-731-0

Typeset in 10pt on 13pt Sabon
Printed and bound in England

Preface

Today, the twin-engined Messerschmitt Me 210 is best known as the worst combat aircraft designed by Messerschmitt. Conceived in 1938, the Luftwaffe had high expectations for the Me 210, which, it was envisaged, was to replace the Bf 110 as the Luftwaffe's prime *Zerstörer* (heavy fighter), and the Junkers Ju 87 Stuka as its prime dive bomber. As such, the Me 210 was destined to become one of the major combat aircraft of the Luftwaffe, serving in the *Zerstörer*, dive bomber, and reconnaissance roles. However, it was not to be. Instead, the Me 210 was plagued by difficult flight and handling problems. Service trials and initial operational experience over Britain, Italy, and North Africa were fraught with difficulties, being largely unsuccessful. With so much time, money, and effort invested in the Me 210, the decision to halt series production in early 1942 was exceptional. However, the Me 210 was also used in Hungary, with the type also being produced under license. The Hungarian Me 210s were mainly used as dive bombers and armed reconnaissance, while a few aircraft saw brief use as night fighters.

In the event, the Me 210 was modified into the basically similar but more capable Me 410. A much better aeroplane than its predecessor, the Me 410 was used from late 1943 until mid-1944 as a daytime heavy fighter against USAAF bombers. A wide range of weaponry was fitted to the Me 410s, including 50-mm cannons and unguided rockets, which, in the end, proved too heavy, reducing performance to unacceptable levels. As a result, the Me 410s proved easy targets for the USAAF escort fighters. During the Luftwaffe's Intruder raids against Britain in 1943–44, as well as Operation Steinbock in 1944, Me 410 units played a large role. Additionally, the Me 410 was used quite successfully as a photo reconnaissance aircraft. Production ended in September 1944.

Both the Me 210 and Me 410 were used on almost every front, with the Eastern Front being a notable exception. Indeed, the Me 210 and Me 410 rank among the very few Luftwaffe aircraft that saw little or no use on the Eastern Front. However, the Hungarian Me 210s were highly active against Soviet forces in 1944–45.

By the end of the war, few Me 210s and Me 410s remained operational. A few Me 410s subsequently underwent cursory inspection and evaluation by Britain, the USA, and the USSR. During the war, the Me 210 and Me 410 had been overshadowed by the Bf 110, which the Me 210 had been intended to replace. When this did not happen, Bf 110 production had to be reinstated, continuing until early 1945.

Although several books and articles have been written about the Me 210 and Me 410, quantatively, these still rank far below the literature available on the Messerschmitt Bf 109 and Focke-Wulf Fw 190. This book is an attempt to cover the design, continued development, and operational use of the Messerschmitt Me 210 and Me 410 in Germany and Hungary.

Acknowledgements

As with all book projects, several people have provided assistance with information and photographs on the Messerschmitt Me 210 and Me 410. Among those people are Gregory Alegi; Csaba Becze Stenge, PhD, for his very valuable input on the Hungarian use of the Me 210; Carl-Fredrik Geust, for information on the Soviet evaluation of the Me 410; Bengt Hermansson (Forced Landing Collection); Ulrich Hild for patiently answering a multitude of questions on German and central European geography; Karsten Lindblad (RDAF Historical Collection); Wolfgang Mühlbauer (DEHLA Archives), for the supply of many photos; Nils Åke Nilsson; Ulf Nyström, for assistance in translating Japanese-language sources; Neil Page of the Falke Eins blog for kindly providing his translation of Dr Gerhard Kaschuba's article (originally published in the German aviation magazine *Flugzeug Classic*) on his uncle, *Leutnant* Paul Kaschuba, and his Luftwaffe career; my good friend, Miro Patocka, for providing valuable contacts and information; Janne Salonen; Hans-Heiri Stapfer; Brett Stolle (NMUSAF); and Hannu Valtonen.

Last but not least, I wish to thank my editor at Fonthill, Jay Slater, for having faith in my writing abilities.

Apologies to anyone I have forgotten.

Contents

Glossary

AGO:	*Aktien Gesellschaft Otto Flugzeugwerke* GmbH
Aufklärer:	Reconnaissance aircraft
BFW:	Bayerische *Flugzeugwerke*
Dipl. Ing.:	*Diplom Ingeneur* (Master of Science)
DVS:	*Deutsche Versuchsanstalt für Luftfahrt* (German Aviation Experimental Establishment)
Dunai Repülögépgyár:	Danube Aircraft Factory, DAF
E-Stelle:	*Erprobungsstelle*—Test establishment for aircraft and equipment
Experten:	Luftwaffe terminology for an ace (a pilot with more than five victories)
FA:	*Fernsteueranlage* (Remote Control System)
FDL 131:	*Fernbetätige Drehlafette* 131 (Remote Control Moving Mount)
Fernaufklärungsgruppe:	Long-range reconnaissance group
FTR:	Failed to return
Gruppe:	Wing
Gruppenkommendeur:	Wing commander
MiA:	Missing in action
MKHL:	*Magyar Királyi Honvéd Legierö* (Royal Hungarian Air Force)
NII VVS:	Nauchno-ispytatel'skij institute Voyenno-vozdushnykh Sily (Research Institute of the Air Force)
RAE:	Royal Aircraft Establishment
RAF:	Royal Air Force
RLM:	*Reichsluftfahrtministerium* (German Air Ministry)
SC:	*Sprengbombe Cylindrisch* (Cylindrical high-explosive bomb. SC 50 indicates a 50-kg bomb).
Schnellbomber:	Fast bomber
S/d:	Shot down
SKG 210:	*Schnellkampfgeschwader* 210 (Fast Bomb Wing 210)

Staffel:	Squadron
Staffelkapitän:	Squadron leader
Stkz Stammkennzeichen:	Factory-applied code
USAAF:	United States Army Air Force
W Nr:	*Werk Nummer*—Construction number
W/o:	Written off
Zerstörer:	Heavy fighter
ZG (*Zerstörergeschwader*):	Heavy fighter wing

Comparative Luftwaffe, RAF, and USAAF Ranks

Luftwaffe	Abbreviation	RAF	Abbreviation	USAAF	Abbreviation
Generalfeldmarschall	Gen. FM	Marshal of the RAF	MRAF	General (Five Star)	Gen. (Five Star)
Generaloberst	Gen. Ob	Air Chief Marshal	ACM	General (Four Star)	Gen. (Four Star)
General der Flieger	GdF	Air Marshal	AM	Lieutenant-General	Lt-Gen.
Generalleutnant	Gen. Lt	Air Vice-Marshal	AVM	Major-General	Maj.-Gen.
Generalmajor	Gen. Maj.	Air Commodore	Air Cdre	Brigadier-General	Brig.-Gen.
Oberst	Ob	Group Captain	Grp Capt.	Colonel	Col.
Oberstleutnant	Oblt	Wing Commander	Wg Cdr	Lieutenant-Colonel	Lt-Col.
Major	Maj	Squadron Leader	Sqn Ldr	Major	Maj.
Hauptmann	Hptm	Flight Lieutenant	Flt Lt	Captain	Capt.
Oberleutnant	Oblt	Flying Officer	Fg Off.	First Lieutenant	1st Lt
Leutnant	Lt	Pilot Officer	Plt Off.	Second Lieutenant	2nd Lt
Unteroffizier	Uffz	Non-Commissioned Officer	NCO	Corporal	Cpl
Fahnenjunker	Fhj	-	-	-	-
Oberfeldwebel	Obfw	Flight Sergeant	FS	Master Sergeant	MSgt
Feldwebel	Fw	Corporal	Cpl	Technical Sergeant	TSgt
Obergefreiter	Obgfr	Leading Aircraftsman	LAC	-	-
Gefreiter	Gfr	Aircraftsman 1st Class	AC 1	Private First Class	P1C
Flieger	Fl	Aircraftsman 2nd Class	AC 2	Private Second Class	P2C

Notes on Luftwaffe Me 210 and Me 410 Unit Identification Markings and Insignia

The Luftwaffe unit structure differed from that of the RAF and USAAF. A *Geschwader* (comparable to a RAF wing) usually consisted of three or four *Gruppen*. Each *Gruppe* (comparable to a USAAF fighter or bomber group) counted three *Staffeln* (comparable to a RAF squadron). Each *Geschwader* and *Gruppe* also had a *Stab* (Staff) unit, usually consisting of three aircraft. The various *Gruppen* and *Staffeln* of a *Geschwader* were able to operate independently of each other on different geographical areas, such as the Western Front and North Africa. Only one *Geschwader*, ZG 26, was completely equipped with Me 410s, although many other *Zerstörer*, bomber, and reconnaissance *Gruppen* operated Me 210s and Me 410s. Brief unit histories appear at the end of the book.

For identification purposes, the *Zerstörer*, bomber, and reconnaissance units employed a four-letter numeric system. This differed from the two-letter (or, in some instances, letter/numeric code) system, with a third letter identifying the individual aircraft, employed by the RAF and the USAAF. For example, the first part of the letter/numeric code, such as F6, indicating *Aufklärungsgruppe* 122 (usually shortened to (F)/122), appeared on both sides of the fuselage to the left of the national insignia. On the right-hand side of the national insignia, the third letter indicated the individual aircraft within the unit, and the fourth the *Staffel*. The respective *Staffel* code letters were 'H' (1.Staffel) to 'Z' (15.Staffel). The letters 'I', 'J', 'O', and 'Q' were not used. Thus, F6+AH indicated an aircraft of 1.(F)/122.

The letters 'A', 'B', 'C', 'D', and 'E' identified the respective *Stab* (Staff) units, 'A' indicating the *Geschwader Stab*, 'B' the first *Gruppe Stab*, and so on.

To complicate matters, all Luftwaffe aircraft were assigned a four-letter *Stammkennzeichen* (factory code) at the respective factory. These codes were used as radio call signs during test and ferry flights. Upon delivery to an operational unit, such *Stammkennzeichen* were usually replaced with the relevant unit code letters/numerals, known as *Verbandkennzeichen* (literally meaning 'unit codes').

Luftwaffe Aircraft Damage Table

During the war, any Luftwaffe damaged or destroyed in combat was surveyed, following which the extent of damage by a rising percentage scale was established. This system also applied to aircraft damaged (or destroyed) in accidents. During the latter stages of the war, many aircraft suffering damage of up to 59 per cent (repairable) may have been declared a write-off anyway, instead being used for spares or as a decoy. By this time, the Luftwaffe did not lack aircraft, but rather trained and experienced pilots and aircrew.

Damage by per cent	Remarks
0–9	Minor damage, which can be partly repaired by the unit's head mechanic
10–24	Minor damage, repairable at unit level
25–39	Major damage, requiring rebuild or repair at unit level
40–44	Damage to engine or aircraft systems (e.g. electrical) requiring replacement at unit level
45–59	Heavily damaged, but repairable by exchanging major components
60–80	Written off, with minor components reusable
81–99	Total loss, over own territory
100	Total loss, either over sea or enemy territory

Introduction

The Messerschmitt Me 210 and its successor, the Me 410, remain two of the most controversial combat aeroplanes of the Luftwaffe. From the issue of the initial requirement for a new *Zerstörer* (heavy fighter)—a two- or three-seat twin-engined aircraft capable of escorting bombers as well as fulfilling the roles of ground attack and aerial reconnaissance—the development of the Me 210 was both protracted and fraught with difficulty. Having begun life in 1937 as a projected replacement for the Bf 110, which at this time had yet to enter service with the Luftwaffe (the Bf 110 prototype had been flown for the first time on 12 May 1936), the new aircraft was intended as a truly multi-purpose combat aircraft.

Assigned the project number P.1060, the Bf 210 was to be capable of serving as a long-range heavy escort fighter, long-range aerial reconnaissance, and ground attack aircraft, as well as being capable of dive bombing.[1] For the latter job, the *Reichsluftfahrtministerium* (German Air Ministry, RLM) wanted the Me 210 to replace the Ju 87 Stuka dive bomber.

Two contenders to the Me 210 as the new Luftwaffe *Zerstörer* were the AGO Ao 225 and the Arado Ar 240 respectively. In the event, the former remained on the project stage, with only fourteen Ar 240s being completed, and only a singular few of these seeing brief service as high-speed reconnaissance aircraft.

In the event, the Me 210 turned out to be an exceptionally problematical aeroplane, plagued with a number of design flaws as well as poor handling and performance characteristics. Nevertheless, in spite of the large number of problems encountered during the flight testing and operational trials, the Me 210 went into large-scale production for the Luftwaffe. Indeed, the Me 210 has been seen as the worst combat aircraft designed and produced by Messerschmitt, being deemed to be far more dangerous to its crews than to the enemy. A large number of Me 210s were used as flying testbeds, with everything from dive brakes to ejection seats being tested. In the event, limited operational trials began in late 1941, with the first operations taking place in late summer of 1942.

Between August 1942 and May 1943, the Me 210 was used with less-than-resounding success over Britain, the Eastern Front, North Africa, and Italy. The initial Me 210 sorties over Britain in August and September 1942 resulted in several aircraft being brought down by RAF Hawker Typhoons. Even less success was recorded on the Eastern Front, from where the aircraft were quickly withdrawn. In fact, no record exists of Soviet pilots encountering Luftwaffe Me 210s or Me 410s.

Looking very purposeful, two Me 210As seen during a test flight. The aircraft on the left, VN+AT, later served with *Erprobungsstaffel* 210. (*Wolfgang Mühlbauer/DEHLA Archives*)

After arriving in Sicily in late 1942, the Me 210-equipped III./ZG 1 engaged in escorting Ju 52/3m transports delivering supplies to North Africa, as well as performing ground attack and bomber intercept sorties. Other Me 210s were used for long-range reconnaissance. Frequently being misidentified as Junkers Ju 88s, several Me 210s were lost to Allied fighters. By the time of the Allied invasion of Sicily and the Italian mainland in the summer of 1943, most Me 210s had been lost or withdrawn from use. Many late-production aircraft were subsequently rebuilt as Me 410s.

During the USAAF daylight bombing campaign against Germany in 1943–45, a few Me 210s were used to shadow to the large formations, reporting their altitude and course to the Luftwaffe fighter units. Few Me 210s remained in Luftwaffe service when the war ended on 8 May 1945.

The Me 210 also entered large-scale production in Hungary, serving with the *Magyar Királyi Honvéd Legierö* (Royal Hungarian Air Force, MKHL), in which service the aircraft was employed rather more successfully. The MKHL used its Me 210s mainly as fast bombers on the Eastern Front between September 1944 and March 1945. However, the MKHL Me 210s first saw action on 3 April 1944 as day fighters against USAAF bombers. Due to heavy losses, the Me 210 was withdrawn as a heavy fighter only weeks later. Apart from combat losses in the air, many MKHL Me 210s were destroyed or damaged on the ground in USAAF raids. Similar to the Luftwaffe, the MKHL conducted tests with different armaments, including a 40-mm cannon. A large percentage of the Hungarian-built aircraft were supplied to the Luftwaffe.

In Germany, the production of the Me 210 was halted on 9 March 1942. Continuous testing had shown that no simple 'quick-fix' solution existed to the various problems exhibited by the Me 210. Nevertheless, following a difficult process of redesign and modification of existing production jigs, the basic Me 210 airframe eventually reemerged as the externally very similar Me 410. Both the fuselage and wings were modified, with more powerful DB 603 engines being fitted.

Although some issues still remained, the Me 410 proved to be a better combat aircraft than its predecessor. Entering service in mid-1943, the Me 410 was mainly used in the *Zerstörer*, fast bomber and reconnaissance roles. In the *Zerstörer* role, the heavily armed Me 410 was pitted against USAAF heavy bombers. A wide array of armament was carried by the Me 410 *Zerstörers*, including heavy air-to-air rockets and the 5-cm BK 5 cannon. Unavoidably, the addition of such heavy armament resulted in reduced manoeuvrability and overall performance, particularly speed and rate of climb.

By the spring and summer of 1944, Allied fighters were roaming the skies of Germany. Against single-seat fighters such as the P-47 Thunderbolt and P-51 Mustang, the Me 410 stood little chance. By late summer 1944, most of the Me 410 *Zerstörer* units had either disbanded or converted to other aircraft.

As a *Schnellbomber* (fast bomber), the Me 410 was used on night intruder raids against Britain, as well as during the Luftwaffe night bombing campaign between January and May 1944

Two decidedly unairworthy Me 410s seen in 1945. Unfortunately, the W Nr on the aircraft on the right is difficult to decipher. The last three digits could possibly be 988 or 989, which does not fit with any known W Nr batch. (*Author's collection*)

known as Operation Steinbock. However, by May 1944, these operational activities had come to an end. In the event, the Me 410 proved more successful as a reconnaissance aircraft, where its high speed and high-altitude performance was essential in avoiding interception.

Attempts were also made to convert the basic Me 410 for maritime strike operations (torpedo-carrying trials were not successful), although some aircraft were fitted with FuG 200 radars. Plans to convert the Me 410 as a night fighter was not proceeded with.

By September 1944, Me 410 production came to an end. Nearly 1,200 had been completed, with many others being converted from Me 210s. By war's end, few Me 410s remained operational.

Today, only two Me 410s survive: one in Britain and one in the USA.

1
The Birth of the Multi-Role Combat Aircraft

The concept of and operational use of the multi-role combat aircraft goes back to the Great War. The idea of the multi-purpose aircraft is to have a single type of aircraft performing different types of jobs continued post-war. Apart from cost savings, the air forces would be able to deploy fewer types of operational aircraft, reducing cost, training, maintenance, and other issues. However, through the decades of aerial warfare, it can be said that designing a true multi-purpose aircraft will (almost) always result in an aircraft that will be able to adequately handle one or possibly two jobs, but rarely any more. The old adage 'Jack of all trades and master of none' can be used to sum up this difficult equation. Two exceptions to this rule from the Second World War era were the DH.98 Mosquito and Junkers Ju 88, both of which operated with great success in the light bomber, aerial reconnaissance, and night fighter roles.

Changing operational requirements through overturning the original specification prior to the first flight, thus more often than not resulting in the redesign of the aircraft, is a common factor. Having to redesign the aircraft (for example, due to poor flight and handling characteristics or lower than expected performance figures) usually results in a long delay in the original delivery schedule. A very important factor from the operator's perspective is the ability to use the aircraft in its intended roles. However, delays brought on through protracted flight testing may result in an aeroplane that has become obsolete before entering service, having been overtaken by requirements, events, or superior technology.

Although still valid today, perhaps one of the best-known historical examples of the above concerns the Messerschmitt Me 210/410. Indeed, the German aviation industry had more than its fair share of costly failures during the Second World War, with the Heinkel He 177 heavy bomber securing second place to the Me 210/410 fiasco. However, the Me 210/410 can be said to be the prime example when discussing unsuccessful combat aircraft of the Second World War Luftwaffe.

However, it must be said that neither American nor British aircraft manufacturers were strangers to failure during the Second World War. Of the American-designed aircraft that did not live up to high expectations, despite the input of massive amount of industrial resources, time, and money, mention must be made of the Curtiss C-76 transport and the General Motors P-75 single-seat fighter.

The British aviation industry managed to design aircraft such as the twin-engined bomber/transport Armstrong Whitworth Albemarle and the seriously underpowered Blackburn Botha, both of which proved to be virtually useless as frontline combat aircraft.

The Early Years

Although aircraft were first used in a war in 1911, it was not until the latter stages of the Great War that the military aircraft really came of age. Single-seat fighters, light bombers, and reconnaissance aircraft were operated in large numbers by the warring powers. Simultaneously with the development of higher-performance aircraft, tactics were being developed. In 1917, the Germans created a new category of combat aircraft. Known as *Kampfflugzeug* (literally, battle aircraft), these high performance aircraft were developed in response to a requirement for the so-called *Schutzstaffeln* (protection squadrons), intended for the bomber escort and reconnaissance roles. These aircraft combined heavy armament with sufficient endurance to fly long-range offensive sorties over enemy territory, thus becoming strategic fighters, as opposed to the single-seat fighter, which had limited range and poor endurance.

Two of the best-known battle aircraft were the Halberstadt CL II and Hannover CL III respectively. Both the Halberstadt and Hannover designs were small, compact twin-seaters, being more than able to hold their own against British and French single-seat fighters. By late 1917, the emphasis had changed to that of ground attack and close support during ground offensives. During the Battle of Cambrai in November 1917, Halberstadt CL IIs strafed British trenches from a very low level using machine guns and trays of anti-personnel grenades with considerable success.

Perhaps the closest British equivalent to the Halberstadt CL II and Hannover CL III was the two-seat (pilot and gunner/observer) Bristol F.2B Fighter. Following an inauspicious beginning in 1917, the Bristol F.2B Fighter went on to serve with great success in the fighter, reconnaissance and light bombing roles. Indeed, the Bristol Fighter (colloqually known as the 'Brisfit') proved so adaptable and versatile that it remained in RAF use until 1932.

Following the German defeat, development of the strategic fighter ended. Between 1919 and the early 1930s, aerial warfare tactics underwent few radical changes. The main strategy involved in securing victory in any future war was by destroying the enemy's military and industrial capacity, as well as breaking the morale of the civilian population, through aerial bombardment. Thus, the bloody business of trench warfare, which had characterised the Great War of 1914–1918, could be avoided. As a result, the bomber was seen as the most important combat aircraft. The single-seat fighter had changed little since the Great War, with biplane designs armed with rifle-calibre machine guns still serving with the majority of the world's air arms. Given the short range of such fighters, their main role was local defence.

The Strategic Fighter Comes of Age

The re-emergence of the strategic fighter began in 1934, when specifications for such aircraft were issued almost simultaneously, albeit largely independently, in France, Germany, and Poland. The concept of the long-range strategic fighter resulted in a new type of combat aircraft.

Aware of the commencement of Bf 110 design and development, the French Service Technique de l'aéronautique (STAé) initiated a requirement for a three-seat heavy fighter. This was to serve in the fighter direction (leading formations of single-seat fighters), daytime ground attack escort for army co-operation and reconnaissance aircraft, and as a two-seat night fighter. Altogether, seven different manufacturers put forward designs, with two (the Breguet 690 and Potez 63 respectively) securing production contracts. The latter was similar in layout to the Bf 110, having a twin tail and elongated cockpit canopy. In the event, heavy fighter, light bomber, army co-operation, and reconnaissance variants of the basic Potez entered service with the *Armée de l'Air* (French Air Force). In its various variants, the Potez 63 suffered greatly during 1939–40 due to low performance and poor tactics, as well as from its similar appearance to the Bf 110. Occasionally, Potez 63 crews found themselves being attacked by RAF and *Armée de l'Air* fighters. Following one such friendly-fire incident, special insignia regulations for the Potez 63s were issued. A broad white band was painted on both sides of the fuselage roundel, with the national insignia also being increased in size.

Far in excess of 1,000 Potez 63s were built, with one batch being completed in 1941 and delivered to the Luftwaffe as operational trainers.

In contrast, about 350 Breguet 690s were completed in three basic variants. Of mid-wing and twin-tail configuration, the Breguet 690 had a rugged, compact appearance, albeit suffering from unreliable engines and a fragile undercarriage. More than 100 were lost to all causes during the desperate fighting of May and June 1940.

The Italian Breda 88 was similar in configuration to the Breguet 690. Designed in response to a 1936 specification from the Italian Air Ministry, the Breda 88 was intended as a fast and heavily armed multi-role combat aircraft. Although one Breda 88 captured the world speed record over a 100-km closed circuit, it proved to be underpowered and too heavy. The addition of military equipment significantly reduced performance. A few Breda 88s were used briefly in North Africa, with very little success. Nearly 150 Breda 88s were built, with a number being relegated for use as ground targets for *Regia Aeronautica* (the Italian Royal Air Force) pilots.

In Poland, discussions between the Polish Air Force and the Department of Aeronautics for a twin-engined heavy fighter capable of performing a multitude of different missions, including bomber interception, dive bomber and ground attack duties resulted in the PZL.38 *Wilk* (Wolf). Similar in appearance to the PZL.37 *Los* (Elk) bomber, the PZL.38 *Wilk* was to have an armament consisting of two 20-mm cannons, four 7.7-mm machine guns, and a bomb load of 300 kg. Two PZL.38 *Wilk* prototypes were built, flying for the first time in 1938. However, emphasis had by then shifted to a developed variant, the PZL.48 *Lampart* (Leopard). Two PZL.48 *Lampart* prototypes were nearing completion when Germany invaded Poland in September 1939.

Notably, none of the aircraft mentioned above were superior or even equal in performance and armament to the Ar 240, Bf 110, and Me 210. It may, however, be of some interest to describe the first Luftwaffe *Zerstörer*: the Messerschmitt Bf 110.

2

The Messerschmitt Bf 110

After the Nazi rise to power in January 1933, military aircraft production in Germany rose sharply. However, the the existence of the reborn Luftwaffe was not proclaimed until 1 March 1935. On 9 June 1936, former Great War ace Ernst Udet was appointed as director of the *Technisches Amt* (Technical Bureau) of the RLM.[1] Udet's formal title was *Generalluftzeugmeister* (Chief of Air Armament), being placed in charge of the development of new combat aircraft. However, Udet seemed less suited to the endless bureaucratic mangling that characterised the RLM, than to actual flying. It was also a job for which he felt out of place. Nevertheless, Ernst Udet was to have profound influence over the future selection of Luftwaffe aircraft.

The specification for a *Zerstörer*-type of aircraft was presented in mid-1934. The specification called for such an aircraft to have two engines, a crew of three or four, the ability to operate up to altitudes of 9,000 metres, have a cruise speed of 330 kph at 6,000 metres, and a range of 2,000 km. The armament would consist of two 20-mm cannons and two rifle-calibre machine guns. The *Zerstörer* would also be able to operate from airfields 500 × 500 metres in size, having a landing speed of less than 100 kph.

It was common *Reichsluftfahrtministerium* practice to distribute the relevant specifications to three companies, thus creating a sense of competiveness in the race to secure lucrative orders. The three companies in question were the Bayerische *Flugzeugwerke* (BFW), Focke-Wulf, and Henschel. The designs of the two latter companies, the Fw 57 and Hs 124, did not win favour with the RLM. Instead, the Bf 110 was selected as the Luftwaffe's new *Zerstörer*. According to *Reichsmarschall* Hermann Göring, the primary role of the Bf 110 was to be bomber escort: 'The Bf 110 and you who fly it will be like Hannibal's cavalry protecting the elephants; the bombers are my elephants.'

Development of the Bf 110 continued rapidly, with the first production Bf 110s being delivered to the Luftwaffe in late 1938. However, this all took place in great secrecy. Incidentally, no Bf 110s were supplied to the Legion Condor, the German air contingent flying in support of the Nationalist General Franco during the Spanish Civil War.

This veil of secrecy changed in August 1938, when the French Chief of Air Staff, General Vuillemin, made an official visit to the Messerschmitt works at Augsburg-Haunstetten. Here, Vuillemin became deeply impressed by the performance of the Bf 110. While viewing 'a part'

The Messerschmitt Bf 110 V1 prototype. (*Wolfgang Mühlbauer/DEHLA Archives*)

of the production line, he noticed completed aircraft taking off at regular intervals. This was part of an elaborate hoax, with the Bf 110s taking off in full view, landing back out of sight, then taxiing back for another take-off. Despite the fact that only three Bf 110B-0s and four Bf 110B-1s had been completed at this time, the impression was that the factory was churning out dozens of Bf 110s every day. Vuillemin's visit resulted in a French attempt to obtain a Bf 110 for evaluation. This cloak-and-dagger operation was set in motion in May 1939, when a bribed German pilot stole a factory-fresh Bf 110C-1. However, due to poor weather, he crashed fatally near Villerssous-Chalamont.

After the war broke out on 1 September 1939, the Bf 110 units operated with great success over Poland, Denmark, Norway, the Low Countries, and France. During the Battle of Britain, however, the Bf 110 suffered badly against the more agile Hurricanes and Spitfires of the RAF. During the battle, single-seat Bf 109s had to escort the Bf 110s on sorties over Britain.

Nevertheless, the Bf 110 served throughout the war on all fronts, both as a long-range heavy fighter, reconnaissance and ground attack aircraft. The basic Bf 110 was also developed into a highly effective night fighter, scoring heavily against RAF heavy bombers. Although it had been planned to replace the Bf 110 with the Me 210 in 1941–42, this did not occur. Production of the Bf 110 was reinstated, continuing until early 1945, when more than 6,000 had been built. The Bf 110 outlived its intended successor, the Me 210, proving itself to be a far more versatile and adaptable combat aircraft.

A late-model Bf 110. (*Wolfgang Mühlbauer/DEHLA Archives*)

3
Messerschmitt Me 210 Genesis

Even though the twin-engined Bf 110 *Zerstörer* was still undergoing flight testing, not yet having entered Luftwaffe service, it was considered to suffer from a number of drawbacks, including insufficient speed and range. Additionally, the Bf 110 was seen as being unable to carry enough bombs and armament required for its role in a future war. As a result, a developed variant of the basic Bf 110 was briefly considered.

However, as future events were to prove, the Me 210 was a poor aircraft from the outset. Instead of developing a faster and more capable variant of the basic Bf 110, it was decided to start from scratch, and develop a completely new aircraft. However, the Bayerische *Flugzeugwerke* (BFW) was not the only manufacturer involved in the design of a new *Zerstörer* for the Luftwaffe. As was common RLM practice, the *Zerstörer* specification was distributed to three different manufacturers; BFW, AGO, and Arado respectively. The latter two companies would present the AGO Ao 225 and Arado Ar 240 designs, as described below.

At BFW's Augsburg factory, work on the Bf 210 began in earnest in mid-1938. A number of large-scale models underwent wind tunnel trials. Interestingly, two different types of tail section configurations were tested, single and twin fins, with the latter configuration eventually being selected. Dimensionally, the Bf 210 was to be similar to the earlier Bf 110. During the design phase, Messerschmitt apparently intervened, ordering the length of the fuselage to be reduced by 90 cm, also having the slats left out. The reasons for this were to save weight as well as cost. On the previous Bf 108 Taifun and Bf 109, wing-leading edge slats had been fitted, greatly contributing to the low-speed characteristics of these aircraft. As will be seen, these changes resulted in poor flight characteristics for the Me 210. The exact reason why these changes were made during the initial design work is unclear, but the main reason behind skipping the slats for the Me 210 is said to have been a cost-cutting measure dictacted by the RLM. It is, however, worthy of note that the company's chief designer, Robert Lusser, resigned in March 1939, apparently due to a conflict with Willy Messerschmitt over the Me 210 design features mentioned above.

The RLM *Zerstörer* specification called for a fast and heavily armed twin-engined heavy fighter, with a range of 2,000 km, closely following the 1934 specification. The heavy fighter would also have a secondary role as a dive bomber. On 7 November 1938, the Luftwaffe

A Me 210 seen during a test flight. (*NMUSAF*)

procurement programme called for around 3,000 heavy fighters to be in active service by 1 April 1942. The lion's share of these combat aircraft was to be Me 210s.

Before returning to the Me 210, it is perhaps of some interest to describe the two *Zerstörer* competitors, the AGO Ao 225 and the Arado Ar 240 respectively, in some detail.

4
The AGO Ao 225

Apart from the Arado and Messerschmitt designs, AGO *Flugzeugwerke* GmbH put forward the highly radical FP-30. Originally founded in 1911, AGO produced a number of two-seat reconnaissance aircraft during the Great War. Having to resort to building cars after the end of the war, AGO became an aircraft manufacturer again following the Nazi rise to power.

Having a wingspan of 21.05 m and length of 19.10 m, the FP-30 (later designated Ao 225) was to be powered by two coupled 1,100-hp DB 601 engines, located in the centre fuselage, driving two propellers (one in each wing). Heavy armament consisting of four MG 131s was to be fitted in the nose section, as well as an MG 151 in a dorsal gunner position similar to that of the Heinkel He 111. A wooden mock-up Ao 225 forward fuselage was completed for engine installation tests. One twenty-four-cylinder 2,400-hp DB 606 engine was also proposed as the power plant for the FP-30 (Ao 225). In the event, the remote drive propeller shafts proved a major stumbling block, so much in fact that AGO considered a more conventional approach by fitting the pair of engines in the wings instead. The Ao 225 was ultimately rejected by the RLM as being too technically advanced as well as difficult to build. Given the problematic development and operational history of the Me 210, these issues would most likely have multiplied had the Ao 225 been chosen for production. Nevertheless, the Ao 225 remains a very interesting 'what if' design of the late 1930s.[1]

The 225 type number was subsequently reassigned by the RLM (a very rare occurence) to the Focke-Achgelis Fa 225 autogyro (with a modified fuselage of a DFS 230 assault glider providing the basis of the Fa 225), of which a single prototype was built.

5
The Arado Ar 240

The Arado E 240 (eventually redesigned as the Ar 240) was another contender. The basic Ar 240 configuration included twin engines, twin fins, and the cantilever wing being fitted along the fuselage centre line. The two crew, pilot and gunner/observer, sat in tandem beneath an elongated canopy. Designed by Walter Blume, the Ar 240 was a highly sophisticated aircraft, including novelties such as a pressurised cockpit (reducing crew fatigue at high altitude) and the 'Arado travelling flap', with the latter, in connection with wing leading edge slats, providing excellent low speed and high lift performance. The small, compact size of the Ar 240 resulted in an unusually high wing loading of 330 kg/m^2. However, the landing speed was reduced by the travelling flaps and slats.

Similar to the Me 210, the Ar 240 would also be fitted with remote-control armament. In early November 1938, General Reidenbach of the *Reichsluftfahrtministerium* visited Arado. Discussing the new heavy fighter with Arado's technical director, Walter Blume, Reidenbach stated:

> This time we have got away with it (a clear reference to the Munich 'Peace in our time' agreement a few weeks previously), but Tommy will be after us next autumn. The 109 is a good fighter, and we are well equipped in that department. But the 110 is not what it should be. It is not fast enough, and the defensive armament is too weak, particularly downward. We need a new destroyer. You and Messerschmitt are to build one each. Messerschmitt is to take the conservative route. You can take more risks. But we must have the aircraft in twelve months time.[1]

Technically speaking, the Ar 240 was far more complicated than its Messerschmitt rival. It appeared as though Arado attempted to put 'all the eggs in one basket' with many of the highly advanced design features being largely untested and far ahead of those of other aircraft manufacturers. Apart from the pressurised cockpit, travelling flaps and FDL 131 remote control armament (similar to that of the Me 210), the Ar 240 also featured a technically advanced fuel system, as well as dive brakes. The wing design excluded the fitting of dive brakes. Instead, the dive brakes were fitted to the tail section of the fuselage, with the two sections opening horizontally. Incidentally, the dive brakes looked remarkably similar to the ones fitted to the Blackburn Buccaneer carrier strike aircraft and the Fokker F28 airliner of the late 1960s.

On 16 May 1939, an order for six Ar 240 prototypes was placed. Designed by a team headed by Hans Rebeski, the Ar 240 first flew on 25 June 1940 (some sources state that the first flight took place on 10 May 1940, but the former date appears to be correct). During taxiing trials, the pair of DB 601A engines, fitted with rotund front radiators, showed themselves prone to overheating. The FA-13 barbette also proved highly problematical, which meant that it was not fitted to the first two Ar 240 prototypes. In the event, the Ar 240 proved very difficult to fly, being unstable in the air. As a result, the third prototype was completely redesigned, taking to the air for the first time on 19 June 1941.

During the early years of the war, Allied knowledge on the Ar 240 was virtually non-existent. The 1942 edition of *Jane's All the World's Aircraft* simply states: 'The Ar 240 is a new twin-engined high-altitude reconnaissance monoplane, of which no reliable information is available for publication.'

Much effort was devoted to developing the Ar 240 into an efficient warplane. Initial operational experience with the Ar 240 in late 1941 and 1942 with the *Aufklärungsgruppe des Oberbefehlshabers der Luftwaffe* (Reconnaissance Group of the Supreme Commander of the Luftwaffe) saw a number of high-altitude reconnaissance sorties being flown over Britain and the Eastern Front. In this role, the Ar 240 carried four Rb 50/30 cameras, two each being fitted in the rear section of the engine nacelles. Reconnaissance flights were also made over Italy, with little recorded success.

Two pre-production Ar 240s—the Ar 240A-01 and A-02 respectively—flew a number of reconnaissance sorties across the Russian frontline. The Ar 240A-03 served with 3./(F)100 in southern Ukraine.[2]

In mid-1943, the Ar 240A-02 was transferred to Italy and 2.(F)/122. Only one sortie was flown, with the aircraft suffering irrepairable damage on landing at Frosione.

It was intended that AGO would build forty Ar 240B reconnaissance variants. Some sources state that thirty-six Ar 240C *Zerstörers* were also ordered at the same time.

The Ar 240 V6 seen while serving with 3.(F)/100 on the Eastern Front. (*Author's collection*)

AGO had, incidentally, constructed some of the Ar 240 prototypes. By December 1942, tooling up and construction of jigs were 80 per cent complete. In the event, AGO did not produce any additional Ar 240s as Erhard Milch ordered the cancellation of the entire Ar 240 programme.

A developed variant, the Arado Ar 440 (essentially an Ar 240C powered by two DB 603 G engines) emerged in 1942. Four Ar 440 prototypes were built, with flight testing at E-Stelle Rechlin showing considerable promise when compared to the Heinkel He 219, Junkers Ju 88S, and Messerschmitt Me 410, exhibiting none of the poor handling qualities that had plagued the earlier Ar 240.

However, the Ar 440 did not enter production. Nevertheless, during the autumn of 1944, reinstating the Ar 440 into production for the *Jägernotprogramm* (Emergency Fighter Programme) was considered. This did not happen, with the twin-engined push-pull Dornier Do 335 being selected instead. Remarkably, studies for a turbine-powered variant of the basic Ar 240 airframe, designated as the Ar 240 TL (TL being short for *Turbinen-Luftstrahltriebwerk*, turbojet engine), were conducted in 1942.

At least one Ar 240 survived the war. Following up rumours that an intact Ar 240 had been located somewhere in the Netherlands, the British test pilot Eric 'Winkle' Brown searched in vain until being told that such an aeroplane was indeed to be found at hangared at Merville in northern France. Arriving at Merville, Brown immediately set about preparing the Ar 240 for a test flight. Unfortunately, no information about which unit the Ar 240 had belonged to was available, but it seems likely that it had been operated for reconnaissance duties as all armament had been removed. Although all identification marks, including the Luftwaffe insignia and *Werk Nummer*, had been painted over, the aircraft was complete and undamaged.

During the test flight, Brown found:

> Longitudinal stability was poor, lateral stability neutral, and the directional stability positive. The rate of climb fell off very little as I climbed to 20,000 ft, where I levelled out and settled into the cruise at what I calculated was a true airspeed of 360 mph.
>
> In the cruise the aeroplane could not be flown hands-off because it diverged quickly both longitudinally and laterally, and would be tiring to fly for a long time. An autopilot was fitted, although not serviceable in my case, but I believe it would have been essential for instrument flying in bad weather. On opening up to full power I estimated that after three min I was hitting an impressive true airspeed of 390 mph, but it was obvious that the Ar 240 was a poor weapons platform. The harmony of control was terrible, with heavy ailerons, light elevators and moderately light rudders.
>
> The stalling characteristics really showed up the nasty side of this aeroplane. Both the all-up and all-down stalls occurred sharply and almost without warning, except for a twitch on the ailerons before the port wing dropped viciously and the aircraft entered an incipient spin unless rapid corrective action was taken. In steep turns, such as would be taken in evasive action, the aircraft could snap over inverted without any warning if too much 'g' was pulled. The best method of recovery in this case was just to relax on the stick and let the aircraft fall into a vertical dive, but a lot of height was lost before recovery could be effected.
>
> The next Achilles' heel proved to be the asymmetric flight characteristics at slow speed. My tests showed that the maximum speed at which the aircraft could be held straight with one engine out was 160 mph. Below that the Ar 240 rapidly entered an uncontrollable spiral dive in the direction of the dead engine.

> The limiting diving speed was placarded as 750 km/h (466 mph) and the aircraft accelerated rapidly to this. On opening the tail airbrakes at that speed the most almighty buffet started on the elevators, but fortunately the deceleration was quite rapid and the buffet decreased commensurately.[3]

Brown's assessment of the Ar 240 was that it was 'an aircraft of outstanding performance for its class and era, but it could not capitalise on this because of inferior and indeed dangerous handling characteristics.'

The Ar 240 was left at Merville, presumably being scrapped soon afterwards. The time, money and effort expended on developing the Ar 240 resulted in a very poor return. Although a few Ar 240s actually entered service, the few sorties flown had no impact on the overall war effort. A list of all Ar 240s built appears in Appendix I.

Arado Ar 240A-0 Technical Data and Performance Characteristics

Engines: two 1,350-hp DB 601 E
Wingspan: 14.30 m
Length: 12.80 m
Height: 3.70 m
Wing area: 31.00 m²
Empty weight: 6.795 kg
Loaded weight: 8.690 kg
Maximum speed: 580 kph at 6,000 metres
Cruise speed: 515 kph
Range: 1,870 km
Service ceiling: 9,300 m
Armament: two 7.92-mm MG 17 (1,000 rounds each), two 7.92-mm MG 81 Z in EDL 81 Z remote-controlled barbettes (1,000 rounds each)

Arado Ar 240 Variants

Ar 240A-0: Bomber and reconnaissance variant. Five built.
Ar 240B-1: Reconnaissance variant. Two prototypes. Powered by DB 605 engines fitted with MW-50 power boost. The Ar 240 V7 served as prototype for the projected Ar 240B-1 series.
Ar 240C-1: *Zerstörer*. Featured longer fuselage and increased wingspan. Not completed.
Ar 240C-2: Night fighter. Not completed.
Ar 240C-3: Light bomber. Not completed.
Ar 240C-4: High-altitude reconnaissance. Not completed.
Ar 240D: Multi-purpose variant. Was to have been powered by DB 614 engines. Project only.
Ar 240E: DB 603 G-powered bomber. Project only.
Ar 240F: DB 603 G-powered fighter. Project only.
Ar 240 TL: Proposed jet-powered variant. Project only.
Ar 440: Four prototypes built. Not proceeded with.

6

The Messerschmitt Me 210

Based on the experience of the preceding Bf 108 Taifun four-seat tourer and Bf 109 fighter, RLM had great confidence in Messerschmitt's abilities in producing high performance aircraft. As a result, an order was placed for sixteen Me 210 prototypes and pre-series aircraft, as well as a production order of no fewer than 2,000 Me 210s. Remarkably, the Me 210 had yet to make its first flight. Incidentally, a future aircraft production plan, dated 25 October 1939, called for the delivery of 1,338 Me 210s.

In this context, it is interesting to note that two preceding Messerschmitt designs—the Bf 108 Taifun and the Bf 109—had both suffered severe criticism from both pilots and the RLM. However, following intense flight tests, the Bf 108 became a huge success with the Bf 109 being selected as the Luftwaffe's standard single-seat fighter. As a result, both Willy Messerschmitt and his company enjoyed an excellent working relationship both with the RLM and the Luftwaffe. Little trouble was expected with the Me 210.

One novel feature of the new destroyer was the remotely controlled FDL 131 barbette system. Originally developed in cooperation between the *Deutsche Versuchsanstalt für Luftfahrt* (German Aviation Experimental Establishment) and the companies Allgemeine Elektricitäts-Gesellschaft (AEG), Arado, Askania, Goerz, Siemens, and Rheinmetall-Borsig, the FDL 131 barbette consisted of twin 13-mm MG 131 machine guns (with 450 rounds each) fitted in the Me 210 rear fuselage. The machine guns were operated by the gunner/observer by means of two handles, which was connected to the guns through a system of linkages, friction drums, and belt drives, with power being supplied by a 1.5-hp electrical motor.

Aiming was assisted by two reflector gun sights mounted on the cockpit walls. Through the movement of the handle, the guns could traverse between 2° inboard and 45° outboard, having an elevation of +/- 75°. A contact-breaker device made sure that the guns could not be fired when aimed at any part of the Me 210 itself. The remote control armament was tested on the Bf 161 V2, as well as a Bf 110C-2/U1.

Regarding this for its time unorthodox armament, it is interesting to note that when the Royal Aircraft Establishment (RAE) examined the wreck of a shot down Me 210 in late 1942, it was concluded that the remote control machine guns and its associated gun sight was of an experimental nature. If the barbettes with its twin 13-mm MG 131s were any more effective than the more conventional rear cockpit armament of the early model Bf 110, a solitary 7.92-mm machine gun aimed and fired manually by the rear gunner, remains unclear. Nevertheless, it must be said that the remote control armament of the Me 210 pointed the way to the future. Apart from the Me 210, the best-known Second World War aircraft using remote control armament was the Boeing B-29 Superfortress.

Apart from the machine gun and cannon armament, an internal bomb bay, located in the extreme lower front fuselage, would also form part of the new design.

High Hopes, Poor Results

However, the first Me 210 prototype had yet to fly. Powered by two 1,100-hp DB 601A engines, the Me 210 V1 (registered as D-AABF, W Nr 210.0001) took to the air for the first time on 2 September 1939. Some sources point to the first flight occurring on 5 September. However, the 2 September date appears to be correct. The day before, German forces had initiated an invasion of Poland. The Second World War had begun.

The Me 210 V1 was fitted with a twin fin tail section, similar to that of the Bf 110. After landing back at Augsburg-Haunstetten, the test pilot Dr.-Ing. Hermann Wurster declared that the Me 210 exhibited serious flaws, stating that 'The aircraft must be lengthened by at least one metre'. This was due to the Me 210 exhibiting a severe lack of longitudinal stability, with the aircraft being unstable in pitch, direction and yaw, making it very difficult to control. In fact, Wurster recommended that the Me 210 prototype should be grounded until these serious problems had been rectified.

The Me 210 V1 was registered as D-AABF. The twin fins/rudders are clearly visible. (*Wolfgang Mühlbauer/DEHLA Archives*)

Upon hearing Wurster's description of the first flight, Messerschmitt is said to have proclaimed that if any changes to the design had to be implemented, he 'would have to throw away jigs worth three million'. However, the removal of the wing leading edge slats was due to the insistence of the RLM. As mentioned previously, the reason for this was said to have been to reduce the overall cost for the Me 210 programme.

Incidentally, another Messerschmitt test pilot, Fritz Wendel, later remarked that the Me 210 featured 'all of the least desirable attributes an aeroplane could possess'.

The twin fins were subsequently removed, being replaced by a large single fin, and a longer-span tapered stabiliser/elevator. The second flight of the Me 210 V1 took place on 23 September. Although the flight characteristics were improved somewhat, they still left much to be desired. One major fault was that the centre of gravity was improperly located, making the aircraft nose-heavy. During the prolonged combat evaluation in 1941–42, this would often result in landing accidents, with the aircraft either ending up perched on their noses or, more seriously, overturning. In the latter case, the crew risked serious injury, with the aircraft usually suffering severe damage.

The Me 210 V2 had also been built with the twin fin configuration from the outset. However, given the severe control issues experienced during the first flight of the Me 210 V1, the second Me 210 prototype was subsequently modified with a single fin, finally taking to the air on 10 October 1939. The Me 210 V2 was also fitted with mockup FDL 131 gun barbettes. The third Me 210 did not fly, instead being used for static tests before being transferred to E-Stelle Tarnewitz for weapons trials. Its outer wings were fitted to the Me 210 V2. As the flight test schedule progressed, the Me 210 V2 underwent a series of modifications. This included fitting larger wing root trailing edge fillets to ease tail buffeting. However, no marked improvement in the flight characteristics could be discerned. The persistent problem of tail flutter would result in the crash of the Me 210 V2.

Further Me 210 prototypes joined the flight test programme in 1940–41. In the event, no fewer than thirty-seven Me 210s were used in the protracted flight test programme, which apart from general flight and handling characteristics also included testing weapons and a wide range of equipment. This number included sixteen prototypes, eight Me 210A-0 pre-production aircraft, and thirteen Me 210A-1s.

A three-quarter rear view of the second Me 210 prototype. Of note is the large canopy and that the rear fuselage cone is missing. (*Wolfgang Mühlbauer/DEHLA Archives*)

A close-up of the Me 210 V2. The bulged rear canopy and numerous pieces of wool tufts, designed to check the airflow over the wings, can clearly be seen. (*Wolfgang Mühlbauer/DEHLA Archives*)

Willy Messerschmitt. (*Wolfgang Mühlbauer/DEHLA Archives*)

Me 210 Prototypes

Prototype	Code/s	Date of First flight	Remarks
Me 210 V1	D-AABF, CE+BY	2 September 1939	Initially fitted with twin fins. Later modified with single fin.
Me 210 V2	WL-ABEO, CE+BZ	10 October 1939	Modified with single fin prior to first flight, and outer wings of Me 210 V3. Used for dive brake tests. W/o near Augsburg on 5 September 1940.
Me 210 V3	CF+BA	-	Used for static testing. Transferred to E-Stelle Rechlin by 30 March 1940.
Me 210 V4	CF+BB		First Me 210 fitted with single fin from the outset. Used for dive brake tests during 29 flights. Dive brakes then removed and transferred to E-Stelle Rechlin in October 1940.
Me 210 V5	ND+VX		Used for DB 601BF engine tests. To E-Stelle Rechlin on 21 November 1940.
Me 210 V6	ND+VY	21 November 1940	Used for flight handling tests.
Me 210 V7	ND+VZ		Used for de-icing and electrical tests
Me 210 V8	NF+LA		Lengthened fuselage. Used for undercarriage tests
Me 210 V9	NF+LB		Used for tail section tests, including internally balanced elevators. Featured smaller wing fillets than the Me 210 V2. Completed forty-one flights before transfer to E-Stelle Rechlin on 28 November 1940.
Me 210 V10	GI+SN	6 December 1940 *	Date indicates commencement of flight tests.
Me 210 V11	GI+SO	1 November 1940	Flight tests began on 24 November 1940.
Me 210 V12	SI+SP		Used for automatic dive brake tests.
Me 210 V13	SI+SQ	17 April 1941	Used for automatic cooling flaps and electrical de-icing tests. Converted as Me 310 V1, and fitted with four-blade propellers and pressurised cabin.
Me 210 V14	GI+SR		Fitted with anti-spin and brake parachutes, and used for spin tests. Also used for ejection seat trials.
Me 210 V15	GI+SS	31 May 1941	Used for radio equipment tests. Powered by DB 601 F engines.
Me 210 V16	GI+ST		Initially used for de-icing tests, followed by comparative stall behaviour tests against the long-fuselage Me 210 V17.
Me 210 V17	NE+BH	3 October 1941	Delivered initially as a Me 210A-0. First prototype fitted with longer fuselage, and first flown as such on 14 March 1942.

Apart from its primary use as a *Zerstörer*, the Luftwaffe also showed interest in night fighter and tropicalised variants of the basic Me 210, the latter being intended for operations over North Africa. In the event, the Me 210 night fighter variant remained a project. Although a number of Me 210 did operate in North Africa and Sicily between late 1942 and mid-1943, it is unclear if any of them were modified with tropical gear, eg engine dust filters.

The Me 210 V2 crashed on 5 September 1940 during dive trials. The pilot, Fritz Wendel, later recalled:

> During the climb I recall the thought flashing through my mind: 'If something goes wrong, remember to avoid baling out over the forest' (Siebentischwald near Augsburg). At 9,000 feet I checked my instruments and started the planned series of dives, my unpleasant thoughts temporarily forgotten. Stick forward ... down went the nose and the needle began to creep round the airspeed indicator. Stick back, and the nose lifted.
>
> Stick forward ... back ... forward, and so on. One more shallow dive and (then) back to the airfield. A thousand feet showed on the altimeter and I began to level off. Then it happened, and right over that blasted Siebentischwald again! The plane shuddered, the tail fluttered, and bang, the starboard elevator broke off! Immediately the plane went into a half-loop downwards. Before I could gather my wits I was flying on my back in the direction from which I had just come. I knew exactly what would happen now, as I had seen the same thing happen to the first prototype some weeks before. The plane would fly inverted for several seconds and then dive straight into the ground.

A highly interesting movie still showing a Me 210 prototype in flight. The resulting film would show the airflow across the wing, made visible due to the numerous wool tufts on fitted to the upper surfaces. (*Wolfgang Mühlbauer/DEHLA Archives*)

> Hanging on my seat straps, head downwards, I automatically grabbed the release pin, but I hadn't jettisoned the canopy. In that split second I fumbled for the roof's emergency release lever, pulled it, and the canopy flew off with a bang. I pulled the release pin … the chute opened with a glorious crack. I looked down, and there were those damned trees almost touching my feet. But I was in luck, for the wind blew me towards the only clearing that I could see, and I escaped with nothing worse than a sprained ankle. I had lost a prototype, but at least I had proved its unsatisfactory characteristics and had lived to tell the tale. But there are few things in the world harder than proving to an aircraft designer that his latest pet creation is simply not good enough.[1]

A seemingly never-ending number of Me 210 accidents continued to occur. Although some aircraft suffered only slight accidents, others were more serious. In particular, the undercarriage seemed to lack strength, folding up during the landing run. Other severe problems included engines being ripped off from their mounts. Having engines falling off in mid-flight apparently occurred on two occasions. Between September 1941 and April 1942, eleven Me 210s were written off in crashes, with an additional sixteen being damaged. Among the latter aircraft, no fewer than fourteen suffered various degrees of damage in landing accidents (a sign of the previously mentioned nose-heaviness and the notoriously weak undercarriage) and one in a take-off accident. Additionally, one Me 210 of I./SKG 210 suffered damage due to engine trouble.

Me 210 SO+MU being recovered following an accident at Augsburg-Haunstetten on 23 March 1943. (*Wolfgang Mühlbauer/DEHLA Archives*)

A frontal view of the Me 210 V1. The fact that the propeller spinners do not cover the whole front of the engines may be due to engine cooling issues.

Protracted Gestation

The many changes, modifications and refinements of the Me 210 that were constantly interrupting the flight test schedule caused Ernst Udet to write several angry letters to Willy Messerschmitt. In the first letter, dated 27 June 1941, Udet wrote:

> As much as I acknowledge the performance of your designs ... the more forcefully I feel constrained to point out that you are, in my opinion, heading in the wrong direction. It is essential to design military aircraft with a margin of safety, especially in the time of war. It is essential to avoid the necessity of adding reinforcements subsequently, as this wastes time ... might I remind you of the wing reinforcements on the (Bf) 109, the undercarriage problems on the (Bf) 109 and (Me) 210 and the protracted tail problems with the (Bf) 110.... This month once again we have received no Me 210s for battle tests, so that the employment of the model has to be postponed for another month. I also have the impression that since the first prototype was built you have made too many changes. The prototypes and the proposed machines in the series are so different that the results of testing are of no use for the question of practical behaviour in action ... One thing, dear Messerschmitt, must be made clear between us. And that is that there must be no more losses of machines in normal ground landings as the result of a faulty undercarriage; this can hardly be described as a technical novelty in aircraft construction. All these unnecessary scandals and this waste of time call for higher standards in the testing of your new aircraft, and I shall report in that sense to my department.[2]

Harsh words indeed, yet with so much already invested in the Me 210, it simply had to be made to work. There was no second option. However, the many inherent problems of the Me 210 had to be solved before the aircraft could actually enter service. It had become a matter of prestige.

Burdened by the ever-increasing demands from Göring, Ernst Udet chose to end his life on 17 November 1941.

A Me 210 seen undergoing maintenance. The airbrake on the upper wing can be clearly seen. (*Wolfgang Mühlbauer/DEHLA Archives*)

A nice view of an early production Me 210. The upper wing splinter camouflage can be clearly seen. (*Wolfgang Mühlbauer/DEHLA Archives*)

7
Service Trials

In November 1941, a small pre-production batch of Me 210A-0s were delivered to *Erprobungsstaffel* 210 (Test Squadron 210) for operational trials. Based at Soesterberg in the Netherlands, the unit was attached to *Stab* KG 6, being known as 15./KG 6. However, the unit would not fly their first operational sorties over Britain until early August 1942. Prior to making the aircraft's operational debut, the Me 210 programme came within an inch of being cancelled altogether. This test and evaluation unit had originally been formed at Cologne-Ostheim on 7 July 1940. Although Bf 109s and Bf 110s of *Erprobungsgruppe* 210 played an active role in the Battle of Britain, the first Me 210s only arrived after the battle had long since come to an end. Nevertheless, the *Erprobungsgruppe* 210 continued nuisance attacks against targets in southern England well into 1941.

In April 1941, *Erprobungsstaffel* 210 was redesignated as *Schnellkampfgeschwader* 210 (Fast Bomb Wing, SKG 210). It had originally been intended to reequip SKG 210 with the Me 210 as soon as possible. However, it was to be another six months before the first Me 210 arrived. On 4 January 1942, SKG 210 was redesignated as I./ZG 1.

One ZG 1 pilot, Johannes Kaufmann, later wrote of his first impressions of the Me 210. Interestingly, Kaufmann provides a rather different picture of the difficult-to-handle Me 210:

> The Me 210 certainly impressed us. However, instruction could unfortunately only be carried out very superficially, as suitable personnel were not available. One had to proceed cautiously in order to capture its novelties as opposed to the Bf 110, and to learn how to deal with them. In comparison with the Bf 110, the Me 210 was faster, the bombs could be housed internally in the fuselage, climb performace was much better, the diving characteristics conformed to the demands placed on it; the weapons were more effective, and the radio and navigational equipment had been improved. Overall, the Me 210 was a more racy aircraft in which we had placed all our hopes and consequently I eagerly looked forward to the first take-off, conducted with extreme caution due to the predicted danger of veering off the runway, took place without any mishap. This warning on take-off was justified, as it needed some corrections to be made with the rudder and the engines in order to stay on a straightline course. The second take-off went off better, and I remained airborne for 26 minutes to test out the new aircraft in flight. The flying characteristics were good, and better than the

An excellent photo of Me 210 NT+CG. This aircraft was delivered to *Erprobungsstaffel* 210 for ETC bomb rack tests. Unfortunately, the ultimate fate of this particular Me 210 is unknown. (*Wolfgang Mühlbauer/DEHLA Archives*)

Me 210A VN+AT seen during a test flight. (*Wolfgang Mühlbauer/DEHLA Archives*)

> Bf 110. In particular, the Me 210 possessed higher manoeuvrability and rapid acceleration. The approach and landing caused no problems, and in this respect it naturally differed from the Bf 110, which in no way constituted a disadvantage. We practised bomb drops, weapons-firing in the air, dives, and formation flying, and soon became familiar with its peculiarities, which led to optimistic expectations....
>
> The first problems were encountered by our younger-generation pilots. As a consequence, we relocated from Landsberg to Lechfeld, in order to have a longer take-off and landing distance at our disposal. Unfortunately, the abundant winter snow crossed through our plans, so that we were only able to fly from Lechfeld between 13 January and 2 March 1942, and on the afternoon of 2 March, we relocated to Tours. The flying programme encompassed 91 flights on the Me 210, to which came an additional 4 hours for the ferry flights from Lechfeld to Tours and from Regensburg-Obertraubling to Tours. In the overall programme of conversion, 82 airfield flights took place, plus 3 for firing practice, 3 bomb drops, 1 dive, and the 2 ferry flights. (It is worthy of note that learning to handle the Me 210 thus accounted for more than 90 percent of the flight training, with actual combat practice flights comprising less than 10 percent.) Coming from Regensburg, on the landing approach to Tours, I saw a most unusual picture. There were some crashed aircraft lying on the airfield which were evidently new and consisted of Me 210s. In the first moments, I could not precisely identify them but upon landing, I came to hear what had happened. These crashes were due exclusively to the young, still inexperienced pilots, so that a revised decision was forced about the aeroplane. This came relatively quickly. The Me 210 was withdrawn, and we had (to) revert to the Bf 110 and go along with it to Russia in the summer offensive of 1942. The whole airfield was gripped with deep disappointment.[1]

According to a re-equipment plan dated 12 December 1941, three new *Schlachtgeschwadern* (ground attack wings) were to be established by 1 May 1942. Two of these were to receive Me 210s, with Bf 109s and the new Henschel Hs 129 equipping the last unit. Adding ground attack to the wide-ranging tasks that the Me 210 was expected to fulfil complicated matters even further. For instance, the dive brakes that were necessary for the dive bomber mission had to be removed. Additionally, increased armour protection for the Me 210 crew, engines, and radiators had to be provided. In the event, it was decided that the first 100 production Me 210s would retain the dive brakes, with all the necessary changes not being fully implemented until the 400th production aircraft. Work was to begin at Landsberg on 15 January 1942. In the end, the ground attack Me 210 remained a prototype. The increased protective armour was eventually introduced on the Me 410.

During the final weeks of 1941, II./ZG 1 was scheduled to receive Me 210s as replacements for their Bf 110s. In the event, no Me 210s were taken on charge. The severe winter conditions on the Eastern Front would not have eased the introduction of a new combat aircraft. II./ZG 1 was withdrawn from operations on the Eastern Front soon afterwards.

In the event, the Me 210 was declared unsuitable for frontline service. Regarding the poor flying qualities of the Me 210, one pilot claimed he had 'one hand on the stick, the other on the (parachute) ripchord'. One major flaw of the Me 210 was its propensity to enter a spin, particularly during sharp turns. The resulting flat spin (in which the aircraft is level with the horizon while rotating either to the left or right) was very difficult to recover from. To

Two factory-fresh Me 210As at Augsburg-Haunstetten. (*Wolfgang Mühlbauer/DEHLA Archives*)

Two Me 210s seen on the rain-soaked tarmac at Augsburg-Haunstetten. (*Wolfgang Mühlbauer/DEHLA Archives*)

Another air-to-air view of Me 210A VN+AT. (*Wolfgang Mühlbauer/DEHLA Archives*)

counter this, as well as speeding up the crew conversion process, nearly fifty Me 210As were subsequently converted by Blohm & Voss as three-seat dual-control trainers. Other sources speak of between five and twenty-six Me 210s being converted.

Despite the many modifications introduced to the basic airframe, the flight and handling characteristics of the Me 210 did not improve significantly. On 9 March 1942, the most difficult decision to end Me 210 production was ordered by Göring, Milch, and *Oberst* i.G. Vorwald. During wartime, such a radical step was almost unheard of. One is reminded of the harsh slogan emblazoned in a Russian factory building Ilyushin Il-2 Shturmovik ground attack aircraft: 'Do not touch the production line'.

The decision was taken following a two-hour meeting between Göring and Messerschmitt:

> *Herr Reichsmarschall* commenced the discussion by listing the main complaints regarding the Me 210. As he has so far only received optimistic reports for the Me 210, it was the heaviest blow (to the Luftwaffe) since its establishment.... *Hauptmann* Diesing then reported on his experience with the Me 210. Operational and accident statistics: a malfunction for every 50 hours flown, with very few gunnery and bombing flights. Lack of operational readiness prevents sufficient training (18 hours before the first sortie), with the most significant complaints involving: (a tendency to) veer off, difficult take-offs and landings, dangerous spin characteristics, problems with the hydraulic and electronic gear, 50 kg bombs can only be released up to an angle of 30°, Me 210 S prototype is not yet available, weapons systems tests are continuing, but large scale tests are lacking. He cannot say anything about the lengthy trials conducted at Lärz, as he was not involved in these.... Prof. Messerschmitt

Two views of Me 210 production. The Me 210 coded DI+NJ was initially used for various tests, later being delivered to *Erprobungsstaffel* 210. (*Wolfgang Mühlbauer/DEHLA Archives*)

> refused to acknowledge any responsibility of equipment damage, apart from damage that had occurred during installation. He recognized that the complaints were very serious, but had no possibility to rectify them within the contracted delivery schedule....
>
> The *Reichsmarschall* declared that the flight tests had failed, having involved either too good or 'lousy' pilots. He announced that changes would have to be implemented. His question regarding the introduction of design changes to the aircraft was answered by Prof. Messerschmitt in a completely unsatisfactory manner. The main points of the debate were:
>
> Major Storp: Already in October 1941, he had declared to the State Secretary that the aircraft could be brought to operational status within the prescribed date. Because this had failed, he must, through Gen. *Oberst* Jeschonnek ask the *Reichsmarschall* for a decision about the early introduction of the Me 210 S.
>
> The *Reichsmarschall* disapproved strongly about the premature halting of Bf 110, Ju 87 and Ju 88 production through the offices of the RLM, in favour of the Me 210.... As the Me 210 even without being modified to the S variant cannot be used as intended (spinning characteristics remain), it raises the question as to why this failure should be continued with as the Bf 110 is already in large-scale service.[2]

Nevertheless, Me 210 production continued until 14 April 1942. Intense flight testing with modified aircraft was then already well underway. The most important changes to the basic airframe involved lengthening the rear fuselage by 95 cm, with the cross section immediately behind the rear cockpit being considerably wider. Additionally, the 5-degree sweepback of the outer wings was reduced. The first aircraft modified in this manner, the Me 210 V17, was flown for the first time on 14 March 1942. However, changing the production line to churning out modified Me 210s was easier said than done. Nine months were to pass before the first Me 410 would be delivered to the Luftwaffe.

On 12 March 1942, Willy Messerschmitt reluctantly agreed that the Me 210 in its present state was not suitable for operations. According to an agreement between the RLM and Messerschmitt, ten modified Me 210s would be completed by 1 April 1942. When this remained unfulfilled, Göring demanded the removal of Messerschmitt as company director, being succeeded by Theo Croneiß. However, he retained a position for design and development work. On 25 April 1942, the RLM issued an order to stop all work on the Me 210.

For Messerschmitt, the financial loss was considerable, amounting to 38 million RM. If the production line had remained open, an additional 600 Me 210s would have reached Luftwaffe units. However, given the amount of problems that the Me 210 had caused since its first flight in September 1939, it was clear to one and all that something must be done. Proceeding with Me 210 production would have meant turning a blind eye on this troublesome aircraft, thus making sure that the flight and handling characteristics would continue unabated.

Until then, 352 Me 210s (including ninety-four at Augsburg and 258 at Regensburg) had been completed, with another 540 aircraft in various stages of completion. The 600 aircraft on order were cancelled. Apart from the Messerschmitt factories at Augsburg and Regensburg, the Me 210 had also been destined for production by the *Lutherwerke* at Braunschweig (Brunswick), Fieseler *Flugzeugwerke* at Kassel, Erla at Leipzig-Mockau, and the Gothaer *Waggonfabrik* at Gotha. In the event, apart from Messerschmitt, only the *Lutherwerke*

A line-up of recently completed Me 210s. The aircraft in the centre of the photo, GT+VZ, was later modified as a Me 410. (*Wolfgang Mühlbauer/DEHLA Archives*)

An early production Me 210 receives attention from a mechanic. Of note are the aerials beneath the fuselage. (*Wolfgang Mühlbauer/DEHLA Archives*)

An excellent close-up photo showing details of the gun barbette, front fuselage, and canopy. (*Wolfgang Mühlbauer/DEHLA Archives*)

A Me 210 seen prior to a test flight. (*Wolfgang Mühlbauer/DEHLA Archives*)

A line-up of Me 210s. The colours of the propeller spinners are of interest, as are the engine exhaust flame dampeners. (*Wolfgang Mühlbauer/DEHLA Archives*)

manufactured Me 210s, and then only in strictly limited numbers. For the Luftwaffe and Messerschmitt alike, the Me 210 experience had proved to be little short of disastrous.

According to one of the Regensburg factory workers, Master Electrician Otto Liebl, chaos reigned:

> From its very beginning, the Me 210 was a much more modern aircraft than the Bf 109. The electric and hydraulic systems alone were far more comprehensive and the aircraft as such was an extremely modern design. As far as I can remember, the Me 210 was a fast aircraft with initially uncomplicated flying characteristics. Because of constant additions such as armament and larger bomb suspensions, the Me 210 became heavier than was probably originally intended. I can still remember quire well that production had to be stopped once again because additional armour-plating had to be added to the cockpit and to the engines. In discussions with our technicians, there were covert whispers about the critical situation with the Me 210. After some serious accidents had occurred with this aircraft in the flying units, the 'big bang' then happened, when some production of this modern aircraft was halted at Regensburg. There was chaos throughout the entire plant. Production of the Bf 109 was to continue immediately whilst at the same time the halls were cleared-out of the Me 210; it was indescribable. Production of the 108 also continued simultaneously. We were occupied for weeks with conversion work until the 210 could again be built at Regensburg. A large portion of the workforce (reportedly about 4,000 persons) thus became unemployed, which

> meant that no aircraft came off the final assembly lines, and the resulting damage for the Messerschmitt plant must have been immense.[3]

Another Messerschmitt employee, Hermann Kronseder, later recalled the fate of some of the already-completed Me 210s:

> I was ordered to go to Obertraubling. The first thing we were ordered to do was to chop up 100 Me 210s. The Luftwaffe had refused to accept this aircraft as it was too nose-heavy and in every third landing, had nosed over. Nothing much happened to the young, inexperienced pilots, and we apprentices were always the first to show up at the wrecks. We sometimes removed the aircraft clock with its illuminated numerals (the paint contained radioactive elements) and took it home, and whatever appeared to be still usable from the 100 aircraft. Engines and tyres were removed, and we then set to work with the axe. Just as we had hacked 12 aircraft to pieces, came the order: 'Stop, stop!' The designers had found another solution: the fuselage was lengthened by one metre, the nose-heaviness had disappeared and the aircraft flew faultlessly. In the shortest possible time, we modified the remaining aircraft.[4]

While chaos reigned at Regensburg, the improved Me 210 underwent tests at E-Stelle Rechlin. On 27 April 1942, Oblt Edgar Petersen provided a glimmer of hope for the Me 210. Petersen stated that the modified Me 210 had improved stability, making it suitable as a Schnellbomber (high speed bomber). One major issue though was the weak undercarriage, which had plagued the Me 210 since its first flight. In his report, Petersen promised that 210 modified Me 210s (designated Me 410s) would be available on 1 December 1942 for daylight bomb raids against Britain.

Options for filling the void left by the substandard Me 210 included asking Focke-Wulf, on 11 June 1942, to restart development of the Focke-Wulf Fw 187 twin-engined heavy fighter as a *Zerstörer*, high-altitude fighter, and night fighter. Six Fw 187s had been built in 1938/40, with a few being unofficially evaluated by *Jagdgeschwader* 5 in Norway. However, no production orders resulted, with the Bf 110 being considered sufficient. Thoughts about developing the Fw 187 came to an end on 18 August, with the RLM declaring that the intended Fw 187C lacked the necessary range and load-carrying capability.

Following a decision in mid-June 1942 to convert the Me 210 into a better aircraft, work proceeded as quickly as possible in modifying production jigs and tools. Modifying the basic Me 210 into the Me 410 involved lengthening and reconfiguring the fuselage and wings, with the DB 601 F engines being replaced by the more powerful DB 603. Introducing such modifications to already-finished Me 210s as well as the production line would involve months of hard work. Nevertheless, the 1 July 1942 RLM Supply Programme called for 1,128 Me 410s to be delivered in 1942–43. In the event, this proved to be highly over-optimistic.

A close-up view of the external bomb racks. Four SC 50 bombs could be carried. (*Wolfgang Mühlbauer/ DEHLA Archives*)

8

The Me 210: Into Service

With the Me 210 having finally been cleared for continued operational trials, *Erprobungsstaffel* 210 resumed flying in July 1942. Soon afterwards, the unit moved to Soesterberg in the Netherlands, being redesignated as 16./KG 2.

Operations over Britain began on 3 August 1942. Flying in pairs, the Me 210s were carrying one SC 500 bomb each. These 'hit-and-run' raids were very similar to those previously carried out by single-seat Bf 109s and Fw 190As. However, it was to be an inauspicious beginning for 16./KG 6.

On 9 August 1942, a Regensburg-built Me 210A-1 (GF+CB W Nr 2322) took off for a reconnaissance flight over the North Sea. The Me 210s were spotted by Typhoons of 266 Sqn. The Typhoon pilots misidentified the Luftwaffe aircraft as being a Ju 88. Literally hugging the waves, the Me 210 was shot down, with Oblt Ernst Haberland and Uffz Heinz Danigel being killed.

> (Enemy aircraft) opened inaccurate green tracer fire and then started to weave to port but this brought him dead ahead of Red 2 (Pilot Officer Lucas); he returned to his original course and presumably decided to rely on his speed as he used his emergency boost.... Red Section was overtaking fast. Red 1 (Pilot Officer Munro) gave a momentary boost and saw strikes low on water. Throttling to plus-2 boost, range was rapidly closed to 200 yards and a three-second burst given. The e/a was flying straight and level. Red 2 also opened fire from port quarter, a very short burst at 600 yards and then 400 yards and a longer burst at 200 yards.... Immediately after opening fire on the last burst, flames appeared inboard of both engines. A hood came off and one of the crew started to climb out, but as fire was continued he slumped back. The enemy attempted a belly landing but bounced, dropped a wing and went in nose first.[1]

Four days later, another 16./KG 6 Me 210 was shot down. During the early evening of 13 August, Lt Heinz Menger and Uffz Erich Rudolph took off in Me 210 2H+VA (W Nr 210.0110.184) for a patrol along the English coast. Just before 7 p.m., Menger and Rudolph were spotted by four Typhoons of 266 Sqn. Following an intense chase, the Me 210 was shot down by Flt Lt Tony Johnston. Rudolph managed to bale out, and then endured six days in his dinghy before being rescued. Menger went down with his aircraft, losing his life.

The same day that Uffz Rudolph was rescued from the English Channel, Operation Jubilee, the amphibious landings at Dieppe, was initiated. Although the Luftwaffe's response largely consisted of Bf 109s and Fw 190s of JG 2 and JG 26, KG 2 was heavily involved as well, with a fairly large number of Dornier Do 217s being lost. It is reported that three Me 210s of 16./KG 2 also took part, with one aircraft suffering undetermined damage.

On 6 September 1942, two Me 210A-1s of 16./KG 6 (coded 2H+CA and 2H+HA) were shot down by Typhoons of 1 Squadron. The first Me 210 (2H+CA) was shot down by P/O Desmond Perrin, crashing near Redcar reservoir at New Marske, with the crew—Fw Heinrich Mösges and Obgfr Eduard Czerny—both baling out. Both parachutes failed to open, with Mösges and Czerny being killed on impact with the ground. Although severely wrecked, the Me 210 was brought to RAE Farnborough for examination. Perrin's Wingman, P/O Tom Bridges, caught the second Me 210, sending it down over Sunnyside Farm, Sledgate, Yorks. The post-action report read in part:

> The e/a continued turning to port and began diving in a south-east direction.... Typhoon closed rapidly and fired two or three bursts at approximately 200 yards from port quarter astern and saw strikes between port engine and fuselage and on top of the fuselage and cockpit cover. He saw pieces fly off and white smoke from port engine.... The e/a then began weaving violently but stopped turning to port. He then fired a final burst from 100 to 50 yards from dead astern and slightly to port. He saw port engine catch fire and more pieces fly off. The aircraft then slowed down and dived steeply to port.

The crew, Oblt Walter Maurer and Fw Rudolf Jansen, baled out successfully, with Maurer ending up in Robin Hood's Bay. He was rescued by a motor launch and brought ashore. Mösges landed near the village Sledgate in North Yorkshire, suffering the ignomy of being captured by a holiday maker. Oblt Maurer subsequently stated to to his British captors that he was uncertain about the future of the Me 210.

Nevertheless, it must be noted that the Typhoon pilots during the intercepts described above had to resort to applying the engine power boost in order to catch the Me 210s, with several of the pilots blacking out when recovering from power dives. If the Me 210 had one advantage over its predecessor, the Bf 110, it was speed.

However, following the lack of success of the Me 210 during the initial brushes with the RAF, *Reichsmarschall* Göring remarked that 'He would have lived longer if the Me 210 had not been produced' would be his epitaph. Thus, Me 210 operations over Britain came to an end. Its successor, the Me 410, would become a more frequent sight in British skies.

Sicily and North Africa

With initial operations over Britain having made it patently clear that the Me 210 was suffering from a number of problems, *Erprobungsstaffel* 210 was transferred to the Mediterranean theatre of operations. Redesignated as III./ZG 1, the unit moved to Trapani on the western tip of Sicily. Commanded by Major Wilhelm Berlin, III./ZG 1 became part of *Fliegerführer Tunis*. Initial operations included flying escort for Ju 52/3m and Me 323 transports, ferrying men and material from Sicily to Tunisia for Rommel's *Afrikakorps*. On 12 November, the coastal areas around Djidelli and Bougie east of Algiers were attacked by 8./ZG 1 and 11./ ZG 1. The only loss occurred when Me 210A-1 VN+AZ (W Nr 0188) suffered light damage when landing back at Trapani.

Another raid was flown the following day, with three Me 210s being brought down near Bougie on the Algerian coast by 154 Sqn Spitfires. The RAF pilots claimed three Ju 88s, a type of aircraft that was similar in appearance to the Me 210. Such misidentification was fairly common during the North African and Italian campaigns. Later on, RAF Mosquito squadrons would resort to painting specific identification markings on their aircraft in order to distinguish them from Me 410s.

It was an inauspicious beginning for III./ZG 1. On 13 November, Allied shipping off Bougie and Djidjelli were attacked. RAF pilots claimed three 'Ju 88s' shot down. Three Me 210s were indeed lost, with one making a forced landing behind German lines. The aircraft was subsequently destroyed to avoid it falling into Allied hands.

On 14 November, a RAF Beaufort was claimed as destroyed near El Aouina, Tunisia. However, this cannot be substantiated in RAF records. The last days of November resulted in a number of successes, but also, inevitably, losses. On 24 November, twenty trucks were claimed as destroyed by ground strafing. The following day proved disastrous for III./ZG 1. No fewer than three Me 210s were lost, with a fourth aircraft landing back at Trapani with heavy damage. Two of the aircraft (W Nr 0051 and 0060) suffered damage from Allied fighters, coming down near Tunis. The third Me 210 (W Nr 0073) was shot down by flak west of Medjez el Bab, with Lt Walter Hanke and Gefr. Heinrich Auer being killed.

On 28 November, USAAF Boeing B-17 Flying Fortresses escorted by P-38 Lightnings bombed Sidi Ahmed and Bizerte. This was possibly the first time that four-engined American bombers had been encountered by Me 210 crews. However, the Me 210 (2N+RV) of Fl.St.Ing. Heinz Pfister and Obgfr Günther Weber was hit by return fire, being forced down 2 km north of Bizerte. A second III./ZG 1 Me 210, W Nr 0164, was damaged in a landing accident at Trapani.

The following day, Hptm Friedrich Plank (the unit's *Staffelkapitän*) and Fw Heinz Pastoors were shot down in Me 210 2N+MV by two 1 FG Lockheed P-38 Lightnings. The USAAF fighter pilots subsequently filed claims for having destroyed a 'Ju 88'.

On 4 December, Heinz Pfister and Günther Weber were shot down by USAAF aircraft for the second time in less than one week. Around 3 p.m., four Me 210s were intercepted by four P-38 Lightnings of the 48 FS near Faid. Two Me 210s were claimed as shot down (one being claimed as a Bf 110), with Pfister and Weber's aircraft (2N+QV) coming down 60 km south of Kairouan. Pfister was unhurt, with Weber suffering injuries. The second Me 210 (W Nr 0071) crashed 50 km east of Faid, with Lt Alwin Meyer and Uffz Karl Morgenröther being injured. During the day, a third Me 210 (W Nr 0099) was destroyed at El Aouina airfield outside Tunis in a bomb raid.

The day before Christmas Eve, Flt Lt Long and Sgt Hunter found six Me 210s over the Gulf of Hammameth. Long eventually shot down one of them 15 km north-east of Sousse, and, together with Hunter, eventually filed claims for destroying another two Me 210s. However, only one Me 210, 2N+BV, was actually lost.

During the six weeks of operations, III./ZG 1 had lost thirteen pilots and radio operators/ gunners killed (including two in accidents). Three more crew members became prisoners of war. Eighteen aircraft had been lost (including three in accidents), with another three suffering repairable damage.

In December 1942, the long-range reconnaissance unit 2.(F)/122 began to receive Me 210s. On 31 December, three Me 210s were serviceable, along with nine Ju 88D-1s. Initially based at Trapani, 2.(F)/122 would remain in Italy until the end of the war, operating both the Me 210 and the Me 410. During February 1943, two 2.(F)/122 Me 210s went missing in the Misrata-Tripoli area.

On 6 March, Axis forces began an offensive against Medenine. The Me 210s of III./ZG 1 strafed ground targets along the Mareth-Medenine road. In conjunction with Bf 109s, Neffatia airfield was bombed by III./ZG 1 aircraft. With 40 (SAAF) Sqn having just arrived at Neffatia, the Luftwaffe attack encountered heavy flak, although no aircraft were lost. The following day, Neffatia was attacked again around noon, with one Me 210 (W Nr 2314) being shot down 50 km west of Gabes.

During a bomb raid against Sfax on 29 March, III./ZG 1 lost four Me 210A-1s, with an additional three aircraft being damaged. The next day, twelve Me 210s escorted by eighteen Bf 109s were intercepted by RAF fighters, which forced the Me 210 crews to release their bomb loads within the German lines.

Resupplying the German units in North Africa required all available transport aircraft: Junkers Ju 52/3ms, Messerschmitt Me 323s, and Italian Savoia-Marchetti SM.82s. Operating out of Sicily, the transports flew at low altitude to avoid Allied fighters. Few Luftwaffe fighters were available to protect the heavily loaded and vulnerable transports.

On 5 April, Allied operations for disrupting these transport flights, codenamed Operation Flax, began. On this day, one solitary Me 210 formed part of the fighter escort for thirty-one Ju 52/3ms. The fighter escort consisted of ten Bf 109s, six Bf 110s, four Ju 87s, one Fw 190, and one Me 210. The Luftwaffe formation was caught at low altitude by Allied fighters north of Cap Bon, resulting in fourteen Ju 52/ms being shot down and others damaged. The solitary Me 210 escort, 2N+FS (W Nr 0134) was shot down by a USAAF P-38 Lightning, with Obfw Herbert Hendrich and Uffz Rudolf Kaiser subsequently being listed as missing. One USAAF fighter pilot claimed an 'Fw 187' as shot down north of Cap Bon at 8 a.m. This was most likely Hendrich and Kaiser's Me 210. Another Me 210, 2N+BR (W Nr 0170), was in fact lost on this day, with Uffz Walter Luttka and his radio operator (name unknown) being killed. Additionally, five more Me 210s were damaged in Allied bomb raids at Chinisia (also known as Bo Rizzo Landing Ground) and Trapani.

The following day, two 9./ZG 1 Me 210s were lost 30 km north-west of Gabes. Both crews—Uffz Gerhard Lemke and Uffz Emil Deleh in 2N+IT and Uffz Walter Lübke and Uffz Rudolf Müttner in 2N+BR—were killed. A third Me 210 was intentionally destroyed by retreating German troops. Yet worse was to come.

On 9 April, USAAF Spitfire Vs of the 52 FG encountered two formations with a total of ten Luftwaffe twin-engined aircraft over the Kairouan area. Although the USAAF pilots identified the German aircraft as Ju 88s, they were, in fact, Me 210s of III./ZG 1. No fewer than nine of the Me 210s were subsequently claimed as shot down. In fact, six Me 210s were lost. One of the Spitfires was shot down by future Me 410 *Experte* Lt Rudi Dassow. However, Dassow's Me 210 was badly damaged moments later, coming down near Bou Thadi. Dassow's radio operator/gunner, Uffz Walter Böhme, was killed when the burning aircraft struck the ground.

Amazingly, Böhme was the only German killed during this rather one-sided battle, although four others were wounded.

USAAF P-38 Lightnings were met north-west of Cap Bon the following day. Two Me 210s were lost, one each from 8./ZG 1 and 9./ZG 1. Another Me 210, of 7./ZG 1, sustained slight damage in combat, but was able to return to base.

On 17 April, USAAF Lightnings made an offensive sweep over the Sicilian Strait, encountering what was identified as Italian Fiat BR.20 bombers. Five of the enemy aircraft were claimed as destroyed. No such bombers are recorded as having been lost on this day. Instead, it appears likely that the USAAF pilots had encountered a formation of III./ZG 1 Me 210s. Three III./ZG 1 aircraft did indeed suffer (repairable) damage, with performing two belly landings at Chinisia.

The following day, 18 April, has since become known as the 'Palm Sunday Massacre'. Scores of Luftwaffe Ju 52/3ms were shot down. The day began rather quietly though, with a B-26 Marauder of 14 Sqn having an argument with two Me 210s. The Marauder received slight damage. Later on, a III./ZG 1 Me 210 was shot down near Cap Bon. The crew, including Lt Fritz Stehle (a future Me 410 *Experte*) and his radio operator/gunner (name unknown), survived. Another Me 210, of III./ZG 26, was damaged beyond repair.

The reconnaissance unit 2.(F)/122 also lost a Me 210. Two Spitfires of 43 Sqn intercepted the Me 210, and claimed it as probably shot down into the sea. Two other Spitfires, of 242 Sqn, were then sent up to search for the Me 210. The Spitfire pilots saw a small patch of fluorescence, as well as a small box some 15 km north of Cap de Garde. A search and rescue Walrus was then despatched, recovering the box (which contained the logbook), a seat, and some other parts. Of the Me 210 crew (Lt Norbert Schiefhauer and Obfw Wilhelm Gisea), no trace was found.

Another 2.(F)/122 Me 210, F6+ZK, was lost off Algiers the following day, being shot down by a RAF Spitfire. Uffz Erich Förster and Gefr. Adolf Hahn were both killed.

On 26 April, Ofw Martin Heinze of 6./ZG 1 achieved a rare success, claiming to have shot down a Spitfire. Although unconfirmed, it is possible that Heinze's victim was P/O Malan of 72 Sqn.

The last actions of III./ZG 1 during the North African campaign appear to have taken place on 10 May. However, both combats took place over Sicily. During the first of these, two 249 Sqn Spitfires encountered three Me 210s in the vicinity of Riposto. One of the Me 210s (identity unknown) was indeed damaged, although further details are lacking. During a USAAF bombing raid against Luftwaffe airfields, Oblt Ferdinand Glanz and Obfw Hermann Schalow of 9./ZG 1 (flying Me 210 2N+NT) intercepted a B-17 Flying Fortress 10 km north-north-east of Catania, but were wounded by return fire.

On 13 May, General Sir Harold Alexander sent a telegram to Winston Chrchill: 'Sir, it is my duty to report that the Tunisian campaign is over. All enemy resistance has ceased. We are the masters of the North African shores.' During the eight months of operations from November 1942 until June 1943, III./ZG 1 lost forty Me 210s, including thirty-three shot down (twenty-eight by fighters and five by flak), with another thirteen suffering various degrees of damage. Additionally, twenty-one aircraft were destroyed in operational accidents with another twenty-two Me 210s being damaged. It was a heavy toll for the new *Zerstörer*. In July 1943, III./ZG 1 left Sicily for France, leaving 2.(F)/122 the sole Me 210 unit in the Mediterranean area.

By the summer of 1943, the Me 210 had largely been withdrawn from first-line operations. However, second-line training and operational conversion units would continue to use Me 210s until the end of the war.

With the beginning of large-scale USAAF daylight raids over Germany, the Me 210 found a new role, namely that of shadowing the bomber formations. For this purpose, a number of *Luftbeabachtungsstaffeln* (Air Observation Squadrons) were formed. To increase range, these Me 210s carried two 300-litre external drop tanks. Additionally, the engines were fitted with GM-1 injection boost, increasing the rate of climb and speed at high altitude. The Me 210s of the *Luftbeobachtungstaffeln* were largely successful in their job of shadowing the USAAF bomber formations, reporting the speed and course of the bombers to fighter and flak units.

According to German records, only one *Luftbeobachtungsstaffel* Me 210 was lost in combat, being shot down on 11 February 1944. However, by April 1944, these Me 210s had been replaced with Bf 110s.

It is interesting to note that during its active operational career, the existence of the Me 210 remained unknown to the German general public. The first Me 210 photographs were not released until nearly two-and-a-half years after production had come to a halt, being published in the 29 August 1944 issue of the propaganda magazine *Der Adler*. By coincidence, this was also the last issue of *Der Adler*.

Although the RAF never air-tested a captured Messerschmitt Me 210, the RAF serial RN231 was assigned on 1 November 1943 to a Me 210. This was made at the request of the Royal Aeronautical Establishment at Farnborough. It is possible that the Me 210 in question had been found in North Africa or Sicily, and if so it was almost certainly a former III./ZG 1 or 2.(F)/122 aircraft. However, no such aeroplane did arrive in the UK.

9
Foreign Operators

Although interest in the Me 210 was shown by a number of foreign air forces, only Hungary would operate Me 210s in quantity. Additionally, the Me 210 was built under licence in Hungary. A solitary Me 210 was delivered to Japan for evaluation. Italy and Sweden also showed interest in the Me 210, although none were delivered.

No Me 410s were supplied to any foreign air arm. However, a small number of Me 410s were evaluated by Great Britain, the USA, and the USSR.

Hungary

Assembling the history of the Me 210 in Hungarian use is a very difficult task, with much contemporary documentation being destroyed during or after the war. It is estimated that more than 98 per cent of the MKHL's administrative records has been lost to history. Much of what is presented here is based on research kindly provided by the Hungarian aviation historian Csaba Becze Stenge, whose knowledge of the Me 210 in Hungarian service is second to none.

In May 1941, *Reichsmarschall* Hermann Göring met with the directors of the Weiss Manfréd (WM) Company. Originally founded in 1882 by the Jewish industrialist Baron Manfréd Weiss (who died in 1922), the Weiss Manfréd company controlled a large part of the Hungarian aircraft and armament industry. According to the negotiations, WM were to supply the MKHL with aircraft of German design. However, a large percentage of the Hungarian-produced aircraft would be delivered to the Luftwaffe.

On 6 June 1941, a contract for the manufacture of German aircraft in Hungary, including the Arado Ar 96, Junkers Ju 52/3m, Messerschmitt Bf 109, and Messerschmitt Me 210, was signed. The company Dunai Repülögépgyár (Danube Aircraft Factory, DAF) was to build the Me 210 at its new Horthy-Liget (today known as Szigetszentmiklós) factory, located south of Budapest.[1]

The DB 601 engines intended for the Me 210s were also to be built by the WM company. In the event, the DB 601 was replaced by the improved and more powerful DB 605 engine, some 1,200 of which were built in Hungary. The Me 210 was primarily intended to operate as a fast bomber, with a long-range reconnaissance variant also being delivered in small numbers. Additionally, some Me 210s were modified as night fighters. There was no change in designation for these aircraft.

One Me 210A-0, W Nr 2100105, was delivered to DAF as a pattern aircraft. Having a lengthened fuselage and leading edge slats, this Me 210 was powered by DB 605 B engines. The MW-1 power boost, as fitted to DB 605 B engines powering Luftwaffe aircraft, was lacking, though. It was envisaged that no fewer than 900 Me 210s (of which 660 were destined for the Luftwaffe and the rest for the Royal Hungarian Air Force, MKHL) would be built by the Dunai Repülögépgyàr.

Despite the cancellation of Me 210 production in Germany, two modified variants, the Me 210C (similar to the Me 210A-1) and the Me 210Ca-1 (similar to the Me 210A-2) would eventually be built in Hungary. These aircraft were all to be powered by DB 605 B engines. The primary role of the MKHL Me 210 was to be that of fast dive bomber.

The first Hungarian-built Me 210Ca-1 rolled off the assembly line in late 1942, taking to the air for the first time on 21 December. At the controls was *Százados* (Captain) Dénes Eszenyi. Test and acceptance flights followed, after which five pre-series aircraft were delivered. A total of 557 Me 210Cs were to be built, of which two-thirds to be delivered to the Luftwaffe with the remainder to the MKHL.

Me 210Ca-1s of the 102/2 FBS. This unit was known as 'Tiger' Squadron. (*Szilaj via Csaba B. Stenge*)

However, the production schedule was revised in early 1943. Only 300 Me 210Cs were to be built, including 200 for the Luftwaffe. These were to be followed by 450 Me 410Ba-1s (300 for the Luftwaffe) and 517 Me 410Ca-1s (including eighty-one for Hungary). The latter type would enter production in March 1945. In the end, only fifty-seven Me 210Cs were delivered in 1943, with Me 410 production being cancelled altogether. The following year, 215 Me 210s were completed (including eighty-five for the Luftwaffe). Production ended in the summer of 1944. A production list of the Hungarian-built Me 210 can be found in Appendix II.

In anticipation of Me 210 deliveries, aircrew training began in 1943 at Budapest-Ferihegy with the *Ausbildungskommando-Zerstörer* (ABK-Z). A Luftwaffe training unit, the ABK-Z was commanded by Oblt Hans-Arnim Weirich. The ABK-Z operated a number of Bf 110C-4s as conversion trainers. However, the Bf 110s lacked dual controls (some dual training was conducted in Focke-Wulf Fw 58s), with the language barrier between the German instructors and Hungarian pilots being somewhat problematical. However, the majority of the latter already had a working knowledge of German, thus being able to assist their colleagues during the course.

Only one minor accident occurred when a Hungarian pilot forgot to open the fuel valve of the port engine of his Bf 110 during take-off. The aircraft suffered minor damage during the subsequent forced landing.

On 19 March 1944, Germany occupied Hungary. The reason behind this was that the Hungarian leader, Admiral Miklos Horthy, had been conducting highly secret peace talks with the Allies. After this became known to the Germans, they moved quickly to secure Hungarian territory. Although Horthy formally remained in command, the Germans quickly installed a puppet regime. As a result of this, the Me 210 conversion course ended prematurely.

Following the German occupation of Hungary, the directors of the WM company (Manfréd Weiss' son-in-laws) bartered the company to the SS in exchange for their lives. As a result, they and their families were allowed to travel to Portugal. However, more than 400,000 Hungarian Jews were subsequently rounded up by the Nazis in the summer of 1944 and sent to their deaths at Auschwitz.

With the Me 210 production production schedule being revised on several occasions, a total of 160 Me 210Ca-1s (s/ns Z001–Z160) were eventually completed, including five prototypes, three tactical reconnaissance aircraft, three long-range reconnaissance aircraft (Z006–Z011), sixteen night fighters, six conversion trainers, and 128 heavy fighters/bombers were delivered to the MKHL. However, the last of these Me 210s, serial Z160, was not officially taken on charge. This particular aircraft did see combat though, as described later.

The DAF-built Me 210s differed in a number of respects from from its German counterparts. The former lacked the longitudinal instability issues so prevalent on the earlier short-fuselage Me 210s. Also, the DAF-built Me 210s were powered by two 1,475-hp DB 605 B engines, giving the aircraft a maximum speed of 560 kph. The main variant was designated Me 210Ca-1, which had an armament consisting of two 20-mm MG 151/20 cannons and two 7.9-mm MG 17s, as well as two remote-controlled 13-mm MG 131s. Up to 1,000 kg of bombs could be carried in the internal bomb bay, with four 50-kg or 70-kg fragmentation bombs being carried on external bomb shackles fitted to the wing roots. The reconnaissance aircraft was known as Me 210Da-1. It could carry two cameras, also being able to carry a third crew member in the modified bomb bay. The rearward firing MG 131s

Crew assembled in front of a MKHL Me 210Ca-1. Note the cameraman standing on the wing. (*Szilaj via Csaba B. Stenge*)

Armourers at work on a Hungarian Me 210Ca-1. (*Csaba B. Stenge*)

were removed on the Me 210Da-1. In addition, a number of Me 210s were bought from Germany in 1944.

In March 1944, a single Me 210Ca-1 (serial Z003) was modified as a *Zerstörer* aircraft. Actual modification work lasted about four months. The pair of MG 17s were deleted, and replaced by a 40-mm Bofors gun. This Swedish-designed anti-aircraft gun was in large-scale use in Hungary during the war. Additionally, three 15-cm *Nebelwerfer* (Fog dispensers) unguided mortars were carried beneath each wing. Actual firing tests began on 24 October. Although thirty Me 210s were to be modified in this manner, only four aircraft are believed to have been completed.

Contrary to the Luftwaffe, the Me 210 was held in quite high esteeem among Hungarian pilots. The Me 210 was considered a modern combat aircraft well suited to the needs for a fast bomber. When operating from primitive airfields with little in the way of ground equipment and support facilities, the DB 605 B engines could provide the mechanics with maintenance problems. Initial combat experience with the Me 210 proved to be disastrous though, when a dedicated night fighter squadron was pressed into service in April 1944 against USAAF daytime heavy bomb raids. Nevertheless, from the summer of 1944, the first of an eventual three dive bomber/close air support squadrons operated Me 210s against Soviet troops and armour. Final operations took place on 1 April 1945.

The pilot's view from a MKHL Me 210Ca-1. (*Szilaj via Csaba B. Stenge*)

A trio of MKHL Me 210s making a low flyby over another Me 210. (*Csaba B. Stenge*)

Night Fighters

Following a Soviet air raid against Budapest on 4–5 September 1942, the MKHL High Command decided to seek the purchase of night fighters from Germany. At the time, the MKHL only possessed single seat-day fighters. As a result, a few obsolete Fiat CR.42 biplanes were pressed into service, with three Bf 110s eventually arriving from Germany. However, the Bf 110s were not fitted with radar, making them virtually useless for nocturnal intercept duties. One early production Me 210Ca-1, serial number Z005, was to have been used as a testbed for the Hungarian-designed Turul radar. However, there is no evidence available that this radar was ever fitted to the Me 210.

A dedicated night fighter unit, the 5/1 éjjeli *vadászrepülő-század* (5/1 Night Fighter Squadron, 5/1 NFS), was formed. Based at Budapest-Mátyásföld, the 5/1 NFS was the first squadron to receive Me 210s, the first aircraft arriving in June 1943. The 5/1 NFS was known as Bagoly (Owl), with the unit insignia being an owl sitting on a tree branch surrounded by a red circle. By 9 March 1944, the 5/1 NFS had seven Me 210s: Z012, Z017, Z019, Z021, Z024, Z026, and Z029.

Another Me 210 unit was the RKI *Romboló század* (Air Experimental Institute Destroyer Squadron, RKIR) based at Budapest-Ferihegy. Formed on 3 April 1944 with twelve Me 210Ca-1, the RKIR was commanded by *Alezredes* (Lieutenant Colonel) Lòrand Dòczy. The unit insignia consisted of a yellow lightning bolt superimposed on a light blue roundel, with the letters RKI at the bottom of the roundel.

However, the 5/1 NFS and the RKIR did not see combat until 3 April 1944, and then only in a day fighting capacity. Incidentally, the MKHL Me 210s all lacked radar, which of course would have made them virtually useless during night interceptions. On this day, the USAAF's 15th AF attacked Budapest. More than 1,000 civilians were killed, with large parts of the city suffering bomb damage.

To counter the USAAF bombers, a dozen Me 210s of the 5/1 NFS took off. One Me 210, flown by *Örmester* (Flight Sergeant) Dezsö Zsámboki and *Örvezetö* (Aircraftman 1st Class) Géza Sallós, was shot down by a USAAF P-38 Lightning over Paks, with both Zsámboki and Sallós losing their lives. Another Me 210, flown by factory test pilot *Föhadnagy* (Flying Officer) Kornél Nagy and István Kuthy (gunner/radio operator), crashed near Bugyi. Kuthy was killed, with Nagy being badly wounded, losing an eye when a Lightning strafed the wreck on the ground. One B-17 Flying Fortress was confirmed as shot down.

On 12 April, USAAF bombers raided targets around Budapest. RKIR Me 210s intercepted the raid, losing one aircraft. The pilot of this Me 210, Akadémikus Sándor Hayden, was seriously injured, dying of his wounds the following day.

A further heavy USAAF raid against Budapest took place on 13 April. Ferihegy airfield was also hit, with several aircraft being destroyed or damaged. The 5/1 NFS lost no less than four aircraft, with seven aircrew being killed. Only one radio operator/gunner, Örmester Ferenc Tóth, survived after baling out. Another three Me 210s were lost by the RKIR. Two P-38 Lightnings and one B-24 Liberator were claimed as shot down, with these claims eventually being confirmed.

For the 5/1 NFS crews, flying sorties against USAAF daylight raids proved disastrous. Four Me 210s were shot down. Of the eight crew members, only one survived. Another two were forced down. The various air combats during this day also resulted in the highest single-day MKHL personnel losses of the entire war.

The RKIR subsequently put forward claims for four B-24 Liberators and two P-47 Thunderbolts. These claims were later approved. As a result of the poor results and heavy losses sustained during the 13 April raid, the 5/1 NFS and RKI *Romboló század* were forbidden to fly any more daylight combat sorties. Nevertheless, night figher training continued. On 15 April, 3/2 Squadron initiated Me 210 training. One accident occurred on 22 April, when Me 210 serial Z079 was slightly damaged in a landing accident. The course ended on 29 April.

In all, these USAAF raids damaged or destroyed fifty-nine MKHL aircraft, of which a large percentage was Me 210s. As a result of the DAF factory having suffered heavy damage, Me 210 production came to an end. A total of 270 aircraft had been delivered.

Fast Bombers

The third MKHL Me 210 unit was the 102/1 *Gyorsbombázó század* (102/1 Fast Bomber Squadron, 102/1 FBS). The 102/1 FBS was known as *Sas* (Eagle), being commanded by *Százados* István Herszényi. The unit insignia consisted of a diving eagle carrying a bomb between its claws. During the work-up phase, the 102/1 FBS was also based at Bilgoraj and Mielec. One interesting episode took place on 8 June 1944, when one of the unit's pilots, Prince Miklós Odescalchi, used Me 210 serial Z088 to fly to Italy. Odescalchi's flight was undertaken to prepare the way for a Hungarian delegation to travel to Italy for secret peace talks. Unfortunately, Odescalchi landed behind German lines near Fermo. Odescalchi was arrested along with his radio operator, *Szakaszvezetö* (Sergeant) Ferenc Bajusz. Indeed, Bajusz was unaware of the real reason behind the flight. Odescalchi's aircraft was probably a Me 210Da-1 photo reconnaissance variant, as it had camera fittings and forward leading edge de-icing gear as well as lacking the forward firing MG 17s. The partly disassembled Me 210 was later discovered by the Allied troops, who misidentified it as a Me 410A.

Odescalchi and Bajusz were both transported back to Hungary, with Odescalchi subsequently being put on trial by a military tribunal. He was executed on 21 January 1945 at Sopronkőhida. Bajusz was acquitted, not having been involved in the secret peace talk plans. Following the end of the war, Odescalchi was rehabilitated, also being promoted posthumously.

Due to the relative inexperience of the 102/1 FBS aircrews, the unit transferred to Poland for operational training. While here, two Me 210s were damaged beyond repair by Polish partisans. Apparently, this was carried out by Polish civilians who were working during the daytime on the airfield.

In July 1944, the 102/1 FBS arrived back in Hungary. Initially based at Hajdúböszörmény in the eastern part of the country, the unit flew its initial combat sortie, against the railway junction at Chortkow, the USSR, on 20 September 1944. The target was dive bombed with great precision from 2,000 metres. Post-raid reconnaissance photographs, taken by the Luftwaffe, showed 80 per cent damage to the target.

MKHL Me 210 serial number Z099 seen at Hajdúböszörmeny in 1944. (*Csaba B. Stenge*)

A second fast bomber unit, the 102/2 FBS (known as *Tigris*, meaning Tiger) was formed at Kecskemét on 20 May 1944 (other sources state 1 June 1944) from 3/2 Squadron. The unit insignia was a leaping tiger. The 102/2 FBS Commanding Officer was *Százados* (Captain) Pál Bodó. The majority of the aircrews were highly experienced, having previously flown parasol-winged Heinkel He 46 reconnaissance aircraft on the Eastern Front. The primary role of the 102/2 FBS was armed reconnaissance, as well as dive bombing.

On 3 June, the 102/2 FBS transferred to Hajdúböszörmény. The Me 210s were picked out of storage at Kenyeri, the first four being ferried to Hajdúböszörmény on 23 June. One of the pilots, Gyula Szilaj Varga, departed the formation, performing an airshow routine over his hometown. Arriving twenty minutes after the other three Me 210s had landed, Varga was met by an irate squadron commander. Another four Me 210s arrived at Hajdúböszörmény on 26 June. Operational training continued until the end of July. On 18 July, 102/2 FBS was visited by a number of war correspondents, with interviews being broadcast on national radio soon afterwards.

According to official records, the first combat sortie was flown on 29 July. On 7 August 1944, *Zászlós* (Cornet) Béla Csapó flew an armed reconnaissance sortie against Kolomea. Csapó dropped four 70-kg bombs against the railway station at Delatin. On the return flight, Csapó spotted between fifty and sixty Soviet aircraft parked at Kolomea airfield in the Mirgorod area. Some sources speak of the aircraft being USAAF four-engined bombers, which had flown a 'shuttle' sortie, attacking oil installations at Trzebinia before heading for Soviet territory. Hours later, six Me 210s of the 102/2 FBS arrived over Mirgorod. A large number

This particular Me 210, serial number Z099, was possibly modified for reconnaissance duties. (*Csaba B. Stenge*)

of aircraft were reportedly destroyed. However, the Hungarian aviation historian Csaba B. Stenge states that MKHL Me 210s never bombed Mirgorod.

Disaster at Hajdúböszörmény

The presence of the Me 210Ca-1 units at Hajdúböszörmény resulted in Allied efforts to destroy or seriously damage the airfield. The first attempt was made by the RAF on 12–13 August, albeit with little success. A fuel bowser was destroyed, with most of the bombs falling over the nearby city of Hajdúböszörmény, killing nineteen civilians and injuring up to forty more. The USAAF raid little over a week later proved far better results.

On 21 August, 102 USAAF B-24 Liberators, escorted by some ninety P-51 Mustangs of the 90th FG and 325 FG attacked Hajdúböszörmény. However, most of the 22,000 fragmentation bombs missed the airfield. Nevertheless, many Me 210s of the 102/1 and 102/2 FBS's were destroyed in repeated strafing runs by 325 FG Mustangs.

After an initial strafing run, during which the Mustang pilot did not encounter any anti-aircraft fire (there were no anti-aircraft guns located at the airfield), a further six strafing runs were made:

> 16 P-51s of the 317th FS, 15 P-51s of the 318th FS, and 18 P-51s of the 319th FS took off at 0700 hours on a Medium Altitude Fighter Sweep over Hajdu Boszormeny [*sic.*] A/D, Hungary. 3 P-51s returned early. 2 P-51s returned from target at 0955 hours and down at base at 1130

The burnt remains of a MKHL Me 210 seen at Hajdúböszörmeny following the devastating USAAF strafing raid. (*Szilaj via Csaba B. Stenge*)

> hours. 44 P-51s remained in target area until 1105 hours. 11 P-51s circled while 33 remained as hi-cover while bombs were dropped. 11 P-51s continued to circle for 10 minutes after bombers left the target. 80 to 100 E/A observed on the ground. One pass was made across the A/D from NE to SW with good results. 6 more strafing passes were made in rapid succession, covering the A/D. The results are believed to be 37 E/A destroyed, 13 probably destroyed, and 17 damaged. 1 Me 109 observed at 1025 hours headed NE was encountered and destroyed by 2nd Lt. Robert H. Brown. 44 P-51s down at base at 1255 hours.[2]

The top scorer was the commanding officer of the 317th FS, Major Herschel H. Green, who claimed eight Me 410s and two Bf 109s destroyed, six Me 410s probably destroyed, and three Me 410s damaged. As the USAAF bombers had been supposed to bomb the airfield, but failed to inflict much damage, the Mustang strafing runs had been 'a violation of the operations order', as the Commanding Officer of the 325th FG bluntly told Major Green upon landing. Nevertheless, Major Green was awarded the Distinguished Flying Cross a month later.

Actual aircraft losses were far lower than those claimed by the USAAF pilots, with about a dozen Me 210s (most of which were from the 102/1 FBS), two Luftwaffe Ju 87Ds of 15./StG 151, and a few MKHL liaison aircraft being destroyed. It seems likely that some of the 'Ju 88s' claimed as destroyed were, in fact, Caproni Ca 135 bombers long since relegated for use as decoys. Additionally, no Bf 109s, Hungarian or otherwise, were based at Hajdúböszörmény. Personnel losses amounted to thirty-five killed and seventy-two injured.

Shortly before the raid, a Me 210 had taken off on a reconnaissance sortie. Returning to the airfield while the raid was underway, the crew were diverted to another airfield. They landed safely after remaining airborne for two hours and twenty-five minutes, the longest MKHL Me 210 sortie during the war.

Three days after the devastating raid, the 102/1 FBS and 102/2 FBS transferred to Tisza. The commanding officer of 102/2 FBS was replaced on 25 August by *Százados* Kálmán Háry. This was due to the earlier-mentioned flight to Italy of one of the squadron's pilots.

Replacement aircraft stored at Tápiószele and Kenyeri began to arrive at Tiszalök. The first combat sortie following the USAAF strafing raid took place on 20 September, when the railway station at Khyriv was attacked. It was also the first sortie for the 102/1 FBS. During this period, it was common for both squadrons to fly together, coordinating their missions. Dive bombing and armed reconnaissance sorties in support of the Hungarian 3. Army were conducted, with the fighting being concentrated around the area between Makó and Nagyvárad. On 28 September, the 102/1 FBS and 102/2 FBS attacked Soviet army columns south of Nagyvárad. On 1 October, Soviet forces crossed into Hungarian territory. On this day, targets south of Kardó were attacked by the Me 210 squadrons. From this point on, MKHL pilots had to fight against Soviet armoured columns and troop concentrations on Hungarian soil. This increased the risk of accidentally hitting Hungarian civilians in towns and villages, something which left the Me 210 pilots with a huge sense of bitterness and anger. On one occasion, a Hungarian assault artillery unit was hit by friendly fire from the MKHL Me 210s.

On 7 October, a solitary Me 210 of the 102/2 FBS was despatched on an armed reconnaissance sortie over the Carpathians. While flying over Ungvár, two Soviet Il-2 Shturmoviks intercepted the Me 210. The Me 210 crew (Kovács and Villám, first names and ranks unknown), managed to shoot down one of the Il-2s also (unsuccessfully) pursuing the second Il-2. This was one of only a few air-to-air victories of the 102/2 FBS. Post-war, a former Soviet Il-2 rear gunner remembered his aircraft being brought down by an 'aggressive' Hungarian Me 210.

Two days later, on 9 October, the Me 210 aircrews attacked Soviet forces crossing the River Tisza. On the same day, a Luftwaffe fighter unit, II./JG 52, arrived at Tiszalök. This resulted in the airfield becoming very congested. As a result, the MKHL Me 210 squadrons began to transfer to Budapest-Ferihegy later the same day. Before the move had been completed, a 6./JG 52 pilot, Hptm Helmut Lipfert, struck two 'Hungarian Bf 110s' (actually Me 210s, as no MKHL Bf 110s were based at Tizsalök) on take-off.

The first sortie from Budapest-Ferihegy took place on 14 October, attacking Soviet forces around Szentes and Mindszent. The next day's events brought confusion to the MKHL Me 210 squadrons.

Since the first months of 1944, the Hungarian leader Miklós Horthy had conducted highly secret talks through representatives in Moscow with the Soviet foreign secretary, Vjatsjeslav Molotov. When learning about this, the Germans occupied Hungary on 19 March 1944. Since then, the war was going badly for the Germans. Within a few weeks in August and September 1944, both Bulgaria and Romania left the Axis and were both now fighting against Germany.

Shortly before Horthy was to announce a truce between Hungary and the USSR on 15 October, German troops arrested his son. Nevertheless, Horthy went ahead with the radio broadcast, announcing the truce. Horthy was removed, with the same radio station broadcasting a message a few hours later that the fight would continue. In Horthy's place, the Germans installed the leader of the Nazi-inspired Arrow Cross movement, Ferencz Szálasi.

The 102/1 FBS and 102/2 FBS continued to fly sorties on 15 October. Five days later, on 20 October, a Soviet airfield at Szarvas was attacked in conjunction with Luftwaffe Ju 87D Stukas of StG 2 and Bf 109Gs of II./JG 52. The Stukas attacked first, at 8 a.m., with the MKHL Me 210s following five minutes later. The II./JG 52 pilots then strafed the airfield. Of the 100-odd Soviet aircraft based at Szarvas, many were destroyed or put out of action.

During the return flight, *Szakaszvezetö* Ferenc Csorba of the 102/2 FBS brought down a Soviet Lavochkin La-5. This was Csorba's second air-to-air victory, having shot down a Lavochkin fighter in 1943 while serving with a Fw 189 squadron.

A second raid against Szarvas was carried out on 21 October. Two days later, the railway station at Oroshása was attacked. During the return flight, the Hungarian Me 210s were intercepted by Soviet La-5s. *Tizedes* (Corporal) József Bilau managed to shoot down one of the La-5s over Túrkeve. The battle was not one-sided, though, with Me 210Ca-1 serial Z140 of the 102/2 FBS, belly landing at Ferihegy.

On 26 October, a 102/1 FBS Me 210 crashed shortly after take-off. Both *Zászlós* János Gyulay and *Szakaszvezetö* István Pál were killed. Four days later, on 30 October, a 102/2 Me 210 (possibly serial Z107) was shot down by flak west of Kecskemét. The pilot, József Kovács, failed to leave the stricken Me 210, with the radio operator/gunner, Mihály Villám, baling out from too low an altitude.

The following day, a Me 210 crew shot up the German gunboat *Bechelaren* (the former President Masaryk) on the Danube River. The exact circumstances of this incident remains unclear.

On 31 October, the 102/1 FBS and 102/2 FBS began to vacate Budapest-Ferihegy for Várpalota. Two unserviceable Me 210s, one from each squadron, had to be left behind.

During the move, the commander of 102/1 FBS, *Százados* Kálmán Háry, 'borrowed' ten Jewish slave workers, hiding them among the squadron personnel. In doing so, he most likely saved their lives.

Intensified Combat Operations

The last two months of 1944 would see intensified combat operations, with several Me 210 crews and aircraft being lost. A third Me 210 squadron, the 102/3 FBS, was formed on 1 November at Várpalota. The 102/3 FBS became known as *Villám* (Lightning). Additionally, the 102. *Gyorsbombázó osztály* (the 102 Fast Bomber Group, 102 FBG) was formed, consisting of the three Me 210 squadrons. The 102. FBG was commanded by Örnagy Albert Martini, with the acting commander of the 102/3 FBS being *Alezredes* Lórand Dóczy. About two weeks later, Dóczy was replaced by *Föhadnagy* Adolf Péterdi. All of the pilots serving with the 102/3 FBS were officers, with the ground personnel consisting of former staff from the Dunai Repúlögépgyàr (DAF).

The first sortie of the month took place on 4 November, with Soviet vehicles in the Sári/Alsónédemi area being attacked. Two Yak fighters were claimed as shot down by 102/1 FBS crews. An aircraft of the 102/3 FBS was badly damaged by flak, with a 37-mm shell hitting the starboard engine, also wounding the pilot. Nevertheless, *Hadnagy* Antal Posgay managed to return to Várpalota.

Two sorties were flown on 6 November, against troop concentrations north of Kecskemét and north of Alsónémedi. The following day, a train loaded with ammunition was destroyed at Szajol.

On 8 November, two Me 210s, one each from the 102/2 FBS and 102/3 FBS, were shot down by flak during an attack on a large troop concentration advancing along the Debrecen–Tiszafüred road. All four crewmembers were killed. One Soviet fighter was shot down over the target by *Föhadnagy* Tibor Béles and Örmester Gábor Kovács of the 102/3 FBS. This was the squadron's sole confirmed air-to-air victory.

Another 102/2 crew lost their lives on 13 November, with their Me 210 being hit both by fighters and flak. Nine Soviet Yak fighters intercepted the half a dozen Me 210s. However, two Yaks were shot down during the same sortie by József Orbán and Tibor Vörös, with the remaining Soviet fighters retreating. According to a contemporary report by a war correspondent, the Me 210s had destroyed an armoured vehicle, some ten–twelve guns, four lorries, and about thirty horse-drawn carts.

On 21 November, the crew of a Hungarian patrolboat on the River Danube reported that a 'Hungarian bomber' had attacked, but that the bombs had missed the ship. It is unclear if the attacking aircraft was a Me 210, but it appears likely that it was.

The following day, the 102/1 FBS and 102/2 FBS attacked railway lines. It had originally been intended that Bf 109s would provide escort for the Me 210s. This did not happen, though, with the Me 210s continuing towards the target without any fighter escort. Relations between Bf 109 and Me 210 pilots/crews were not always cordial. The Me 210 crews stated that they occasionally had to perform their missions unescorted, with the fighter pilots in their turn complaining about difficulties in escorting Me 210 formations, stating that the fast bomber formations were usually too widely scattered for any effective escort. Before reaching the target, a dozen Yaks intercepted the Hungarian Me 210s. Although one Yak was shot down by Örmester Lajos Poós of 102/2 FBS, the Me 210 also sustained damage. Another Me 210 was shot down by flak, with *Zászlós* Béla Csapó and Örmester Györö Szente force landing behind Soviet lines. Both Csapó and Szente became prisoners of war, returning to Hungary in 1947.

On 28 November, two locomotives were destroyed. However, one 102/3 FBS aircraft was downed by flak, with the crew, *Föhadnagy* Kornél Majoros and *Tizedes* Károly Szüts, being killed in the ensuing crash. At the time of his death, Majoros was the most successful MKHL bomber pilot.

Several more train-busting sorties were flown in the following weeks. By early December, Soviet forces had managed to cross the River Danube. On 4 December, several sorties against Soviet troops south of Lake Balaton were flown in conjunction with Luftwaffe units.

On 8 December, the 102 FBG left Várpalota for Lesvár. The first known sortie from Lesvár took place on 11 December. Very poor weather kept the Me 210s grounded for several days, with many of the ground staff being recruited by the MKHL Rifle Regiment as infantrymen. Additionally, the stocks of fuel were severely depleted, sharply reducing active operations.

Nevertheless, two sorties were flown on 21 December with one 102/1 FBS Me 210 being shot down by flak near Seregélyes, killing *Hadnagy* Sándor Brányi and Örmester Miklós Gergovácz. Two days later, another Me 210 was brought down by Soviet flak near Szete (present-day Kubáňovo, Slovakia). The Me 210 was flown by *Föhadnagy* Adolf Péterdi, the commanding officer of the 102/3 FBS, with Örmester Károly Mészáros as radio operator/gunner. Péterdi was an experienced reconnaissance pilot, having previously completed seventy-four sorties over the Eastern Front. However, this was only his second fast bombing sortie. In the event, Péterdi was captured, eventually being released by Soviet authorities in 1945, while Mészáros, who had been wounded, later died in captivity. According to Soviet sources, Mészáros was killed during an air raid against a military hospital at Deménd.

Their Me 210 was serial Z160, the final Hungarian-built example. Following completion, the aircraft had been ferried to the 102/3 FBS without undergoing any pre-acceptance test flights. Several vital pieces of equipment had been missing, these being installed by the unit mechanics. However, during the sortie, Péterdi experienced trouble with the Me 210s bomb bay doors as well as the dive brakes.

On Christmas Eve, Soviet forces encircled Budapest, effectively putting the capitol under siege. Despite of the increasing lack of fuel, the 102. FBG continued to fly ground attack and close air support sorties, which inevitably brought further losses of personnel and aircraft. On 25 December, a Me 210 of the 102/3 FBS was damaged by Soviet fighters, with the radio operator/gunner, Örmester Imre Szukis, being fatally injured. Nevertheless, the pilot managed to land back at Lesvár. Apparently, new regulations issued around this time stated that due to the shortage of fuel, aircraft that had sustained damage in air combat would have to fend for themselves—keep formation and leave the stragglers behind.

On 26 December, a Yak fighter was shot down over Drégelypalánk by Örmester János Klug and *Tizedes* Mihály Elezsánsky of the 102/1 FBS. This was the last confirmed air-to-air victory of the MKHL Me 210 units. Poor weather conditions resulted in the last sortie of the year being flown on 29 December.

The Final Year

The first month of 1945 saw German and Hungarian forces make three attempts to break the siege of Budapest. These counteroffensives were supported by the Me 210s of the 102. FBG. Operations continued during January and February 1945 in increasingly difficult conditions. On 1 January, a bridge over the River Garam (in Slovakia)was attacked. One of the Me 210s returned with engine trouble, being damaged beyond repair in a belly landing. On 3 January, one Me 210 was lost (the exact cause of this loss is unknown, but it is presumed that the aircraft was brought down by flak), with another being badly damaged in an encounter with a Soviet fighter, during which the radio operator/gunner was injured by shrapnel from a 20-mm cannon shell. Nevertheless, the pilot managed to return to base.

On 19 January, a Lavochkin La-5 was shot down by Jószef Bilau, a radio operator/gunner of the 102/2 FBS. Bilau had previously shot down a Soviet aircraft. However, Bilau's victory was not confirmed due to the collapse of MKHL administrative records keeping.

Three days later, nine Me 210s attacked a pontoon bridge over the River Danube. Four Bf 109Gs of the 101/I FG provided escort for the Me 210s. Things appeared not to have been particularly cordial during the sortie, with the Bf 109 pilots subsequently filing a complaint that the Me 210s had flown in a 'scattered' formation, making escort duties more difficult. In all probability, this was in retaliation to earlier complaints by the Me 210 crews about their escorting Bf 109s during previous sorties.

Several train-busting sorties were carried out between 22 January and 5 February (or possibly 4 February), usually flown by two Me 210s each, with fourteen locomotives being claimed as destroyed.

On 1 February, the 102. FBG was renamed as the 1. FBG. The commanding officer of the 102/2 FBS, *Százados* Pál Bodó, was replaced by *Százados* László Tomor. The exact cause behind this remains unclear, but it could have been due to a 'friendly fire' incident earlier in the year, when a German unit was attacked by MKHL Me 210s. Another possibility was due to the fact that Bodó had been hiding a number of Jews, claiming them to belong to the squadron's work force. Bodó was also known to show open disregard for the Arrow Cross movement.

On 4 February, no fewer than twenty-one sorties were flown. One Me 210 (W Nr 150064) was lightly damaged in landing accident. This particular Me 210 had not been built in Hungary. Instead it was one of nineteen aircraft purchased from Germany. The Me 210s were transferred to Hungary from Fl. Gast 5/VIII. Celldömölk (Pàpa in Hungary) and Fl. Gast 7/ VIII. Wiener Neustadt in Austria. Negotiations for the purchase of these aircraft had been initiated in October 1944. However, the first aircraft of this batch did not arrive in Hungary until early 1945. For details on these aircraft, please refer to Appendix II. It seems likely though that some of these Me 210s were not delivered to Hungary.

On 14 February, nine Me 210s attacked targets around Lake Velencei. Following this large-scale effort, three train-busting sorties were flown until 20 March.

With Soviet forces fast approaching Lesvár, the 1. FBG was transferred to Parndorf in Austria on 28 March. At least six Me 210s were intentionally destroyed at Lesvár, along with most of the unit's administrative records. During the flight to Austria, a Soviet armoured column was attacked, this being the last time the MKHL Me 210s were used in anger. Due to lack of fuel, no more operations were flown.

On 1 April, Soviet tanks encircled Parndorf. The Me 210s were intentionally destroyed to prevent them from being captured, along with all the remaining unit records. The 1. FBG personnel retreated to Waldhof, Rohrbach, and Taubenbach, surrendering to US troops. In all, some 750 combat sorties had been flown, including 250 to 300 by the 102/1 FBS, more than 300 by the 102/2 FBS and more than 150 by the 102/3 FBS. A former Me 210 pilot remarked: '[they] could hit a target the size of a bed-sheet' during the dive bomber sorties. Thirteen Soviet aircraft had been shot down by the Me 210 fast bomber units, with countless Soviet vehicles being damaged or destroyed.

However, losses had been severe. Twenty-three crew members were lost on combat operations, with only three of these returning to Hungary after the war. As previously mentioned, one Me 210 pilot was executed during the war. Additionally, three air crew were wounded in combat, with one of the ground staff being killed during an air raid.

MKHL personnel photographed sitting in and on a Me 210Ca-1 (*Fortepan.hu*)

Italy

On 5 May 1943, the *Regia Aeronautica* requested the supply of fifty Me 210s. None were delivered.

Japan

The first production Me 210A-2 (W Nr 2350) was delivered to Japan in January 1943, as part of the Japanese–German Technical Exchange Agreement.[1]

Apart from the retention of the DB 601 F engines, the aircraft had otherwise been brought up to Me 410 standard. Upon arrival, the Me 210 was assembled by Kawasaki at its Akashi factory prior to evaluation by the Imperial Japanese Army Air Force (IJAAF). During one of the test flights, the undercarriage and engine mounts of the Me 210 sustained damage. No further Japanese interest in the Me 210 ensued. The Me 210 did not receive an Allied code name, unlike some of the other German aircraft evaluatated in Japan. The Me 210 did, however, influence the design of the Rikugun Ki-93 twin-engined heavy fighter and ground attack aircraft. Two Ki-93 prototypes were built at Tachikawa in 1944–45, but the design never entered series production.

Sweden

Negotiations for the supply of Me 210s, as well as licence production by Saab, were initiated in the spring of 1941. The possible delivery of Me 210s to *Flygvapnet* (Swedish Air Force) were reflected in a preliminary plan, dated 12 July 1941. It was envisaged that the light bomber Wings F-7 and F-14 would receive Me 210s, or the indigenous Saab B 18. Two prototypes of the B 18 were flying by mid-1942, with an initial production order for sixty-two B 18As, powered by two Pratt & Whitney Twin Wasp engines, being placed in June of that year.

The sole Me 210 supplied to Japan for evaluation. (*Author's collection*)

Nevertheless, negotiations for Me 210s continued, as well as obtaining a licence agreement for the DB 605 engine. If these negotiations had been successful, it was estimated that only ninety-six B 18s would be built before being replaced on the Saab production line by the Me 210. In the event, no Me 210s reached *Flygvapnet*. The DB 605 engine was, however, built under licence in Sweden, powering both the B 18B bomber and J 21A fighter.

Me 210A-1 Technical Data and Performance Characteristics

Engines: two 1,350-hp DB 601 F
Wingspan: 16.40 m
Length: 12.15 m
Height: 3.70 m
Wing area: 36.20 m^2
Empty weight: 7,270 kg
Maximum weight: 9,690 kg (Destroyer)
Maximum speed: 573 kph at 5,900 m (Destroyer)
Range: 1,820 km (Destroyer)
Service ceiling: 9,150 m
Armament: two 13-mm MG 131 machine guns in remote-controlled barbettes; 1,000-kg bombs

Messerschmitt Me 210 variants

Me 210A-0: Pre-production variant.

Me 210A-1: *Zerstörer* variant. The armament consisted of two forward-firing 20-mm MG 151/20 cannons, two 7.9-mm MG 17 machine guns, and two 13-mm MG 131 mounted in remote control barbettes.

Me 210A-2: Proposed fighter-bomber variant. The armament was remain the same as that of the Me 210A-1. Additionally, two 500-kg bombs could be carried in an internal bomb bay, with two more 500-kg bombs on external underwing bomb racks. Bombs weighing 250 kg or 1,000 kg could also be carried on the external bomb racks.

Me 210B-0: Pre-production photographic reconnaissance variant. Two converted from Me 210A-1s.

Me 210B-1: Photographic reconnaissance variant, only two built. The MG 17 machine guns were removed, with a pair of Rb 75/30, Rb 50/30 or Rb 20/30 cameras being fitted in their place. Armament consisted of one MG 151 and one MG 151/20. Both machine guns were forward-firing. Six LC 50 F or ETC 50 bombs could be carried. In addition, two 900-litre auxiliary fuel tanks were fitted, replacing the internal fuselage tank.

Me 210B-2: Similar in most respects to the Me 210B-1, except for the provision of a motorised hand camera. Additionally, two SC 250 bombs could be carried.

Me 210C-1: Powered by DB 605 B engines with MW-1 boost. Conversions of previous variants. One 1,800 kg bomb could be carried externally.

Me 210Ca-1: Built under licence in Hungary. The 'a' suffix indicated *ausland* (foreign). Powered by two 1,475-hp DB 605 B engines. Also had different radio equipment. Three sub-variants of the basic Me 210Ca-1 were proposed: heavy fighter, night fighter, and command platform. Although none of these variants entered production, some design and development work was initiated.

Me 210C-2: Powered by DB 605 B engine with MW 1 boost. Conversions of previous variants. Had the ability to carry one SC 1800 bomb.

Me 210D-1: Photographic reconnaissance variant. Powered by DB 605 B engines with MW 1 boost. The Me 410 V17 was converted as the sole Me 210D-1, with other conversions remaining unconfirmed. Armament consisted of two MG 151s and two MG 131s. One Rb 20/50 or two Rb 75/50 cameras carried in bomb bay.

Me 210Da-1: Photographic reconnaissance variant based on the Me 210Ca-1. Powered by DB 605 B engines with MW 1 boost. Two aircraft, s/nos Z006 and 007, were converted. The forward-firing armament consisted of two MG 151s and two MG 131s. One Rb 20/50 or two Rb 75/50 cameras carried in bomb bay.

Me 210E-1: *Zerstörer* and dive bomber, based on the Me 210A-1. Only one (Me 210 W Nr 027) converted. Was to have been powered by DB 603 engines. The future Me 410 was based on the Me 210E-1.

Me 210F-1: Photographic reconnaissance variant, based on the Me 210B-1. Project only. Was to have been powered by DB 603 engines.

Me 210F-2: Photographic reconnaissance variant, based on the Me 210B-2. Project only. Was to have been powered by DB 603 engines.

Me 210S-1: Ground attack variant with armour protection in cockpit, bomb bay, engines and oil radiators. Similar in appearance to the Me 210A-1. The bomb load was to have consisted of one 500-kg bomb or two 250-kg bombs carried in the internal bomb bay and ninety-six SD 2 anti-personnel bombs carried externally. The fuel capacity was to have been reduced by deleting the pair of 170-litre capacity tanks in the outer wings. The armour protection was to include crew positions, engines, radiators, and undercarriage. This subsequently became standard for the Me 410. Project only.

Me 210S-2: DB 605 engines Similar to the Me 210S-1, but was to have been powered by DB 605 engines.

Me 210 Conversion trainer: Some forty-eight war-weary Me 210s were converted by Blohm & Voss into three-seat conversion trainers. The forward-firing armament was removed, with a third seat and double set of flight controls fitted. One had been delivered in January 1944 (against a planned five examples), with a total of sixteen having been delivered by 31 March 1944. This was below expectations, with twenty-six having been planned for delivery by this date.

10

The Messerschmitt Me 310

With the Me 210 proving a disappointment, a developed variant fitted with a pressurised cabin, a high aspect ratio wing, four-blade propellers and more powerful 1,750-hp DB 603 A engines was proposed. To a large extent based on the Me 210E-1, albeit having a longer fuselage, the resulting aircraft was designated Me 310. The new aircraft was anticipated to have a maximum speed of 660 kph (419 mph) and a service ceiling of 11,000 metres (36,090 feet). The Me 210 V13 was subsequently modified with a pressurised cabin and four-blade propellers. The first flight occurred on 11 September 1943. However, the Me 310 progressed no further. Instead, a rather less radical solution was put forward, resulting in the Me 410.

Me 310 Technical Data and Performance Characteristics

Engines: two 1,750-hp DB 603 A
Wingspan: 17.90 m
Length: 12.20 m
Height: 4.30 m
Wing area: 37.70 m²
Empty weight: N/A
Maximum weight: 11,050 kg
Maximum speed: 660 kph
Range: 1,900 km
Service ceiling: 11,000 m
Armament: two forward-firing 20-mm MG 151/20 cannons, two forward-firing 7.92-mm MG 17 machine guns, and two 13-mm MG 131 machine guns in remote-controlled barbettes

The Me 210 V13 was modified with a pressurized cabin and four-bladed propellers. It underwent brief flight tests as the Me 310 V1. A Bf 110 and Bf 109 can be seen in the background. (*Wolfgang Mühlbauer/DEHLA Archives*)

A full-frontal view of the Me 310 V1. According to German records, this aircraft carried the code letters SI+SQ. However, the letter 'G' can clearly be seen beneath the right wing, and 'Q', or possibly 'O' beneath the left wing. (*Wolfgang Mühlbauer/DEHLA Archives*)

11
The Messerschmitt Me 410

With the troublesome Me 210 providing both Messerschmitt and the Luftwaffe with severe problems, something had to be done to rectify this very serious matter. With the decision to develop the basic Me 210 airframe into a more acceptable combat aircraft, Waldemar Voigt was appointed as chief designer. In the event, the redesign and re-entry into service of the twin-engined *Zerstörer* was to last almost exactly nine months. Interestingly, the Me 410 was one of only a select few Luftwaffe aircraft to receive names, with the Me 410 being unofficially known as the *Hornisse* (Hornet). Incidentally, the unit insignia of the Me 410-equipped II./ZG 26 was a hornet, resulting in the unit being widely publicised in Nazi propaganda as the *Hornissengruppe* (Hornet Group).

The Me 410 V1, which was a modified Me 210A-0 (coded DI+NW), first flew in early 1942. As related above, the most noticeable changes included fitting a lengthened rear fuselage, with the sweepback of the outer wings being reduced. Additionally, the geometry of the flaps was modified, with the radiator flaps and ailerons being redesigned.

The engine chosen for the new Me 410 was the liquid-cooled twelve-cylinder inverted V12 Daimler-Benz DB 603. Other aircraft powered by the DB 603 included the Dornier Do 217M and 217N variants, the Dornier Do 335, the Heinkel He 219, and the Focke-Wulf Ta 152C. Nevertheless, following a period of intense redesign, constructing new jigs, and otherwise preparing the new aircraft for production, the first five Me 410s were delivered on 8 December 1942. In January 1943, the *Erprobungsstaffel* 410 was formed. Based at Lechfeld, the role of *Erprobungsstaffel* 410 was to evaluate and prepare the Me 410 for combat operations.

The Commander of E-Stelle Rechlin, Obstlt Edgar Petersen, had submitted a positive report on the improved handling characteristics of the modified Me 210. With the necessary redesign of the airframe implemented, the aircraft re-entered production. There was a difference, though. With the Me 210 having acquired an extremely difficult-to-erase reputation for being a substandard combat aeroplane, it was redesignated as the Me 410. Although the Me 410 was externally similar to its predecessor, it was to all intents and purposes a new type of aircraft.

With Petersen having stated that no fewer than 210 Me 410s would be available for a daylight bombing campaign of Britain by December 1942, this proved overly optimistic. In the event, the baptism of fire for the Me 410 would not take place until the summer of 1943.

Two views of the Me 410 V1. On the second photo, the pieces of wool tufts attached to the wings to check the airflow are clearly visible. (*Wolfgang Mühlbauer/DEHLA Archives*)

Due to its high speed, the Me 410 was considered to be a '*Schnellbomber*' (fast bomber). However, Luftwaffe operations had, by this time, been forced to change emphasis from offensive to defensive operations.

From 4 July 1942, USAAF heavy bombers were beginning to appear in steadily increasing numbers over German-occupied Europe, as well as over Germany itself. What was required was a twin-engined heavily armed fighter able to knock down bombers. With its speed and load-carrying capability, the Me 410 fitted the bill.

In the event, the Me 410 would not only serve with the *Zerstörer* units fighting against USAAF heavy bombers, but also as an intruder and reconnaissance aircraft over southern England, as well as with reconnaissance units in Italy, France, and Germany. During the latter stages of the war, a few *Seenotstaffeln* involved in maritime operations in the North Sea Baltic Sea coasts were equipped with Me 410s. In late 1944, the Norwegian-based 10./ZG 26 received a few Me 410s.

First of all, we will look at the Me 410 operations against USAAF heavy bombers.

An early-production Me 410, W Nr 10046, GH+YK. Note that the background has been heavily retouched. (*NMUSAF*)

12

The Me 410: Into Service

With USAAF heavy bombers starting to appear in German airspace in 1943, a special *Luftflotte*, *Reichsverteidigung* (Defence of the Nation), was established. The four-engined B-17 Flying Fortresses and B-24 Liberators were known as '*Dicke Autos*' (fat cars) or '*Viermots*' (short for 'four engines'), while the escorting P-38 Lightnings, P-47 Thunderbolts, and P-51 Mustangs were referred to as '*Kleine Indianer*' (little Indians).

Having converted to the Me 410, I./KG 51 flew their first sortie on 6 September 1943. A total of 334 B-17 Fortresses attacked Stuttgart. However, the raid was a failure due to poor weather, resulting in the USAAF formations being scattered over a wide area. Only one B-17 was claimed by a Me 410, with I./KG 51 losing one aircraft.

This inauspicious beginning did not improve significantly, with the *Gruppenkommendeur* of I./KG 51, Major Klaus Haeberlein, telling *Reichsmarschall* Göring during an official visit in October that the Me 410 did not have sufficient high-altitude performance to catch the high-flying Americans. This was partly due to the reduced performance of the DB 603 engine when operating at such altitudes. Göring subsequently accused Haeberlein of 'cowardice', relieving him of his command.

One Me 410 pilot, Oblt Fritz Stehle, later recalled:

> You really had to work on those bombers; it was very seldom that you knocked one down with the first burst ... Though it was much better than the Me 110, the Me 410 was still not good enough. It was too heavy and not manoeuvrable enough. And carrying full armament its overtaking speed on a bomber formation was so low that it took a long time to get into a firing position. If Me 410s were caught by enemy escorts they were in almost as difficult [a] position as the Me 110s. If your Me 410 was attacked by a Mustang you could only pray. And hope your gunner shot well! ... My Viennese gunner, Feldwebel Alois Slaby, was very experienced and knew exactly when the enemy fighter was about to open fire. He would say 'Not yet, not yet,—NOW!' and I would chop the throttles and the Me 410 would decelerate rapidly; if we were lucky the enemy fighter would go screaming past. Or sometimes I would put the Me 410 into a skid with the wings level and the enemy rounds would flash past the wingtip. We knew if we could buy a little time that often meant survival; once American escorts had dropped their (external drop) tanks they could not fight long near Berlin, before

Me 410A-1 PP+VO (W Nr 420.098) seen at Augsburg-Haunstetten soon after completion. (*Wolfgang Mühlbauer/DEHLA Archives*)

> they had to break off and head for home. But the Me 410 was useless as a dogfighter, it could not turn or do anything like that. We felt as if we had been entered for the Kentucky Derby on a carthorse![1]

During his Luftwaffe career, Stehle shot down a total of twenty-two aircraft, including three B-17s and three B-24s while serving with 5./ZG 26. In late summer 1944, Stehle was transferred to JG 6. During the later stages of the war, he flew Messerschmitt Me 262 jet fighters with JG 7, scoring one Russian Yak-9 shot down on 8 May 1945. This was reputedly the final Luftwaffe aerial victory of the war.

Prior to his posting to II./ZG 26, in late 1943, Fw Fritz Buchholz was a flight instructor:

> There came the day when Göring remarked, at some airfield in north Germany, that he would make use of the instructors from the flying schools if the rate of success in shooting down enemy aircraft did not improve. In accordance to this reasoning I was, together with about ten other instructors, posted to ZG 76 in the Reich Air Defence. There they were baffled by this new fangled and wasteful idea and, after some checking back, directed us to the *Zerstörer* school at Bad Aibling. Here we were rushed through our training in a special course ... I was then posted with two other instructors via the Replacement *Gruppe* Braunschweig to II./ZG 26 (of Hptm Eduard Tratt) at Hildesheim. My joy to have achieved my dream of becoming

operational at last soon received a damper. We former instructors did not feel welcome in the community of this suicide commando. Some bright spark had had the absurd idea to convert the Me 410 to a single-seater. By dispensing with the radio operator, the radio gear and the rearward guns, they thought to make the machine so fast that attacks from behind no longer needed to be considered.

What a deadly error! The proponents of this idea soon found that the extra 20 km/h was not enough to make up for the experienced eyes of a rear gunner and the moral effect of having the guns. To place the meanwhile despised aircraft in the hands of us instrument flyers crowned it all. I flew my first sortie on 11 February 1944, led by Hptm Tratt; as newcomer at the tail-end of course (incidentally a wonderful feeling). Our formation consisted of 12 aircraft. We met up with a bunch of Me 110s and went onto SW course trailing long condensation trails. For Hptm Tratt our retarded progress due to the slower Me 110 soon got too boring and he increased power in order to make sure of catching the 'Fat Cars' on their way home. Meanwhile I had moved up to nr. 4; the others had taken their leave because of 'lame horses' etc. I had no radio contact, only concentration on keeping good formation (Hptm Tratt) was very critical in this respect) and awaited the things to come. Vibration in

A Me 410 seen following a forced landing. The forward fuselage has been covered with a tarpaulin, with a mechanic attaching it to the gun barbette. The code letter 'F' can be clearly be read, followed by a very faint 'X'. Unfortunately, the exact circumstances behind this incident are unknown. The NMUSAF caption states: 'Unintelligible German writing on caption'. (*NMUSAF*)

the starboard engine tore me from my dreams. I went spiralling down (full power on the port engine and idling with the starboard), trailing white smoke. The white snowscape offered no means of orientation. So I 'got myself a ticket' (a pinpoint fix) at the railway station of Bad Kreuznach and swindled myself to Wiesbaden-Erbenheim on one engine and a red light. In the evening my kite was serviceable again. Flying Control did not want to allow me to take off for Hildesheim because of snow showers and clouds covering the Taunus hills. I showed them my instrument rating and my last piece of chocolate helped me to secure permission for take-off. I took off at 1630 hours, pulled up and flew above the clouds in the direction of home. After my calculated time had elapsed, I went down through a fortuitously discovered gap in the clouds. I was swallowed up by the dark and the Mittelland Canal became my saviour, enabling me to find Hannover and the railway line to Hildesheim. In a two-seater with radio operator this flight would have been easy. The single-seater made it punishable carelessness. I was cured. Hptm Tratt was already back with two or three more Lightnings shot down. His wingman was down on his belly at Hanau.

After further more or less successful operations with and without 'Dödel' we were reequipped at Oberpfaffenhausen with new aircraft mounting a 5 cm cannon. The BK 5 weighed some 1600 kg and made the Me 410 very clumsy, supposedly had a recoil of seven tons, had a magazine of 21 rounds which were mounted in a ring around the breech and were fed by compressed air. After this re-equipment we were moved, because of enemy fighter cover, to Königsberg/Oder. From there we operated, partly with fighter escort, against all attacks on the Reich from the Baltic to Bavaria and Silesia. The BK 5 was a dangerous weapon with its high-explosive mine ammunition. Bombers hit with it burst like a balloon, but, due to its fast and far-reaching trajectory and telescopic sight, there was the temptation to commence an attack too soon. Apart from that, it mostly jammed after the first or second shot, and this could not be rectified during flight. The successes did not reach the hoped for expectations. Added to which we lost the most successful *Zerstörer* commander, Hptm Tratt. He was shot down (on 22 February 1944) during a daring single-handed attack on a bomber formation over Nordhausen. Oblt Prokopp, the only witness, was some time later, while flying beside me, rammed by a Thunderbolt and killed.

Lt (Rudi) Dassow, dissatisfied with the poor results with his BK 5, had eight 2 cm cannon mounted in the nose of his aircraft. It was a pleasure to see his successes with that lot. With that 'watering can' missing was impossible. Re-equipment of this sort might have resulted in a reprieve for the already doomed Me 410, for the losses were out of all proportion to the successes. When the bomber formations got the idea to drop their bombs through a complete cloud cover and the *Zerstörer* units were unable to take off due to bad weather and the lack of instrument flying training, a six-seater Junkers W 34 crew trainer was quickly obtained and I had to instruct the flight leaders in instrument flying in between sorties. On occasion it also happened that I led the formation through the cloud layers and then handed over to the formation leader. When however the 'Red Indians' had got onto our formation, all closed up wingtip to wingtip and a change of position was no longer possible. Then it was mostly course east, descending fast, full throttle and avoiding clouds whilst speeding towards home. Many comrades were shot down under such circumstances. In view of the burning comrades who were no longer to be helped, I frequently pulled back the stick and swung myself sidewards into the clouds. Using the direction indicator of the airfield radio beacon I then got home along the shortest route. My instinct for self-preservation was not of course welcomed by the *Gruppe*, but I had damned little inclination to go to the dogs because of the inability of others in instrument flying, especially as I had seen far worse examples.

On 29 June 1944 for example, we were directed to a bomber formation in the area of Dessau. We flew at 8,000 m, when suddenly I saw the bombers below me flying at 6,000 m and called: 'Fat Cars to starboard' and turned on my guns. For a while nothing happened. Suddenly the tails rose and in an almost vertical dive and an impossible angle for firing we went through the formation in the direction of home. I pulled up again, followed by eight others, and tried to get at the bomber stream from head-on. Due to the lengthy overtaking process the enemy fighter relief came along and prevented a second attack. I dived into cloud with the others and landed under Flak fire at Magdeburg-East. At the evening debriefing I was the whipping boy because a) I had not reported: 'Fat Cars below us', (which for me, due to the known height difference, was obvious) and b) had broken off the second attack. The fact that the commander of the *Gruppe* with about 20 aircraft had gone home after the botched first attack (without fighter defence) was played down.

On 13 June 1944 we were directed onto a bomber stream consisting of Liberators flying on a south-east course over the Baltic. Having made out the bombers, we flew on a parallell course within sight of the formations, even though no 'Red Indians' were to be seen, until east of Frankfurt/Oder. From base we received the report: 'Hanni (height) 8,000, course south-east.' After a few minutes we were attacked by 20 Mustangs. I was forced to bail out and my parachute opened over the military exercise area at Reppen. That evening 12 Me 410s had to be struck off the list of available aircraft. The Liberators were able to bomb the factory at Posen undisturbed.

Our engineers had fitted the valuable aircraft clocks with a hinge and a nail in order to enable pilots to pocket the timekeepers before baling out. I have never seen a clock which had been saved by this method. In August 1944 we converted to Fw 190s and were renumbered II./JG 6.[2]

Another Bf 110 and Me 410 pilot of ZG 76, Walter Ibold, later recalled these operations:

[In early 1944] we had taken over the Me 410 in Prague. During this time I flew some 25 to 30 sorties with two *Viermots* confirmed shot down, two Mustangs damaged in air combat and three other indecisive combats. I was shot down twice, once I had to crash-land near Ingolstadt with a hard belly landing. Helmut and I had been lucky again. On our first sortie over Hungary there were Viermot formations flying in from the south. During my first attack I was able to finish off a Boeing, it was already damaged. On our return flight we were chased by two Mustangs. They came closer but did not fire, they had probably exhausted their ammunition. One of them flew in a curve to dead ahead of my Me 410, the pilot waved and I instinctively pressed my firing button. He burst apart. I could weep even today when I think about it.

We handed over our Me 410s after our operations over Slovakia (in July 1944) and proceeded to fly some training sorties in Me 109s at Bonn-Hangelar.[3]

On 20 February 1944, the 8th AF began Operation Argument, a series of raids against aircraft manufacturing plants in Northern Germany and occupied Poland. More than 1,000 heavy

A line-up of Me 410s of an unknown unit. (*Wolfgang Mühlbauer/DEHLA Archives*)

bombers were involved. Only twenty-one USAAF bombers were lost, with the Luftwaffe losing more than fifty single-seat fighters and twenty-five Bf 110s and Me 410s. One of the Me 410s lost was W Nr 420.037 of 6./ZG 26, shot down over the Isle of Fyn, Denmark. During the intercept, Obfw Siegfried Haase and Uffz Fritz Schröter's aircraft was hit by return fire from the USAAF bombers. Both Haase and Schröter baled out of their stricken aircraft, with the Me 410 coming down in a farmer's field east of Faaborg. Haase had suffered a slight head injury, being taken to hospital. Uffz Schröter's parachute failed to deploy, and he was killed on impact.

This particular crash has an interesting postscript, which clearly shows the attitude of the German troops in occupied territories. A Danish farmhand picked up Schröter's wristwatch, lying close to the body of the German airman, and handed it over to a nearby German soldier. The farmhand was immediately arrested for attemting to steal the watch, being sentenced to one year in prison. He was then transferred to a prison at Rendsburg in Northern Germany, not being released until the summer of 1945, weeks after the end of the war.

On 6 March 1944, the first large-scale USAAF raid against Berlin took place. The raid saw 814 (702 effective) B-17s and B-24s, escorted by 943 (832 effective) fighters strike against the German capitol. On this day, II./ZG 26 had a dozen Me 410s based at Hildesheim, and EKdo 25 five Me 410s at Achmer. In comparison, the Luftwaffe fighter force available included some 450 Bf 109s, 180 Fw 190s, and no fewer than 237 Bf 110s, with many of the latter belonging to nightfighter units.

Led by Oblt Stehle, ten of the II./ZG 26 Me 410s took off from Hildesheim at 11.25 a.m., joining formation with thirty-three Bf 110s of III./ZG 26, I./ZG 76, and II./ZG 76, and seventy-two Bf 109s and Fw 190s over Magdeburg, south-west of Berlin. The Me 410s were

A Me 410 is prepared for towing. The aircraft is most likely coded PP+VO. (*Wolfgang Mühlbauer/ DEHLA Archives*)

armed with four 21-cm rockets each. Having spotted the rapidly approaching bombers, the Luftwaffe pilots prepared themselves for battle. Just as the Luftwaffe fighters closed in for the attack, thirty-three P-51 Mustangs of the 357th FG appeared, seemingly out of the blue. Other USAAF fighters were flying high above the bombers, out of sight for the Luftwaffe pilots. At 12.42 p.m., the *Zerstörer* units attacked the USAAF formation over Tangerhütte, 12 km north of Magdeburg.

The Me 410 pilots fired off their 21-cm rockets, also raking the bombers with cannon fire. Oblt Stehle's aircraft passed very close to a B-17, with Stehle's radio operator/gunner, Fw Alois Slaby, being able to hear the roar of the engines of the USAAF bomber. During the second firing pass, Slaby saw a Me 410 flown by Fw Willi Bonnecke collide in mid-air with a B-17. The out-of-control Fortress struck another B-17, with both aircraft being destroyed. Whether Bonnecke hit the USAAF bomber by accident or intent has never been established.

The action against the USAAF formation lasted about twenty-five minutes. During this time, II./ZG 26 lost six Me 410As, with a seventh aircraft being severely damaged. Three pilots/ radio operators had been killed with another four wounded. All in all, it was a disaster for II./ZG 26. Other Luftwaffe losses during the battle included ten Bf 110s shot down and two more damaged, as well as five Bf 109s and two Fw 190s shot down.

The USAAF had lost eleven B-17s (including eight shot down and three in mid-air collisions) and four P-51 Mustangs.

After dropping their bombs over Berlin, the USAAF formation turned westward. At 2 p.m., a Me 210 of *Luftbeobachtungsstaffel* 2 took off from Stade, joining the USAAF bombers near Hannover, shadowing them on their way back to East Anglia, reporting course and altitude to ground stations.

In April 1944, the *Erprobungskommando* 410 was evaluating the Me 410 as a night fighter. In the event, no Me 410s were used operationally by the *Nachtjagdgeschwadern*, albeit a few aircraft were formally on charge with I.NJG 5. In this context, mention must be made of frequent sightings made by RAF bomber crews in 1943–44 of 'Me 210s' performing night interceptions. This included the massive raid against Nuremberg on 30–31 March 1944, where a Me 210 was reported to have damaged an engine of P/O Cyril Barton's Halifax. However, in all likelihood, these sightings were erroneous. Misidentification with the similarly configured Junkers Ju 88C was most likely to blame.[4]

On 11 April 1944, an incident with a tragic result took place when a Me 410B-1 of 8./ ZG 76 was shot down by Swedish anti-aircraft artillery (W Nr 420622). The aircraft was approaching the airfield with undercarriage down, with the engines loudly backfiring. The anti-aircraft gunners misinterpreted the noise of the backfiring engines with gunfire, and opened fire against the Me 410.

Luftwaffe Me 410 units, 31 May 1944

I./ZG 26 20 (six serviceable)
II./ZG 26 52 (twenty-four serviceable)
I./ZG 76 47 (twenty-five serviceable)
II./ZG 76 36 (none serviceable) forming
I./KG 51 0 (none serviceable) forming
IV./KG 51 12 (five serviceable)
II./KG 51 24 (seventeen serviceable)
FAGr. 121 9 (three serviceable)
FAGr. 122 8 (four serviceable)

Above and below: The remains of Me 410B-1 from 8./ZG 76 seen after being shot down by Swedish Flak on 11 April 1944. (*Bengt Hermansson/Forced Landing Collection*)

13
A Famous Photo

One much-published photograph shows a Me 410 peeling away from a B-17. The date, location, and identity of the Me 410 and B-17 has been previously often been incorrectly identified. This famous photo was in fact taken on 12 May 1944 during the raid against Brüx by 1Lt Victor LaBruno of the 388 BG. The Me 410 was flown by Lt Paul Kaschuba of (Z)./EKdo 25.

Since 1942, the *Sudetenländische Treibstoffwerke* AG had produced synthetic fuel at Brüx. On this day, the USAAF began a bombing campaign against the German oil and petroleum industry. Among the 470 Luftwaffe fighters that saw action that day were *Zerstörers* of I./ZG 26 and II./ZG 26 as well as two Me 410s from the *Erprobungskommando* 25. Following the end of the war, Brüx returned to Czech control, being renamed as Most.

Born on 22 February 1922 in the small village of Tost near Gleiwitz (present-day Gliwice in southern Poland), Paul Kaschuba joined the Luftwaffe in late 1940. Having received training as a fighter pilot, *Leutnant* Kaschuba was assigned to (Z)./EKdo 25 on 2 May 1943. This *Zerstörer* Staffel was involved in testing different types of weaponry, from cannons to unguided rockets, designed to bring down USAAF heavy bombers. While serving with (Z)./EKdo 25, Lt Kaschuba flew at least twenty-five operational sorties against USAAF bombers. On 8 October 1943, Lt Kaschuba shot down a B-24 Liberator. Two days later, he was himself shot down over Osnabruck. During a visit to Achmer on 17 November by Hermann Göring and the *General der Jagdflieger* Adolf Galland, Lt Kaschuba was awarded the *Eisernes Kreuz zweiter Klasse* (Iron Cross Second Class, EK II). Exact details of Kaschuba's subsequent combat career are sparse, but on 19 January 1944, he was awarded the *Frontflugspange* in Bronze (Fighter pilot's Bronze combat clasp), signifying twenty-five combat sorties.

One difference was that the Me 410s of (Z)./EKdo 25 and those of other units was that the former did not have the BK 5 cannon fitted. Instead, their main armament consisted of the 37-mm Flak 43 cannon. The Flak 43 was a development of the FlaK 18, featuring an increased rate of fire. Externally, the Flak 43 differed slightly from the BK 5 cannon, having a longer barrel and wider muzzle brake. A telescopic gun sight, the *Zielfernrohr* ZFR 4a, was also fitted. By April 1944, several of the (Z)./EKdo 25 Me 410s had been fitted with a Flak 43 cannon with a ZFR 4a. That same month, two of these Me 410s were transferred to II./

The last moments of *Leutnant* Paul Kaschuba and Fw Karl Bredemeyer. Taken on 11 May 1944, this photo was released to the press on 6 June. (*National Archives (NARA) via Robert Pęczkowski*)

ZG 26 for further operational testing. It is likely that the aircraft of II./ZG 26 were of the Me 410A-1/U4 variant, armed with the 50-mm BK 5 cannon.

On 12 May 1944, the two EKdo 25 Me 410s temporarily assigned to II./ZG 26 took part in intercepting a heavy USAAF raid directed against the German oil and petroleum industry. One of these was flown by Lt Paul Kaschuba and his *Bordfunker* (radio operator/gunner), Fw Karl Bredemeyer, were flying Me 410A-1/U4 W Nr 10241. This particular aircraft had originally been constructed as an Me 210, later being rebuilt as an Me 410.

The targets included five plants and refineries producing synthetic fuel, with the USAAF's 8th AF committing 621 B-17 Flying Fortresses and 265 B-24 Liberators, escorted by 735 fighters. This was the first USAAF raid against the German oil industry.

The Luftwaffe's response included some 470 single-seat fighters and fifty-one twin-engined *Zerstörers* (including both Bf 110s and Me 410s). On this day, II./ZG 26 had about thirty Me 410s based at Königsberg-Neumark. Regarding the other two ZG 26 *Gruppen*, I./ZG 26 at Gabbert did not have a single serviceable aircraft, while half of the III./ZG 26 pilots had been transferred to Munich-Riem for conversion training on the Me 262.

Right: Lt Paul Kaschuba served with (Z)/ Ekdo 25 between 2 May 1943 and January 1944, completing at least twenty-five combat sorties. (*Neil Page via Kaschuba*)

Below: On 17 November 1943, *General der Jagdflieger* Adolf Galland visited Achmer. He is seen here shaking hands with Lt Paul Kaschuba, who on this day received the Iron Cross Second Class. (*Neil Page via Kaschuba*)

The aerial combat actions on 12 May were intense, with many casualties on both sides. During the raid, the USAAF lost forty-three B-17 Flying Fortresses, three B-24 Liberators, four P-47 Thunderbolts, and three P-51 Mustangs. Although several claims were filed, it would appear that only a single heavy bomber, a B-17G of the 452nd BG, was shot down by a Me 410. Nearly 100 Luftwaffe aircraft were destroyed or damaged, with many aircrew being killed or wounded. II./ZG 26 lost four Me 410s with another six sustaining varying degrees of damage. (Z)./EKdo 25 lost one Me 410, with the second aircraft landing at Parchim, reporting problems with its Flak 43 cannon. The Me 410 that was shot down was flown by Lt Paul Kaschuba. Through years of diligent research, Dr Gerhard Kaschuba was finally able to piece together what had happened to his uncle.

A post-mission report provided an emotional insight into the last moments of Kaschuba and Bredemeyer:

> I [Manuel Head] was a 1st Lt and pilot in the 388th BG. Our ship was named 'Lady Godiva' because it wore no camouflage paint. As I recall the 388th BG was attacked from the rear—I saw nothing of the combat with the exception of this Me 410 peeling away just off my starboard wing. I well remember my exclamation, 'what the hell is he doing here?!' and in a fraction of a second he was gone. Victor LaBruno took the pic from the right hand window in the radio compartment. Eugene Crossin in the upper turret told me later that his tracers poured into the belly of the Me 410 and a 'kill' was subsequently credited to him. Another crew member recalled how the Me 410 streamed a trail of smoke as it dove away.[1]

An excellent view of Me 410 W Nr 10241, which was flown by Lt Paul Kaschuba and Fw Karl Bredemeyer on their last flight on 11 May 1944. (*Neil Page via Kaschuba*)

One II./ZG 26 pilot who took part in the fight, *Gefreiter* Richard Wilde, later stated:

> The sortie was flown at noon. My position in our formation was immediately to the right of the *Gruppenkommendeur*. When we caught sight of the bomber formation, we were heading on a southernly course. The bomber formation was flying about 500 metres lower down and heading west. The *Kommandeur*, *Haupmann* Günther Weyl, set up the attack by bringing us in behind the B-17s on a wide curving right-hand turn with a slight height advantage allowing for accurate firing. Following a corresponding order, he broke his own attack very early, while the rest of the group continued the attack to the closest range. During our closing approach my right neighbour caught fire. Dark red flames with a deep black smoke appeared in the front under the hull. The flames billowed out about one or two fuselage lengths behind the tailplane. Almost certainly the cannon rounds were burning which also happened to me shortly thereafter. As I recall the aircraft peeled away to the right with a half-roll. I managed seven or eight firing rounds with the heavy cannon on the approach with no problems. Not a single jam. Even the smaller cannon worked well that day. I could see the impacts of my firing on the right inboard engine of the B-17 and now fired the cannon hoping for a direct hit in the fuselage. As I was attacking I took numerous hits as we closed in. I could see their impacts and see their effects on the port wing. There were streaks of oil around the port engine. Above the din, my radio operator, Karl Lapsie, shouted that very hot oil was coming into his compartment, burning his legs. As I continued my attack, oily smoke started to fill the cabin, hampering my vision. As I unleashed my last cannon shell, flames erupted in the cockpit. We had to get out. We were right alongside the B-17's huge tail fin when I rolled the aircraft away to port, jettisoning the canopy at the same time. Karl Lapsie must have been torn out by the slipstream. While I threw off my straps and unplugged the ooxygen and cable connections, the machine went over in a steep dive, quickly picking up speed. The negative G was pinning me down, so I had to pull the plane up again, despite the fire, before I could pull myself up out of my seat. As I fell away from the machine I pulled the ripchord but as my chute deployed I could see that it was largely burned away—large sheets of silk flapped wildly on the lines. Because I was falling too fast, the impact when it came was very heavy, resulting in three vertebrae fracturing. I was unable to move. The burning rubber from my life jacket and lifeboat set the surrounding grass on fire. I had come down in a wood near a small dam at Scheibe-Alsbach and was taken to the *Reservelazarett* (Auxiliary hospital) in Sonneberg. Karl Lapsie also came down with his chute intact at Scheibe-Alsbach in a heavily wooded area. In the hospital I was told that he must have fallen into the crown of a very tall tree. The branches at the top were broken away. Karl must have fallen and plunged to the ground. The immediate cause of death was a broken neck, but he also had severe burns.[2]

Gefreiter Hans Steckler later recalled the sortie:

> I was a *Gefreiter* and *Bordfunker* in 4. *Staffel*. My pilot was Lt. Günther Schmale. Schmale and I had got through the first attack of our *Gruppe* on the Flying Fortresses unscathed. Afterwards, some of our machines dormed up again and we closed on the bomber formation once again with some four to six aircraft. It was what you would describe today as the height of insanity! In the midst of heavy defensive fire from the bombers, I suddenly heard an

explosion in the front cockpit. The pilot screamed out. Then the machine plummeted sharply downwards. I quickly jettisoned the cabin roof, and, as the machine's rate of descent appeared to ease a little, took the opportunity to jump clear. I quickly tugged on the ripchord and then swung under the chute for quite a while. Finally I landed in a meadow near Veilsdorf. I was received by the country population with initial hostility as they thought I was an American. I was eventually taken by car to the hospital in Hildburghausen. While my pilot had taken an explosive round in the stomach, I had only minor injuries. Schmale failed to get out of the aircraft and the Me 410 was completely destroyed on impact with the ground.[3]

Yet another II./ZG 26 Me 410 *Bordfunker* that saw combat that day was Walter Fritz:

I belonged to 6. *Staffel* and was *Bordfunker* to Uffz. Otto Höllinger. When we sighted the Fortress formations in the Dresden area, *Hauptmann* Weyl called out over the radio 'Pauke-Pauke'—the code word to attack—and ordered us to re-assemble 1,000 metres below the bombers. Otto Höllinger loosed off some shells from the BK 5 and we made a split-S very early on behind the American formation. I recall now what Fritz Buchholz did. He went straight back into the climb and launched a second attack from below the bombers. Two other Me 410s—without the BK 5—closed up as the No. 3 and 4, and Fritz Buchholz led the Schwarm into the second attack. I had time to look around several times, since we encountered no Indians (US fighters) in the skies on this mission. We climbed from below into the bombers, Otto firing only with his 2 cm weapons. We were very close to the formation

Another view of Me 410 W Nr 10241. (*Neil Page via Kaschuba*)

> by this stage and Otto shouted out, 'hits in the outer port engine which is burning and hits in the inboard port engine'. Suddenly above me loomed the lower fuselage of a Fortress, very close and large. By now we were in trouble—on the starboard wing I could see three or four big holes and then a stream of white smoke formed. Our starboard engine was on fire. As we dove away I heard Otto call out over the FT (radio telephone): '*Aussteigen*!' Get out. Because of the G-force I had the greatest difficulty unfastening my belt straps. Otto, however, was able to pull the machine up—we were already very low. At that point I threw off the cabin roof and went out. According to eyewitness reports—there were soldiers nearby—we were lower than 200 m. After the chute deployed, I came down on the edge of a wood near Gerstungen an der Werra, landing on my side. The left side of my face was black and blue, which was later diagnosed as severe concussion. It would appear that on baling out I had struck the tail fin. The steel helmet that we wore during combat had been torn off. Otto Höllinger put the machine down for a belly landing in the vicinity of Gerstungen. In the end the damage to the aircraft was assessed as only relatively minor—about 20 per cent. There were impact holes in the wings. Otherwise the machine was in good condition. Otto Höllinger fell in combat just weeks later on another sortie.[4]

The net result of the 12 May raid was that about 25,000 tons of fuel was destroyed, with production at the various oil installations and refineries being halted or reduced to a great extent. One historian, Don Caldwell, subsequently described it as 'the worst single day of the war for Germany.'

This and subsequent raids against the oil and petrochemical industries greatly reduced the operational effectiveness of the Luftwaffe. By the end of the war, the fuel reserves had dwindled to almost nil.

It was a disastrous day on 8 July 1944 for the Me 410 *Zerstörer* units, and, in particular, I./ZG 76. On this day, units of the Italian-based 15th AF were scheduled to bomb the oil refinery at Korneuburg, Austria. The fighter escort consisted of forty-eight Lockheed P-38 Lightnings of the 82nd Fighter Group. Charles Pinson noted:

> It didn't take long to find some action as we counted 16 Me 410s below us. They were flying 90-degrees to our path, which meant they would cross in front of us. I radioed the others and told the 97th Squadron to remain with the bombers while the 95th and 96th would go after the '410s.... Fortunately for both squadrons, the Luftwaffe pilots were not expecting the P-38s to be riding point for the bombers. Another factor in this encounter was that there were also nine '109s in the area who would jump into the fight once it had started.... We went into a steep dive and as the Me 410s passed under us, we turned and hit them from the sides. Thus, we had a two-pronged pincer attack. The timing was perfect as we struck from two sides simultaneously.... We all fired as we came into range. This split the enemy formation, with eight breaking to the left and the remainder going to the right as they were making an obvious attempt to form two defensive circles. They didn't have time as we were on their tails for zero-degree deflection shots.... Every enemy aircraft had a P-38 chasing it and all of them were forced to defend themselves with evasive action. As we attacked from the right side, I set my sights of the trailing '410, which was in the third flight of their box formation. Firing at 300 yards out and closing fast, my rounds impacted on his fuselage nacelle, wing root and

A close-up of the BK 37-mm cannon, as fitted to Lt Kaschuba's Me 410. (*Neil Page via Kaschuba*)

A forward view of BK 37-mm cannon. (*Neil Page via Kaschuba*)

> fuselage, causing the rear gunner to collapse out of sight. A split second later, his engine failed and a huge puff of grey smoke shot out, followed by flames. The stricken German fighter did a 90-degree turn to the right, entering into a 60-degree diving turn. I was behind him firing short bursts at his port wing and engine. Solid hits started a fire in the engine and it began to falter.
>
> At that moment, I noticed another Me 410 coming my way with two Lightnings in hot pursuit. To keep him from firing at me with a good deflection shot, I turned into him and he passed by me with two of our guys giving chase. I did a 360-degree turn to pick up my original quarry and it was easy because of the smoke he was trailing. He was about 3,000 yards ahead of me and I followed him into a valley where he levelled off and crash-landed in a freshly-cultivated field. I turned around to get back into the action. When the mission was over and the dust had settled, the 82nd Group had scored one of its biggest days of the war. We were credited with 21 confirmed 'kills' and four 'probables'.[5]

Due to the large Me 410 losses suffered by the *Zerstörer* units between late 1943 and the summer of 1944, I./ZG 26, II./ZG 26, and ZG 76 either disbanded or converted to other types of aircraft. The Me 410 had served in the *Zerstörer* role for less than one year. It had enjoyed both successes and disasters against the USAAF bomber formations. Although heavily armed, with the BK 5 cannon in particular being able to bring down a bomber with a few rounds, the Me 410 stood little or no chance against single engine fighters such as the P-47 Thunderbolt and P-51 Mustang. On one occasion, the crew of a ZG 76 Me 410 managed to shoot down a USAAF twin-engined P-38 Lightning. However, incidents like that were exceptions, and not the rule.

Against such adversaries, the Me 410 lacked the necessary performance, being too slow and not nearly as manoeuvrable as the USAAF fighters.

On 21 July 1944, Berlin and the surrounding areas were subjected to a heavy USAAF raid, involving no fewer than 1,234 bombers and 1,269 escorting fighters. The Luftwaffe claimed to have shot down forty-four bombers. Several USAAF bombers sought refuge in neutral Sweden, including B-17G 42-38194 of the 381 BG/533 BS (named Baboon McGoon). The co-pilot of this Fortress, 2Lt R.H. Irwin, later reported: 'We were shot down by [a] Me 410 during the attack against Berlin. Our aircraft force landed in Sweden without injuries to the crew.... An Me 410 was also shot down by our crew.'

Although singular successes against USAAF B-17 Flying Fortresses and B-24 Liberators occurred, these became fewer and fewer until the summer of 1944. The days of the Me 410 *Zerstörer* were numbered. The final *Zerstörer* unit to operate the Me 410 was II./ZG 76, which between June and November 1944 was based in East Prussia.

Two II./ZG 26 Me 410s about to take off. (*Wolfgang Mühlbauer/DEHLA Archives*)

Me 410s of ZG 26. (*Wolfgang Mühlbauer/DEHLA Archives*)

14
Night Intruder Operations

Already in 1940, the Luftwaffe General Josef Kammhuber remarked: 'When I want to kill wasps, I smoke out their nest. I don't swat the insects in the air one at a time, I go to the nest when they are in!'[1]

Intruder raids over Britain, designed to search for, and if possible shoot down bombers over their own airfields, originally began in 1940, but gradually petered out the following year. It is interesting to note that Hitler was opposed to such operations 'on principle'. With the RAF and USAAF performing increasingly destructive bomb raids against Germany, the aerial defences were charged with knocking down as many bombers as possible. However, Hitler had ordered that the night fighter units would only intercept bombers over Continental Europe. Since 1940 the RAF had performed nightly raids on a regular basis against Luftwaffe airfields in France and the Low Countries, destroying a large number of aircraft, as well as disrupting operations.

By mid-1943, Kammhuber was replaced by *Generalmajor* Josef Schmid. Schmid began to consider restarting intruder operations over Britain. However, to effectively follow formations of bombers at night, new radar equipment was an absolute necessity. The Me 410 was to be one of the new intruder aircraft.

The first unit to receive Me 410s was II./KG 40, with the initial aircraft arriving in May 1943. Soon afterwards, II./KG 40 was redesignated as V./KG 2. During the night of 13–14 July, V./KG 2 was briefed to attack airfields in the Cambridge area. One Me 410A-1 of 16./KG 2 (U5+KG, W Nr 0238), flown by Fw Franz Zwissler and Obfw Leo Raida, was intercepted by an 85 Sqn Mosquito, flown by F/L E.N. Bunting and P/O F.G. French. Having caught the Me 410, Bunting and French shot down the German intruder 5 miles east of Felixstowe at 11.59 a.m. Both Zwissler and Raida were killed when their aircraft crashed into the North Sea. This was the first of many encounters between the Me 410 and the Mosquito.

A total of sixty Me 410s (including twenty-one in 1943 and thirty-nine in 1944) were destroyed RAF Mosquitoes, with another two being claimed as probables and one as damaged. The final RAF Mosquito victory over a Me 410 occured on 23–24 December 1944.

By the third week of August, V./KG 2 Me 410s had visited British shores on several occasions. In the early hours of 23 August, Me 410 U5+HF of 15./KG 2 was shot down near Ipswich by Sqn Ldr Howitt, DFC, and P/O J.C.O. Medworth of 85 Sqn.

Two SC 500 bombs being hauled aboard a Me 410. With the aircraft lacking both engine cowlings and propeller spinners, this photo possibly shows bomb loading training or an exercise. (*Wolfgang Mühlbauer/DEHLA Archives*)

This was the first Me 410 to come down on British soil, crashing at Church Farm, Chelmondiston.

However, the battle was not completely one-sided. Shortly after midnight on 24 August, a 97 Sqn Lancaster (serial number EE105) was shot down just prior to landing at RAF Marham by a 15./KG 2 Me 410 (W Nr 420.214), flown by Hptm Wilhelm Schmitter (*Staffelkapitän*) and Ofw Heinz Graeber. Interestingly, the Lancaster was brought down by the rear gunner using the remote control machine guns. This was the first victory of the night intruder Me 410s. Soon afterwards, Schmitter attacked an airfield 'west of Cambridge', dropping eight bombs. However, on the return flight, the Me 410 was shot down off Knokke by a 29 Sqn Mosquito. Both Schmitter and Graeber baled out, with Graeber striking the tail section of the Me 410, breaking both his legs. Unable to get into their dinghies, they fired flares, which were spotted by a Flak unit. Schmitter and Graeber were very lucky indeed to be picked up by a rescue vessel only ninety minutes after coming down into the North Sea. Schmitter subsequently went missing on 8 November 1943.

A Rare Success for the Intruders

What was arguably the Me 410's finest hour (at least when discussing night intruder operations) occurred on 22 April 1944 over East Anglia. On this day, the USAAF attacked the marshalling yards at Hamm. Most unusually, the USAAF B-24 Liberators took off at 4 p.m. and were due to return to their bases in East Anglia after darkness. It was far more common for the USAAF bombers to take off well before noon, landing back during the afternoon or early evening in broad daylight. On the return flight, the bombers were shadowed by half-a-dozen Me 410s of II./KG 51, led by Hptm Dietrich Puttfarken. A twenty-three-year-old recipient of the Ritterkreutz, Puttfarken was a highly experienced pilot having flown hundreds of sorties.

With the English coast only minutes away, the USAAF crews began to relax. The raid was over, and the darkness of the blacked-out Norfolk and Suffolk countryside was dotted with runway lights anticipating arrival of the bombers. At 10.07 p.m., a B-24 was seen to burst into flames and crash into the sea off Hopton.

The next B-24 to come under the attention of the Me 410s was named 'Cee-Gee II'. Its bombardier, Lt Arthur Orlowski, later recalled the last moments of the Liberator:

> We couldn't open the bomb bay door. No 2 gas tank and the hydraulic systems were shot out. A fire was burning just in the back of the wing. Conway kicked out the bomb bay doors but Munsey told me to keep him in while he made a run for the coast. Crale, the second pilot stayed with Munsey. The discipline was perfect. The radio operator said that he was hit in the eyes by some debris. Munsey then called Helfand (the navigator) and Laux (the front gunner) up on to the flight deck. McClure was hit on the head and came forward to tell us that McKinney was hit. We went back and found Brown jacking up his ball turret. McClure and Brown attempted to attach the static line to the rip chord of McKinney's parachute, but they could not break it loose. The gas tank then exploded and blew all three of them out of the tail hatch. We were over land at this time and the interior of the 'plane was in flames. I shoved Grady ahead of me, then looked back and saw Crale starting to get out of his seat. I don't think that Munsey had his parachute pack snapped on to his harness at that time. Conway, Helfand, Laux, Grady and I jumped through the bomb bay in that order. We were at about 4,000 feet.[2]

Five of the crew baled out safely, with a sixth landing about 15 metres offshore. He drifted out to sea, his body never being found. The B-24 crashed at Reydon Marsh, taking both pilots with it.

By now, chaos reigned in the skies over Norfolk and Suffolk. B-24 gunners as well as anti-aircraft artillery were firing indiscriminately. When the smoke cleared, two Me 410s had been lost. However, no fewer than fourteen B-24s had been destroyed, either through direct action, or indirectly, by the Me 410 crews. This included nine that had been shot down, three that crashed on landing, and two in a mid-air collision. Sixty-eight airmen had been killed and another twenty-three wounded. An RAF Armstrong Whitworth Albemarle (serial number V1610 of 42 OTU), engaged in a cross-country navigational exercise, had also been brought down by the roving Me 410s. The following day, the BBC broadcast a report, stating:

'There was slight enemy action over the United Kingdom last evening. One American bomber was reported damaged.'

The first of the two Me 410s lost on 22 April was 9K+HP of 6./KG 51, which was shot down by return fire from a B-24. The crew, Oblt Klaus Krüger and Fw Michael Reichardt, were both killed. The second Me 410, 9K+MN of 5./KG 51 is believed to have crashed into the North Sea, possibly after having sustained damage during the attack. Both Hptm Dietrich Puttfarken (*Gruppenkommendeur*) and Ofw Willi Lux were posted as 'Missing in Action'.

Over the next couple of nights, II./KG 51 returned to British skies, shooting down two RAF heavy bombers. On 27 April, one II./KG 51 Me 410 collided with a twin-engined Airspeed Oxford advanced trainer. The Oxford was approaching Church Lawford near Rugby, when struck by the Luftwaffe aircraft. All aboard perished.

During inspection of the Me 410 wreck, it was discovered that the forward firing armament consisted of four MG 151/20 cannons (two more than usual) and a pair of MG 17 machine guns. The aircraft was also fitted with two external drop tanks, something which had not been seen before on Me 410s.

Shortly after 2 a.m. on D-Day, 6 June 1944, a Me 410 was claimed shot down by a 214 Sqn Fortress II. Having taken off from Oulton shortly before midmight for a radio jamming sortie, Wg Cdr D.J. McGlinn and his crew were attacked by a Luftwaffe aircraft off Sidmouth, provisionally identified as a Me 410. During the combat, the turbo-supercharger of the Fortress No. 2 (left inner) engine was hit, forcing McGlinn to abandon their sortie. Nevertheless, the Me 410 was claimed to have been shot down by return fire.

During the same night, a Mosquito crew, Fg Off. LeLong and Sgt McLaren of 605 Sqn, claimed a Me 410 shot down near Evreux. On 7 June, Me 410s and Fw 190s managed to penetrate the flak and fighter umbrella covering the invasion fleet. Two ships were sunk, including a US Navy destroyer. For a few weeks, Me 410s continued to attack the Allied beachheads in Normandy, until losses reduced the effectiveness of the Luftwaffe units.

Following D-Day, the night intruder raids over Britain reduced sharply. Instead of conventional aircraft, Hitler's 'Wonder weapons', the V-1 and V-2 missiles became a major threat to the British cities. The final night intruder sortie of II./KG 51 took place on 25 July 1944. A total of twelve Me 410s had been lost along with their crews. Nevertheless, the Me 410s had been able to harass and destroy Allied bombers over their own airfields with relative impunity, bringing a sense of insecurity to the Allied airmen. However, the small number of Me 410s involved in these raids could not stop the tidal wave of Allied bombers bringing death and destruction to Germany. If anything, the night intruder raids proved to be a minor nuisance to the RAF and USAAF.

Mention must be made of the final Luftwaffe night intruder sortie over Britain, on 3–4 March 1945. Codenamed Operation Gisela, this involved shadowing returning RAF bombersback to their airfields in Lincolnshire. The Luftwaffe force consisted of Junkers Ju 88Gs, drawn from several night fighter units. The Me 410 had long since disappeared from such operations. Although some thirty RAF aircraft were destroyed or damaged, Luftwaffe losses amounted to thirty-four Ju 88Gs. It also marked the final Luftwaffe losses over Britain.[3]

15
Operation Steinbock

The final Luftwaffe bomber offensive against Britain began on 21 January 1944. Codenamed Operation Steinbock, it came to be known as the 'Baby Blitz'. With RAF and USAAF heavy bombers striking against German cities on an almost daily basis, Hitler ordered a retaliatory series of raids against targets in and around the Greater London area. However, when Operation Steinbock ended in May 1944, very little had been achieved. No fewer than 524 Luftwaffe aircraft had been lost to all causes, and, more importantly, many experienced pilots and other flight crews.[1]

Luftwaffe operations over Britain in 1944, began on 2 January, when Me 410s of V./KG 2 and Fw 190s attacked targets in southern Britain. On the night of 2–3 January 1944, two KG 2 Me 410s were brought down by RAF night fighters. One was shot down by Wing Commander John 'Cat's Eye' Cunningham. Two more Me 410s were lost between 13 and 15 January.

Among the Luftwaffe units available for Operation Steinbock was V./KG 2, which on 20 January 1944 had a strength of thirty-five Me 410As (all serviceable). Another Me 410, II./KG 51, would also be involved in Operation Steinbock. Otherwise, the force consisted of Do 217, Ju 88 and Ju 188 medium bombers, Heinkel He 177 heavy bombers and Fw 190 single-seat fighter bombers.

The first raid, on the night of 20–21 January, was a failure. Of the 430 Luftwaffe aircraft of taking part, only forty managed to find London. Operational losses were thirty-eight aircraft, including one Me 410. In London, seventy-four civilians were killed and seventeen were injured. Material damage was limited, although the Vickers Armstrong factory at Dartford was severly damaged.

A second night raid, on 28–29 January, saw sixteen Me 410s and ten Fw 190s attack various targets. None of the Luftwaffe raiders were shot down, with damage being minimal.

On 3 February, twenty-six Me 410s and nineteen Fw 190s crossed into British airspace around 7.30 p.m. Yet again, damage was limited. No Me 410s were lost, although two of the Fw 190s failed to return. A second wave in the early hours of 4 February, consisting of 235 bombers, resulted in minor damage to targets in and around London.

On 18–19 February, what can be considered to have been the most successful Luftwaffe raid during Operation Steinbock took place. Some 179 civilians were killed, with nearly 500 being injured. This solitary raid was judged to have been the most 'damaging' Luftwaffe operation against Britain since 31 May–1 June 1941.

At daybreak on 21 February, twenty-one Me 410s of V./KG 2 and thirteen Fw 190s dropped SC 500 bombs and incendiaries against a variety of targets. Little damage was done.

In the early hours of 23 February, yet another Luftwaffe raid arrived over Britain. V./KG 2 contributed fifteen Me 410s to a force of 185 bombers. Two of the Me 410s failed to return, one of which was shot down by Branse Burbridge of 85 Sqn:

> After a frustrating sortie we were over the sea and heading back home when Bill gained an AI (Airborne Intercept) contact, so I quickly pulled into a starboard turn and descended and eventually saw a Messerschmitt 410. I managed to get directly behind him and gave a long burst and, as I had not got this close since my Havoc days, I wanted to make sure of it. I need not have worried as its left hand engine promptly burst into flames, which quickly spread and with a mixture of sadness and elation we saw it explode with considerable violence and go down. After the first hits Bill and I saw one of the crew bale out and he went just over the top of us. I was glad that someone did get out. That was my first one.[2]

On this night, a Me 410A of 14./KG 2 (W Nr 420.463, U5+CE) was shot down over Bentley Farm, Framfield near Uckfield, Sussex by Sqn Ldr Caldwell and Fg Off. Rawling of 96 Sqn. After being hit, the Me 410 dived into the ground, exploding on impact. The crew, Uffz Reinhard Eggers and Ogfr Stefan Bednorz, were both killed.

Sqn Ldr Caldwell's post-action report read:

> I was patrolling over the Channel at 24,000 feet under Wartling Control when I was warned of a bandit 15 miles south at 21,000 feet on a vector of 290°. I obtained contact crossing port to starboard, range 5 miles slightly below. E/a now on Northerly vector. At 2,000 feet I obtained visual of blue exhausts. Evasion was regular and hard. I was forced to break away to avoid overshooting and momentairily lost contact. This was regained at 2,000 feet after e/a had been seen to pass beneath at 40 to 50 feet, 220 ASI. I closed to 800 feet and fired a burst with 1½ ring deflection, no strikes resulted. I was temporarily illuminated by Sqn Ldr's (searchlights) but bandit was not apparently aware of our presence. I closed to 4/500 feet and fired second burst with ½ ring deflection. Strikes and flashes appeared, followed by an explosion and sparks, in what was believed to be starboard engine. Time 0013 hours, height 15,000 feet. E/a turned starboard and dived vertically, soon afterwards I saw an explosion on the ground to starboard.

During the brief combat, Caldwell had fired off 120 rounds from the Mosquito's four 20-mm cannons, with the gun camera exposing some 3 feet of film.

The Sussex Police subsequently provided a report of the gruesome findings at the site of the crash:

> This plane was attacked by a night fighter and was seen falling in flames. When it crashed, the bombs on board exploded, throwing portions of wreckage and pieces of the bodies of the airmen nearly 300 yards away. Only small portions of bodies were found (Sufficient to fill a

> sack quarter full). A military Medical Officer examined the hands and feet which were found and said without question they were from two different bodies. Also portions of two mens identity cards were found.[3]

One Me 410 lost in early March in a crash. By this time, operations were beginning to take a toll on the Luftwaffe units. During this month, II./KG 51 had a total strength of twenty-six Me 410s, of which a mere seven were serviceable.

By mid-March, the Luftwaffe bombers moved their attention away from London to northern England and Scotland. A raid on Hull became a total failure, with the Hull residents being unaware of the attack. However, London again became a priority target within a week. On 12–13 April, 3./KG 51 lost a Me 410, shot down by a 96 Sqn Mosquito.

During the night of 18–19 April, KG 51 lost three Me 410s, including some to RAF night fighters. Apart from the aircraft of V./KG 2 and II./KG 51, reconnaissance Me 410s of 1.(F)/121 flew a number of post-raid sorties in April. Two aircraft were lost, one being downed by Branse Burbridge of 85 Sqn.

This particular reconnaissance unit suffered significantly on 20 April, when no less than three out of five Me 410s were shot down during a ferry flight. Having taken off from Le Buc in France, the Me 410s headed towards Soesterberg in the Netherlands, from where they were to participate in a raid against Hull. One 1.(F)/121 pilot, Ofhr Werner Meyer, later recalled the disastrous flight:

> We had to get five aircraft ready for a big operation. The CO always insisted on sending as many aircraft as possible ... We transferred five aircraft from our airfield to Soesterberg: that must have been between 5 and 8 o'clock. They went off ... At nine o'clock in the evening one of them rang ... to say that he was at such and such a place, approximately WNW of PARIS, and had been shot down there by two Mustangs. He had baled out with his W/T operator, the aircraft had caught fire, they had got down safely ... Shortly afterwards we rang up Soesterberg: 'How many aircraft have arrived?' 'Two aircraft.' They had shot down the other two as well ... Neither of the remaining aircraft flew on the operation ... we had two men killed, a pilot and a W/T operator from two different aircraft, the other two from the same two aircraft were injured, one of them badly and the other not so badly, and two were not injured at all.[4]

During Operation Steinbock, a total of 27 Me 410s were lost to all causes. At this juncture, the Luftwaffe was overstretched, fighting on several fronts, and, as a result, lacked the resources to conduct a sustained bombing campaign. As was the case with the night intruder raids, Operation Steinbock failed to stop, or even delay the Allied war effort. Losses among the civilian population had been high, it was nothing like the 'Blitz' of 1940–41.

Following the Allied landings in Normany on D-Day, 6 June, Luftwaffe raids against Britain became a rare occurrence. However, during the summer of 1944, a new menace in the shape of V-1 'doodlebugs' began to rain down on southern England. Although many of the V-1s were brought down by British defences, nothing could be done against the supersonic V-2 rocket. These *Vergeltungswaffen* (Vengeance weapons) would cause far more death and destruction than the conventional bombers used in Operation Steinbock. The V-1 and V-2 menace would not disappear until early 1945, when the German forces had finally been forced to withdraw from the rocket firing sites along the North Sea coast.

Over Sicily and Italy

Having driven Rommel's *Afrikakorps* out of North Africa, Operation Husky (the invasion of Sicily) began on 10 July 1943. Although the Me 210s of 2.(F)/122 continued in service (III./ZG 1 transferred to France in July 1943), the new and improved Me 410 had begun to arrive. During the summer and autumn of 1943, the Me 410 supplanted and eventually replaced the Me 210.

During Operation Husky, several Me 210s and Me 410s were captured intact or in various stages of disrepair on Sicily, including one 2.(F)/122 Me 410 at Trapani. This aircraft eventually found its way to the USA as FE-499.

A III./ZG 1 Me 210, coded 2N+HT, was captured intact at Gerbini on 25 August. This Me 210 was taken over by the Spitfire-equipped 601 Squadron, with RAF roundels and fin flash being painted on the aircraft. The ZG 1 unit insignia, however, was not painted over. It appears unlikely however that the Me 210 was test flown by any 601 Sqn pilots. When 601 Sqn moved on, the Me 210 was taken over to the USAAF's 12th Bomb Group (BG), which decided to test fly the former Luftwaffe aircraft. The 12th BG's Operations Officer, Lt-Col. G. E. Hall would make the first flight. During the take-off run on 1 October 1943, one engine appeared to 'run away' causing the aircraft to veer off the runway. A war photographer, Howard Levy, just managed to escape being hit by the Me 210. Apparently, Lt-Col. Hall fired off the nose guns as a warning before ending up in a personnel area. Hall was killed, with the Me 210 being destroyed by fire.

Since July 1943, 2.(F)/122 was the only Luftwaffe Me 410 unit in Italy. Part of *Fernaufklärungsgruppe* 122, which also included 1.(F)/123 (equipped with Ju 88s) and *Wettererkundungsstaffel* 26 (Weather Reconnaissance Sqn 26), 2.(F)/122 were flying high-altitude reconnaissance sorties against Allied-controlled harbours and landing grounds. The tactics used involved approaching the target area at altitudes between 7,620 and 8,534 metres (25,000 to 28,000 feet), and then fly on a straight course before heading back to base. Usually, the Me 410 crews managed to escape interception. At this juncture, many of the Me 410 crews were former flight instructors with much combat flying experience as well.

However, an increasing number of Me 410s were lost. Not all of the losses however were due to combat-related causes. On 27 November, *Oberleutnant* Stubbe of 2.(F)/122 landed by mistake at Monte Corvino. Stubbe's Me 410 was subsequently evaluated by the RAF.

On 31 May 1944, 2.(F)/122 had seven Me 410s, of which only three were serviceable. Another source speak of eight and four Me 410s respectively. The other two aircraft of the unit was a solitary Ju 88D-1 and a Fieseler Fi 156.

By early June, 2.(F)/122 operated from Perugia and Bergamo, flying almost daily sorties. One memorable sortie occurred on 6 June, when Oblt v.d. Daele and Uffz Blaschek flew the unit's No. 3,000 sortie. Reaching its 500th or 1,000th sortie was always a cause for great celebration for the relevant Luftwaffe unit. Remarkably, a second recorded No. 3,000 sortie was completed two days later by Hptm Dietse and Fw Bendorf.

German radio traffic was monitored on a regular basis, and on 12 June, a message that a Me 410 would take-off from Piacenza at 4.45 a.m. the following day, routing over Corsica and the Tyrrhenian Sea before landing back at Bergamo. Taking off at 4.48 a.m. (three minutes later than briefed), Ofw Jackstadt and Uffz Stauch were intercepted in the vicinity of La Spezia shortly after 7 a.m. by RAF Spitfires. Nevertheless, the Luftwaffe crew managed to return to base. Their badly shot up Me 410, F6+FK, was a write-off. On 14 June, German forces attacked Italian partisans north west of Varese, with a 2.(F)/122 Me 410 providing aerial reconnaissance.

Oblt v.d. Daele and Uffz Blaschek were to have another narrow escape during the morning of 19 June. At 5.22 a.m., they were caught at very low level off the Island of Elba by USAAF P-47 Thunderbolts. During the combat, which lasted until 5.45 a.m., the Me 410 was badly hit. However, v.d. Daele and Blaschek managed to land at Bergamo unscathed.

At this time, the Me 410 reconnaissance aircraft were under close surveillance by the RAF, with RAF radio intelligence enjoying the: 'fullest details of routes to be followed at least one hour before (reconnaissance) flights commence.'

Following the start of Operation Dragoon on 15 August, the Allied invasion of southern France, one 2.(F)/122 Me 410 was seconded to Flieger Division 2 in France. The scarcity of reconnaissance Me 410s may be seen from the fact that *Luftflotte* 2 (which controlled all Luftwaffe units in Italy) demanded its immediate return already on 17 August. During this month, 2.(F)/122 flew some eighty-five sorties, excluding training and ferry flights. On 9 August, 2.(F)/122 moved from Bergamo to Ghedi, where they were to remain for the rest of the war. One of the 2.(F)/122 pilots became a prisoner of war in August, revealed to his Allied captors that the unit had ten crews, most of which were 'young and inexperienced'. Dreams of receiving Me 262s were mentioned during the interrogation, but: 'P/W was filled with praise of the Me 262. Unfortunately his knowledge was not commensurate with his enthusiasm'. Regarding the Me 410s, the German pilot stated that all aircraft were fitted with GM-1 boost. Interestingly, he also mentioned rumours of a jet-powered Me 410, which increased speed with 150 kph. It is unclear if the PoW was referring to a pure jet aircraft, or a standard DB 603-powered Me 410 to which auxiliary jet engines had been fitted.

Losses continued to occur at an alarming rate. On 13 August, Fhr Richard Hesse and Uffz Helmut Seegert were brought down near La Spezia by RAF Spitfires. Although both Hesse and Seegert baled out of their Me 410, F6+GK, only Hesse survived. He was eventually picked up by a USAAF OA-10A Catalina.

Two days later, on 15 August, Me 410B-3 F6+DK crashed 20 km north-west of Mantua. The pilot, Lt Fischer, was killed, with the radio operator/gunner, Uffz Kemna, being injured. Later the same day, another Me 410 sustained 15 per cent accidental damage at Treviso.

With the presence of Allied fighters becoming more frequent, many sorties had to be aborted. For instance, of the six sorties attempted on 22 September, three had to be aborted.

On 12 October, USAAF fighters strafed Bergamo-Seriate, claiming several Me 410s, Ju 88s, and one Do 217 destroyed or damaged. Nevertheless, on 2 October, 2.(F)/122 had eight Me 410s, six of which were serviceable. Since August, operational activities had declined sharply. During November, a mere twenty-eight daylight sorties were flown. Although the Allies were keeping a sharp eye on the Luftwaffe presence in northern Italy, the occasional erroneous report could still filter through. One example of this was a report, dated 6 November, of 'at least 21 Me 410s' over the Ligurian Sea. On this day, 2.(F)/122 managed three sorties. No further sorties took place until 10 November.

A well-known photo showing Me 410 F6+QK of 2.(F)/122 under close scrutiny by RAF personnel. The Me 410 had force landed near the River Sangro, Italy, on 26 November 1943. (*Author's collection*)

In late November 1944, the Commander of 1° *Gruppo Aerosiluranti*, Magg (Major) Marini, met *General der Flieger* Maximilian Ritter von Pohl (the Commander of all Luftwaffe units in Italy), requesting that a Me 410 be placed under his control. Marini had previously requested Luftwaffe cooperation in providing up-to-date information on an Allied convoy sailing from Corsica. The Savoia-Marchetti SM.79 torpedo bombers of 1° Gruppo Aerosiluranti would then attack the convoy. When no such information was forthcoming, Marini demanded an Me 410 to be transferred. No Me 410 was forthcoming though.

The number of sorties continued to dwindle, with fourteen sorties being flown during December 1944. Three of these sorties took place on 10 December. The last of these, the No. 3,300 sortie for 2.(F)/122, ended prematurely when Ofhr Spöntjes and Fw Ziélenkiewicz were shot down by a USAAF P-47 near Mariana Mantovana. Following a two-hour sortie on 13 December, the Me 410s of 2.(F)/122 did not fly operationally again until 20 December.

On 29 December, two sorties were flown. The first of these was uneventful, but the second sortie resulted in the loss of Ofhr Spöntjes and Uffz Schmausser in Me 410B-3 F6+GK. Having received warnings over the radio of Allied fighters, Spöntjes and Schmausser crashed fatally near Ancona. It proved to be the final operational sortie in 1944.

New Year's Day 1945 saw a single sortie being flown in F6+AK. Only fourteen sorties would be flown by 2.(F)/122 between 1 January and 20 March 1945. By 1 January, the unit was down to two serviceable Me 410s. Two days later, a single replacement Me 410B-3, F6+KK, arrived. However, no operational flying would be done until 20 January.

The following day, Oblt v.d. Daele and Uffz Blaschek were ordered to fly a sortie over the Ligurian Sea. When returning to Bergamo, they were warned that USAAF P-38 Lightnings were in the vicinity of the airfield. However, v.d. Daele and Blaschek managed to land safely.

On 2 February, 2.(F)/122 received a considerable boost, when no less than three replacement Me 410s arrived at Ghedi. Six days later, Ofw Wilhelm Zimmerman and Uffz Wilhelm Lenecke were shot down in F6+KK by a 93 Sdn Spitfire:

> The first sensation came at lunch-time when an Me 410 stooged gently over the coast road at about 200 feet while many unbelieving eyes blinked with surprise. A section … was diverted from a bombing mission and after a chase Lt (H. P.) Anderson attacked it. The Hun was last seen diving into cloud at fifty feet with its starboard engine on fire. This is claimed as probably destroyed and it is hoped the gun camera will produce sufficient evidence to step up the claim.[5]

Very little operational activity occurred in the following weeks. The final combat-related loss of the war for 2.(F)/122 happened on 23 February, when Lt Franz Girlich and Uffz Walter Kemna were shot down in Me 410B-3 F6+NK near Ghedi by 2Lt Jim Young, of the P-47D Thunderbolt-equipped 347 FS, 350 FG:

> It was my 15th mission … we were getting low on gas and ammo, so started home at 10,000 feet. Somebody in the flight spotted a bogey at 2 or 3 o'clock at the same altitude, so we turned and gave chase. When the German saw us he hit the deck. Flight Leader (Lt John E.) Powers fired the rest of his ammo and there was a thin stream of grey smoke coming from (the German's) port engine.
>
> I remember using water injection to get 'enuf' speed to keep up with the 410. The enemy 'plane tried to use evasive action by pulling straight up from the deck to 900–1,100 feet, then pushed the nose back to the deck. I kept firing small bursts … and could see some hits on the 410. I remember we flew 10–15 minutes (it seemed that long) at top speeds … and I kept firing short bursts at him. Finally he was at treetop level with his port engine trailing smoke, and my ammo finally hit his starboard engine. The plane dipped his right wing and hit the ground in a big ball of flame.[6]

By early March, 2.(F)/122 had three Me 410B-3s, all of them serviceable.

On 14 March 1945, orders arrived to disband 2.(F)/122. The job of high-altitude reconnaissance would from then on be performed by Arado Ar 234 jets. Such aircraft had been present in Italy since January 1945, being operated by Kdo Sommer. However, 2.(F)/122 remained operational until 20 March, when its final (3,326th) sortie was flown. One Me 410, coded F6+EK, took off during the morning of 20 March, but had to abort after flying a mere eight minutes. At 11.27 a.m., Fw Bayer and Uffz Lensing took off in Me 410 F6+BK, landing back two hours later.

On 1 April, 2.(F)/122 counted four Me 410B-3s, all of them serviceable. On this day, two of the Me 410s, F6+BK and F6+DK, were flown back to Munich-Riem. The other two Me 410s followed a couple of days later. The thirty months of Me 210/Me 410 operations over Italy had ended. Five wrecked Me 410s were subsequently found at Ghedi (two), Vicenza (two), and Villafranca (one).

Maritime Escort and SAR Duties

Beginning in August 1944, a number of *Seenotstaffeln* (Sea Rescue Squadrons) were formed. Among these units were *Seenotstaffel* 80 based at List on the island of Sylt and *Seenotstaffel* 81, based at Parow near Stralsund on the Baltic Sea coast. These two *Seenotstaffeln* retained Me 410s until the end of the war. Additionally, it was planned to establish the *Seenotstaffel* 100 at Bug on the island of Rügen on the Baltic Sea coast. However, it seems that this unit was not formed.

These Me 410s, possibly of the B-2/U2 variant, were fitted with FuG 200 'Hohentwiel' radar. The exact purpose of introducing Me 410s to the *Seenotstaffeln* are not entirely clear. However, their possible missions most likely included escorting search and rescue (SAR) flying boats and seaplanes against enemy fighters, protecting *Kriegsmarine* submarines, as well as locating enemy surface vessels and submarines. With the evacuation of wounded troops and civilians from the Courland pocket (in present-day Latvia) and other areas along the east coast of the Baltic Sea, one hypothesis is that it was intended for the Me 410s to protect the sealanes against Allied aircraft and Soviet submarines.[7]

In this context, mention must be made of plans of modifying the Me 410 as a torpedo bomber. Although trials were conducted in the autumn of 1944, they were not successful. It was also planned to introduce the Me 410B-6/R2 anti-shipping variant. The Me 410B-6/R2 variant was very heavily armed with two MG 131s, two MG 151/20s, two MK 108 cannons as well as two rearward-firing MG 131s. A FuG 200 'Hohentwiel' radar was also fitted. However, the Me 410B-6/R2 did not enter production.

During the final weeks of the war, the 2./*Seeaufklärergruppe* 126 received a number of Me 410s as well as a few Siebel Si 204Ds, the latter presumably used for the training of radar operators. Incidentally, a Si 204D of this unit was flown to Sweden by defectors in April 1945. As this aircraft was fitted with a FuG 200 'Hohentwiel' radar, it may be presumed the Me 410s were also equipped likewise. With 2./SAGr.126 being a dedicated maritime reconnaissance unit, it seems likely that their Me 410s would be used in this manner.

The End

By the late summer of 1944, most of the remaining Me 410s would serve in the high-altitude reconnaissance role, and, to a lesser extent, for anti-shipping patrols. Only one *Zerstörergruppe*, II./ZG 76, retained Me 410s by the end of 1944.

In August 1944, the *Fernaufklärungsgruppe* 3 (FAGr. 3) was formed, supporting the operations of *Heeresgruppe Mitte* (Army Group Centre). By early 1945, FAGr. 3 consisted of three *Staffeln*; 4.(F)/*Nacht*, 2.(F)/100 and 4.(F)/121. A fourth *Staffel*, 1.(F)/122, was transferred to Kbely and Ruzyne air bases near Prague, later moving to Vysoké Mýto.

Several Me 410s were located in Czech territory in May 1945. Although many former Luftwaffe aircraft were pressed into service with the reformed Czech Air Force, these did not include any Me 410s.

On 4 October 1944, a P-61 of the 422nd Night Fighter Squadron (NFS), flown by 1Lt Paul A. Smith and 2Lt Robert E. Tierney, claimed one Me 410 shot down over Belgium. Other P-61

Black Widow intercepts of Me 410s met did not go as planned. On Christmas Day 1944, Lt Van Neiswender was vectored towards an unidentified intruder over Bastogne:

> As soon as we had a lock on him, the bogey did a quick half-roll and dived for the dark wooded area below. I pushed the throttle wide open and the chase was on! It was a fight that should have entered the record books. We started close, but not close enough to fire the guns. We were finally ablie to get a positive i.d. and it was an Me 410. This pilot had his airspeed over 400 mph and was pulling away quickly. I was wide open and it was as if we were standing still! Seconds later, we lost radar contact and at the same time, the tailcone at the rear of the crew nacelle caved in from the pressure. We had been up for over three hours and now we were headed back to Etain, with nothing to show![8]

Only one other Me 410 victory was claimed by a USAAF P-61 pilot. This occurred on 8 April 1945, when a P-61 of the 414 NFS (flown by Capt. Albert Jones and 2Lt John Rudovsky) shot down a Me 410 that was about to land at Halle.

During the final months of the war, encounters between Allied fighters and Me 410s had become a rare occurrence. In one instance, on 16 April 1945, sixteen P-51 Mustangs of the USAAF's 4 FG/334 FS attacked Gablingen airfield near Augsburg just after 5 p.m. Spending some forty minutes over the airfield, the Mustang pilots claimed no less than forty-four aircraft destroyed (including five Me 410s) and twenty-one more damaged (including two Me 410s).

On 10 January 1945, very few Luftwaffe units were still operating Me 410s; IV./ZG 26 had forty-one aircraft (thirty-five serviceable), with other units being *Fernaufklärungsgruppe* 3, *Fernaufklärungsgruppe* 122, *Seenotstaffel* 80, and *Seenotstaffel* 81.

By the spring of 1945, the Me 410 had largely disappeared from front line service, with only a few long-range reconnaissance units and two *Seenotstaffeln* still retaining Me 410s. Acute fuel shortage had grounded many Luftwaffe units, with any fuel reserves available being allotted to single-seat fighter units. The final Me 410 sortie in Italy took place 20 March 1945, with Ar 234 jets having taken over reconnaissance duties two months previously. The remaining Me 410s were flown back to Germany in early April. Another reconnaissance unit still operating Me 410s was 1.(F)/122. Based at Vysoké Mýto in eastern Bohemia, this unit moved to Kbely and Ruzyne near Prague in late April 1945. In Germany itself, 3.(F)/22 as well as *Seenotstaffeln* 80 and 81 also had Me 410s on charge. Operational activities at this late stage of the war of the *Seenotstaffeln* were in all likelihood very limited.

On 1 April 1945, the following Luftwaffe units still operated Me 410s:

Stab/Fernaufklärungsgruppe 3: Two Me 410s (both serviceable) One crew (cleared for operations)

2.(F)/100: Two Me 410s (both serviceable) and eight Ju 88s (all serviceable) Ten crews (nine cleared for operations)

4.(F)/121: Three Me 410s (two serviceable) and ten Ju 188s (seven serviceable) Eleven crews (five cleared for operations)

1.(F)/122: Twelve Me 410s (ten serviceable) Thirteen crews (ten cleared for operations)

5.(F)/122: Seven Me 410s (six serviceable) and ten Ju 188s and one Ju 88. Twenty crews (sixteen cleared for operations)

Above: A completely destroyed Me 410 at a former Luftwaffe airfield in Belgium in September 1944. A USAAF P-38 Lightning of the 485th FS, 370th FG of the Ninth AF can be seen in the background. (*National Archives (NARA) via Robert Pęczkowski*)

Below: Me 410 7A+EH of 1.(F)/121 was destroyed at Villacoublay in an Allied bomb raid. (*National Archives (NARA) via Robert Pęczkowski*)

2./*Seeaufklärungsgruppe* 126: Eleven Me 410s (none serviceable) Also five Siebel Si 204s (two serviceable). Twelve crews (ten cleared for operations)

A few 3.(F)/22 Me 410s did fly one sortie in early May 1945.

Just before midnight on 4 May, orders were dispatched to all Luftwaffe units in north-western Germany. Instead of surrendering to British forces, the Luftwaffe crews were ordered to transfer to Prague and Norway. Take-off time was scheduled before 6.30 a.m., with the deadline being set at 8 a.m. Plain and simple, the fight was to continue on the Eastern Front as well as in Norway. A total of 114 Luftwaffe aircraft, including three Me 410s of 3.(F)/22, headed north, arriving in Norway during the morning of 5 May. Two of the aircraft were damaged in landing accidents. It was all in vain. On 8 May 1945, the German forces in Norway, finally surrendered. The war in Europe was finally over.

Three Me 410s, all surrendered at Værløse, Denmark, were subsequently brought to the UK, and subjected to brief evaluation. All received Air Ministry 'AM' serial numbers. It must be said that the Me 410 did not envince much interest within the Royal Aircraft Establishment, particularly when compared with the new Arado Ar 234 and Messerschmitt Me 262 jets and the Messerschmitt Me 163 rocket fighter. By this time, the Me 410 was outmoded.

A US soldier sitting in a Jeep is taking a closer look at a Me 410 camouflaged by trees somewhere in Germany. (*National Archives (NARA) via Robert Pęczkowski*)

One derelict Me 410 found in Denmark in May 1945. (*Karsten Lindblad/RDAF Historical Collection*)

A BK 5 cannon-equipped Me 410 seen 'somewhere in Germany' in early 1945. (*Wolfgang Mühlbauer/ DEHLA Archives*)

A Me 410 in RAF insignia photographed in Denmark in mid-1945. (*Karsten Lindblad/RDAF Historical Collection*)

A Me 410 surrendered in Denmark being inspected by RAF personnel. (*Karsten Lindblad/RDAF Historical Collection*)

16
Armament Diversification

A huge variety of weaponry was fitted to the Me 410. Although some of these were used operationally, particularly the 50-mm BK 5 cannon and the W.Gr21 unguided rocket, others were merely tested but, for different reasons, never put into operational use on the Me 410. What follows is a brief overview of some of the main heavy weapons carried by the Me 410.

The 21-cm Wfr.Gr. 21 (*Nebelwerfer* 42)

Originally an army mortar grenade, the *Wurfgranate* 21 (W.Gr.21) was initially fitted to Bf 109Gs and Fw 190As and first used operationally during the summer of 1943. Some success was achieved, with three B-17s being brought down on 13 June. The shell weighed 112 kg, having a 40-kg warhead, being carried inside a tube, known as the *Ofenrohr* (stovepipe). The weapon also acquired the unofficial name of '*Dodel*', meaning fool in Austrian-German. The W.Gr.21 was an unguided rocket, aimed by the pilot through a Revi 16B gun sight and fired electrically.

The Commander of EKdo 25, Hptm Horst Geyer, later recalled:

> Unlike other missiles, the 21-cm Werfer, which came to us from the Army, was not equipped with fins or stabilizers. Rather, this weapon was stabilized by its own spin, which, in turn, was created by the blast from initial ignition and the subsequent velocity. The 21-cm shell turned two or three times per second after leaving its launch tube, but speed increased rapidly thereafter.
>
> We observed that the shell did not run straight to its intended target, but rather spiralled, and therefore often missed the target. To overcome this, the manufacturer built in a time fuze intended to detonate the shell at a pre-set time. We usually fired the weapon from a range of 400 m (1,300 feet) and from our experience with it, we were able to set the fuze correctly, compensating of course for the approach-speed of the target. However, the closer to the target you were, so the greater the blast and the success of the weapon.[1]

The major advantage of the rockets was that it could break up the large bomber formations, afterwhich the B-17 and B-24 stragglers could be dealt with by conventional cannon fire. The new weapon did indeed cause major concern within the 8th AF, which at the end of August

1943 reported that the W.Gr.21 seemed: 'to be the most dangerous single obstacle in the path of our bomber offensive'.

During a raid on 10 October 1943, Bf 110s and Me 410s armed with four W.Gr.21 each (two tubes beneath each wing) caused much destruction among the USAAF bombers. The major drawback of the W.Gr.21 was that Me 410 performance was considerably reduced, making them easy targets for the enemy's single-seat fighters.

A rearward-firing variant of the W.Gr.21 was also tested. After passing through a bomber formation, the rearward-firing W.Gr.21 would provide a surprise 'Parthian shot', detonating 1.5–two seconds later. Known as the *Krebsgerät* (Crab Device), this weapon underwent ground tests during which 'positive results' had been achieved. The *Krebsgerät* was to be fitted to twenty Fw 190s and one (Z)./EKdo 25 Me 410, the latter at the orders of *Oberst* Hannes Trautloft. Only one airborne firing was carried out, which resulted in the Me 410 suffering badly from the weapon's recoil. Smoke filled the cockpit, with the hydraulic systems suffering severe damage.

The Wfr.Gr. 42 was modified with a six-round drum magazine. Renamed BR-Gerät Drehring (BR rotating chamber apparatus). Ground tests involving a Me 410A-2 were initiated at E-Stelle Tarnewitz, but the were not concluded before the war ended. During the actual ground firing tests, the airframe suffered extensive damage.

The Bordkanone 3.7 Cannon

Originally used as an anti-aircraft weapon under the designation Flak 43, it had a calibre of 37 mm. Built by Rheinmetall-Borsig, it became known as Bordkanone 3.7 (literally onboard cannon 3.7). In Luftwaffe service, the BK 3.7 was fitted to the Ju 87G, Ju 88P, and Hs 129B ground attack aircraft, and used for tank busting on the Eastern Front. It was also tested on the Me 410. Having a length of 3,630 metres and weighing 295 kg, the BK 3.7 had a rate of fire of 160 rounds per minute. However, the magazine only twelve rounds. The BK 3.7 was tested by the (Z).EKdo 25.

The Bordkanone 5 Cannon

Originally produced by Rheinmetall-Borsig as the Kampfwagenkanone 39 (KWK 39) anti-tank weapon, the BK 5 cannon was adopted for use against USAAF heavy bombers. The BK 5 cannon was developed specifically for use in the Me 410 *Zerstörer*. Having a calibre of 50 mm, the BK 5 was 4.342 metres in length, a weight of 540 kg, with the firing rate being forty-five rounds per minute. Each round weighed 1,585 kg, having a muzzle velocity of 860 metres/second. However, the magazine could only fit twenty-two rounds. Only about 300 BK 5s were produced, and fitted to the Me 410A-1/U4. It was also tested on the Me 262. Problems abounded during ground and air tests with the BK 5. The sole *Zerstörergruppe* to be fully equipped with BK 5-armed Me 410s was II./ZG 26.

The first sortie took place on 8 February 1944. Soon afterwards, four USAAF P-38 Lightnings were claimed as destroyed by II./ZG 26. However, this remains doubtful. Whatever the case, visual observation of hits stated that the BK 5 cannon shells appeared to have only an incendiary effect, with the enemy aircraft catching fire but not breaking apart or blowing up. Another worrying aspect was that the Me 410 pilots had been forced to fire at distances between 100 and 700 metres. All of this appeared strange, particularly as during ground tests, the various aircraft used as targets had all suffered a high degree of structural damage when the shells exploded on impact. It was soon found out that the Allied aircraft shot down, had in fact been brought down by MG 151 machine gun fire, using incendiary ammunition. The BK 5 cannon fire had missed their intended targets.

In the end, it took great marksmanship to down USAAF bombers using the BK 5. When Hermann Goering was interrogated on 10 May 1945, he was disdainful of the BK 5:

> You might find around Germany some jet airplanes equipped with anti-tank guns. Don't blame me for such monstrosities. This was done on the explicit orders of the Führer. Hitler knew nothing about the air. He may have known about the Army or Navy, but absolutely nothing about the air. He even considered the Me-262 to be a bomber and he insisted it should be called a bomber.

A BK 5 cannon-equipped Me 410A. (*Neil Page via Kaschuba*)

MK 103

Developed by Rheinmetall-Borsig, the 30-mm MK 103 was originally intended for use both as an anti-tank and air-to-air weapon. The MK 103 had a barrel length of 1.34 metre, weighing 141 kg. It was intended to fit the MK 103 to the Me 410A-2, as well as the Me 410H. Tests were performed at E-Stelle Tarnewitz, but the MK 103 was not cleared for use in the Me 410. A few Luftwaffe aircraft were armed with the MK 103, including the Dornier Do 335 and Focke-Wulf Fw 190F-8.

MK 108

The 30-mm MK 108 was also developed by Rheinmetall-Borsig. The Me 410B-6 anti-shipping variant was armed with two MK 108s. It was also planned to fit two MK 108s to the Me 410H.

17
The Enemy's Opinion

Three air forces—the RAF, the USAAF, and the VVS—performed test flights of captured Me 410s. From surviving evidence, it would appear that the most exhaustive flight test and evaluation was performed by Britain. Nevertheless, apart from testing a captured Me 410A-3 in 1944–45, the performance and handling characteristics of Messerschmitt's *Zerstörer* was of little interest to the RAF and Royal Aircraft Establishment (RAE).

Although a detailed technical description was made of Me 210s and Me 410s captured in Sicily in August 1943, few, if any such aircraft were air-tested by USAAF pilots. One notable exception was the Me 210 handed over by RAF's 601 Sqn to the USAAF's 12th BG. On 1 October 1943, Lt-Col. G. E. Hall of the 12th BG was killed when attempting to take off in the Me 210. In 1944, one Me 410 was brought to the USA, but it seems that this aircraft remained firmly grounded.

The VVS evaluated a captured Me 410B, with particular emphasis being placed on the BK 5 cannon and its associated equipment.

RAF Evaluation

As far as is known, no Me 210 was ever test flown by RAF pilots. However, the 11 February 1943 issue of *Flight* included a detailed description of the Me 210, as well as illustrations of the remote-controlled armament, fuel tanks, dive brakes and engine mounts. It seems likely that the aircraft had originally belonged to III./ZG 1 before being captured in North Africa sometime in late 1942–early 1943. It is unclear though if the Me 210 in question had been brought to the UK. A few Me 210s had been brought down over the UK in late 1942, with the wreck of at least one subsequently being examined at the RAE. However, the *Flight* article appear to discuss an aeroplane that had been captured in at least semi-complete state.

The article from the 11 February 1943 issue reads, in part:

> The armament comprises two fixed 7.9 mm and two fixed Mauser 20 mm guns in the nose. A notable departure are the two 13 mm guns in remotely controlled 'barbettes' and sighted by the rear gunner. A large quantity of ammunition of all calibres is carried. The bomb

> compartment is in the nose of the fuselage, below the pilot's cockpit, and provision is made for carrying a variety of bomb loads up to a total of 2,200 lb. weight. Protection of the pilot and crew, as well as vital parts, is exceptionally replete, approximately 900 lb. of armour plate being used. Radio equipment comprises the normal FU.G 10 ground/air set complete with D.F. and B.A. facilities and also the FU.G 16 air/air set fitted for remote tuning....
>
> Diving brakes are fitted to both upper and lower surfaces, the upper brake comprising three slats of extruded 'L' section aluminium alloy, and the lower brake comprising four slats. An ingenious feature of these brakes is the method of retraction, which is hydraulically operated with a parallel motion. They fit flush with the wing profile, as shown in the illustration, drag being reduced to a minimum in normal flight. A most interesting feature are the six flexible self-sealing fuel tanks fitted in the wings with a total capacity of 550 gallons. Oil tanks are also of this type.
>
> As already stated, the fuel and oil tanks are completely flexible and appear to approach the ideal of a crash-proof tank. The fibre sheet previously used on German tanks is completely dispensed with in this aircraft, the flexible skin taking the form of a self-sealing rubber compound of approximately 3/8 in. Thickness, this being again reinforced at the outer and longitudinal seams by additional thicknesses. As a result the tank is heavy in comparison with normal construction. Fuel tanks are housed within the wing and centre section, and are slung from the upper skin from two main attachments. These take the form of a circular bracket on the tank, with four raised lugs, which are bolted to the metal skin of the wing....
>
> The engine mounting is particularly interesting, as the principle of design, as can be seen from the sketch, is a complete reversal of previous German practice. The main supporting members are welded steel box girders in compression and incorporating the standard type of shock absorber mounting held in position by large-diameter circlips at the two pick-up points on the engine. They extend to the fireproof bulkhead, where the attachment takes the form of a ball joint. A diagonal tubular member in tension runs from the top of the engine are protected, also the engine cooling system. The pilot is exceptionally well screened by armour, both under and at the back of his seat, with additional protection in the nose of the aircraft. The rear gunner is protected by a large bullet-proof panel 2.5 in. thick, below which is a further armour apron.
>
> Speaking generally, the machine embodies many interesting design features, and, moreover, the construction and workmanship are good. As a dive bomber it may be efficient, but the general layout as a long-range fighter aircraft does not strike one as being equal to British designs of this type.

The first opportunity to properly air-test the Me 410 arose in November 1943. During a reconnaissance sortie on 27 November, *Oberleutnant* Stubbe of 2.(F)/122 landed at Monte Corvino near Salerno, Italy, by mistake. Stubbe's Me 410A-3 was shipped to the UK for evaluation by the Royal Aircraft Establishment (RAE), arriving at Farnborough on 14 April 1944. Finished in RAF camouflage, and assigned the RAF serial number TF209, the Me 410 also had a large 'P' surrounded by a thin yellow outer ring (indicating prototype) was painted on the fuselage.

On 1 May, the Me 410 took to the air for the first time in RAF hands, being flown by Sqn Ldr R. J. 'Roly' Falk.

The Me 410 was slightly damaged on 5 June when landing at Boscombe Down after one of the undercarriage legs failed to lock in the 'down' position. Subsequently returned to Farnborough by road, TF209 was repaired and air tested on 12 August. At the RAE, the Me 410 had been

A nice air-to-air photo of Me 410 serial number TF209. (*Author's collection*)

Me 410 TF209 seen undergoing maintenance. (*Author's collection*)

flown on sixteen occasions for four hours and fifty minutes. Two days later, the Me 410 was flown to Wittering by Sqn Ldr Howard-Williams for comparative evaluation against the DH.98 Mosquito. On 19 August, the Me 410 was formally transferred to the Fighter Interception Unit (FIU). Four days later, the FIU returned to RAF Ford, the Me 410 arriving at Ford on 25 August. The RAF's Central Fighter Establishment (CFE) was formed at Tangmere on 4 September by the amalgation of the FIU and other units. On 21 September 1945, TF209 was transferred to 6 MU at Brize Norton for storage, eventually being struck off charge on 14 August 1947 and scrapped.

Following the end of the war, three Me 410s were brought to the UK:

AM 72 Me 410A-1/U2 W Nr 420430: Preserved RAF Museum, Cosford (a complete history of this aircraft appears on p. 153)

AM 73 Me 410A-1 W Nr 130360: The operational Luftwaffe history of this Me 410 is, unfortunately, unknown. Following RAF takeover, the aircraft was allocated the identity Air Min V-2. On 20 August 1945, the Me 410 was ferried from Værløse to Kastrup near Copenhagen by Sdn Ldr Ian 'Curly' Somerville. Soon afterwards, it was flown to Schleswig. However, it was not until 11 November that it was flown, by Sqn Ldr Lancaster, to Farnborough. Following a brief test flight on 14 December, the Me 410 was flown to 6 MU at Brize Norton by Eric 'Winkle' Brown a week later. Upon arrival at Brize Norton, the Me 410 was placed in storage, eventually being struck off charge and scrapped on 14 August 1947.

AM 74 Me 410B-6 410208 Similar to the other two Me 410s brought to the UK, no information on the Luftwaffe use of this aircraft is available. However, as it was fitted with the FuG 200 anti-shipping radar, one hypothesis is that it belonged to *Seenotgruppe* 80 or 81. Following surrender, it was allocated the identity Air Min V-3. Ferried to Kastrup by Sdn Ldr Somerville on 19 August, the Me 410 was subsequently flown to Gilze Rijen. It did not arrive at RAE Farnborough until 17 September. During the German Aircraft Exhibition, held at Farnborough in November/December 1945, this Me 410 was on public display. It is possible that the aircraft remained grounded following arrival at Farnborough. On 15 December 1946, it was noted in the Farnborough scrapyard.

The British test pilot Eric 'Winkle' Brown later said of the Me 410:

> There was a superficial resemblance between the Me 410 and the Mosquito at a distance and they were broadly similar in configuration, apart from wing positioning and seating arrangement for the two crew members, but the German aircraft was more functional in appearance, lacking any pretensions of elegance. The steeper angle of ground sit adopted by the Messerschmitt resulting from the lower position of its wing combined from the fact that the engines protruded further ahead of the cockpit than did those of the Mosquito rendered view for taxying somewhat restricted other than dead ahead.... (The) undercarriage had to be retracted before 150 mph (240 km/h) was reached. This was a critical period as an engine failure under 155 mph (250 km/h) meant almost certain disaster as the Me 410 could not be prevented from falling away in an uncontrolled spiralling dive.
>
> Once a speed of 155 mph (250 km/h) and an altitude of at least 500 ft (152 m) had been attained, the flaps could be tucked away, the throttles eased to 1·3 *atas*, the propeller pitch coarsened to give 2,500 rpm, the radiators almost closed and a sigh of relief released as the aircraft settled into the climb at 180 mph (290 km/h)The climb to 20,000 ft (6 095 m) took slightly more than 12 minutes, and at that altitude, with 1·2 atas and 2,500 rpm, the cruise

> was 330 mph (530 km/h). I soon discovered that the controls were not well harmonized, the elevators being heavy, the ailerons fairly heavy and the rudder moderately so. The Me 410 was therefore a rather poor aircraft to manoeuvre, and it manifested a very sharp stall with a severe wing drop, particularly if stalled in a tight turn. Furthermore, the stalling speed was high.
>
> The Me 410 was very clean aerodynamically and therefore it accelerated extremely rapidly in a dive, use of the parallel-bar dive brakes above and below the outer wing panels being essential. The maximum speed permitted in a dive was 466 mph (750 km/h) below 4,000 ft (1 215 m), but it was exceedingly difficult to keep the propellers from over-speeding and the engines from over-cooling....
>
> (The Me 410) fell short of the Mosquito in most performance respects and far short of its British contemporary on the score of manoeuvrability. It was one of those aeroplanes that gave, in my view, a knife-edge feeling to its pilot; it was certainly about the last aeroplane that I would have wished upon myself if returning to base in bad weather after losing an engine![1]

USAAF Evaluation

Of the three Me 410s found in Sicily in August 1943, the US War Department's publication *Tactical and Technical Trends* published a brief résumé of the twin-engined *Zerstörer*.

> The airframe appears to be approximately the same as the 210, which is a two-place, twin-engine, low-wing monoplane, the wings having a pronounced taper to rounded tips. The slim fuselage has a blunt nose, a humped cockpit inclosure [*sic.*] in the forward end, and a large fin and rudder. The tail wheel and landing gear are both retractable, the latter into the engine nacelles. Dive brakes are fitted on the upper and lower wing surfaces, outboard of the engine nacelles.... The major difference is found in the engine. The Me-410 is powered with the new Daimler-Benz 603A-2 motors, developed from the DB 601 used in the Me-210 but somewhat larger. Those examined had 12 cylinders rather than the 16 cylinders thought to be in the 603's. They had inverted 'V' liquid-cooled units with no turbo-blower system.
>
> The DB 603 is probably de-rated, as are most of the newer German engines, and estimated performance figures have therefore been made for a de-rated version. The maximum emergency power at 19,000 feet is estimated to be about 1,800 hp with a normal fuel capacity of 608 U.S. gallons. This indicates an estimated maximum speed of 390 to 400 mph at 22,000 feet, with a normal cruising speed of 335 mph and an economical cruising speed of 260 mph. A service ceiling of 33,000 feet and a normal range of about 1,100 miles appears possible.
>
> The armament of the Me-410 was expected to be heavier than that of the 210, which consists of two 20-mm fixed cannon and two 7.9-mm fixed machine guns located in the forward fuselage, and two 13-mm machine guns firing to the rear each with a 50° traverse, mounted in blisters on each side of the fuselage just aft of the trailing edge. However, while this proved in general correct, the two 7.9-mm forward machine guns were not actually installed in the aircraft examined and the apertures were blocked off.
>
> The armor in the new aircraft is similar to that of the 210, which is very heavy, varying in thickness from 4 mm to 13 mm and protecting the pilot's seat, cockpit, engine and radiators. There is also a bullet-proof glass protection for the radio operator.

> The 410 is seen more and more frequently, and is possibly being used as a substitute for for the Fw-190 as well as replacing the Me-210. There has been some indication that this model may also have been equipped for use as a bomber.

As described elsewhere, one 'liberated' Me 210 crashed on its first flight in late 1943, killing its USAAF pilot.

Following the end of the war in Europe on 8 May 1945, American, British, French and Russian teams scrambled to locate and secure German aircraft and associated equipment for evaluation purposes. A USAAF team, led by Colonel Harold Watson, and known as 'Watson's Whizzers' managed to secure a large number of aircraft for shipment to the USA. A telegramme from the RAF HQ 2 Tactical Air Force, dated 16 June 1945, noted:

> Col Watson of D OF I USSTAF authorised to take over these aircraft (located in the British sector, consisting of north-eastern Germany, Denmark and Norway) and fly out ... Request that you release aircraft and afford all possible assistance to render serviceable to enable shipping schedule to be met.

Among the aircraft mentioned were four Me 410s located at 'Westland'—Westerland on the island of Sylt. These aircraft could possibly have belonged to *Seenotstaffel* 80. However, on a list of the aircraft selected, the Me 410s had been crossed over. Although no explanation is given, the reasoning behind rejecting these aircraft was presumably due to lack of shipping facilities, with priority being given to jet aircraft such as the Arado Ar 234 and Messerschmitt Me 262. Additionally, by mid-1945, the Me 410 was an obsolete design, although its weapons, radar and other miscellaneous equipment may have been of some interest.

As noted elsewhere, only one Me 410 actually arrived in the USA. However, this aircraft remained unflown, with little in the way of evidence of formal evaluation surviving. Nevertheless, this particular Me 410 was selected for preservation.

USSR Evaluation

A captured Me 410B-2 (W Nr 130379 of II./ZG 26), most likely captured at Posen (present-day Poznan in Poland) in East Prussia, was evaluated by the NII VVS (*Nauchno-ispytatel'skij institute Voyenno-vozdushnykh Sily* (Research Institute of the Air Force)) at Ramenskoye outside Moscow, with the tests being completed following the end of the war in Europe. The Russian evaluation team, which included Lieutenant Colonel V. Y. Magon and Major I. P. Piskunov, noted that performance dropped considerably when the heavy 50-mm BK 5 cannon was fitted. Nevertheless, the aiming control system was considered excellent, with the cannon having a range of more than 1,000 metres. This made it possible for the Me 410 crews to destroy enemy bombers well out of range of the bombers machine gun defences. With its superior speed and manoeuvrability, the Me 410 was considered having the edge over the Petlyakov Pe-2 and Tupolev Tu-2 light bombers. Against single-engined fighters, however, the Me 410 was clearly inferior, with its sole chance of survival being a head-on attack. Nevertheless, the evaluation report stated:

The Me 410 seen at Wright Field on 7 October 1944. To its left is Typhoon serial number MN235. (*NMUSAF*)

This is the sole Me 410 brought to the USA seen soon after the end of the war. (*Wolfgang Mühlbauer/ DEHLA Archives*)

> Individual structural elements and aggregates of the propeller engine group, armament, and special equipment are of interest from a technical point of view and must be the subject of study by the design bureaus within the People's Commissariat of the Aviation Industry.

Interestingly, no confirmed reports of encounters between Soviet pilots and Luftwaffe Me 210s and Me 410s exist. As described elsewhere, MKHL Me 210s clashed with Soviet fighters on a number of occasions.

Unconfirmed reports speak of captured Me 410s being used by VVS units in the spring of 1945. This appears highly unlikely for a number of reasons. With the Petlyakov Pe-2 and Tupolev Tu-2 medium bombers and Ilyushin Il-2 Shturmovik close support aircraft being in large-scale use, the need to field captured Luftwaffe aircraft against its former owners seems non-existent. One possible reason for doing just that would have been for propaganda purposes. In the event, the obvious need for pilot training, as well as severe maintenance and spares issues would most likely have outweighed any advantages of using Me 410s. However, during the Great Patriotic War, other captured Luftwaffe aircraft, including Bf 109s, Fi 156 Storchs, He 111s, and Ju 52/3ms were indeed used operationally by the VVS.

A Me 410B-2/U4 seen soon after falling into Russian hands near Posen (Poznan) in early 1945. (*Carl-Fredrik Geust*)

18
Luftwaffe Messerschmitt Me 210 and Me 410 units (1941–1945)

This chapter contains brief, concise histories of each known Me 210/Me 410 unit. Information regarding the formation of each unit, base/s, Orders of Battle, significant events and disbandment have been included.

I./*Schnellkampfgeschwader* 210: Unit code S9+, it was formed on 24 April 1941 at Abbeville, France, from *Erprobungsgruppe* 210. During the Battle of Britain, *Erprobungsgruppe* 210 flew a number of low-level attack sorties, being equipped with Bf 110s and Bf 109s. The very nature of such sorties occasionally resulted in very high losses. For instance, one Bf 109 and six Bf 110s were lost on 15 August 1940 during an attack on Croydon. The losses included the unit's *Gruppenkommendeur*, Hptm Walter Rubensdorffer. Although the designation of the unit was derived from the Messerschmitt Me 210, the first of these did not arrive until November 1941. At this time, the unit was based at Landsberg-Lech. On 4 January 1942, I./SKG 210 was redesignated as I./ZG 1.

No. 3.(F)/22: Unit code 4N+, it was formed on 1 October 1937 at Prenzlau from 3./Aufkl. *Gruppe* 122. On 1 November 1938, the unit was redesignated as 3./Aufkl.*Gruppe* 121, but it reformed on the same day as 3./Aufkl.*Gruppe* 121. Yet another redesignation resulted in the unit becoming 3.(F)/22. Initially operating reconnaissance variants of the Dornier Do 17, these were supplemented by Bf 110s in 1940. In June 1941, 3.(F)/22 converted to the Ju 88D. The Ju 88s were replaced by the improved Ju 188 in late 1943. In December 1943, 3.(F)/22 moved to Spilve in Latvia, remaining there until October 1944. A few Me 410B-3s arrived in mid-1944, operating alongside Ju 188s. 3.(F)/22 ended the war at Zabeln in May 1945. Three Me 410s of 3.(F)/22 were flown to Norway on 5 May 1945.

No. 1.(F)/33: Unit code 8H+, it was formed in December 1940. In July 1941, 1.(F)/33 was based at Baranowicze in Poland, being equipped with Ju 88Ds. The unit saw action during Operation Barbarossa, being based at Minsk and Smolensk respectively until returning to Germany in December 1941. By late spring of 1942, 1.(F)/33 deployed to Toussus-le-Buc in France, moving to Istres in November. 1.(F)/33 remained at Istres until September 1943, moving to Saint Martin. By this time, different subvariants of the Ju 88 (including A-4s, A-14s, A-17s, D-1s, and T-1s) were on charge. The first Ju 188s began to arrive in early 1944. In June 1944, one Me 410A-1 and four Me 410A-3s were taken on charge. Before the month was out, the solitary Me 410A-1 had been transferred to another unit. Me 410s never completely superceded the Ju 188s, both types remaining in use until early 1945. Following the Allied invasion of France, 1.(F)/33 moved to Munich-Riem in August 1944, remaining there until 4 September. On that date, 1.(F)/33 transferred to Leck. It did not remain at Leck for long, moving to Perleberg in early October. Soon afterwards, yet another transfer was made, to Jüterbog-Waldlager, where 1.(F)/33 remained based until February 1945, when the unit was disbanded.

No. 1.(F)/121: Unit code 7A+, it was formed on 1 May 1934 at Neuhausen as *Fliegerstaffel* Neuhausen, being redesignated on 1 October 1935 as *Fliegerstaffel* 1 Neuhausen. Another unit redesignation, this time to 1./Aufkl.Gr. 11, occurred on 1 October 1937. Thirteen months later, on 1 November 1938, 1.(F)/121 was reformed at Prenzlau from 1./Aufkl.Gr 22. In July 1940, Aufkl. *Staffel* (F)/H *Flakkorps* was absorbed into 1.(F)/121. At this time, the main type of aircraft was the Ju 88D. In July 1943, 1.(F)/121 transferred to Toussus-le-Buc. While based here, a small number of Me 410A-3/B-3s began to arrive in December 1943. During Operation Steinbock, a number of sorties were flown over Britain. The unit remained at Toussus–Le Buc until August 1944, when a move to Florennes in Belgium was made. With Allied forces approaching Belgium, 1.(F)/121 transferred to Langendiebach on 4 September. Less than one month later, on 2 November 1944, 1.(F)/121 was disbanded.

No. 1.(F)/122: Unit code F6+, it was formed on 1 May 1934 at Prenzlau from 1./Aufkl. Gr. 222. During the war, 1.(F)/122 operated a fairly diverse types of aircraft, including the Ju 88A-5, Ju 88D-1, Ju 88D-5, Ju 88T, Bf 109E-9, Bf 109F-4/R3, and Bf 109G-4/R3. In late 1942 and early 1943, a single Fw 200C-3 was on charge with the unit. In May 1944, six Me 410A-3s arrived, alongside solitary examples of the Bf 110C-5 and Bf 110E-1. Additional Me 410B-1 and B-3s were taken on charge in mid-1944. By early 1945, 1.(F)/122 had become part of *Fernaufklärungsgruppe* 3, which had been formed in August 1944 to conduct photo reconnaissance operations for *Heeresgruppe Mitte* on the Eastern Front. No. 1.(F)/122 was based at Vysoké Mýto in eastern Bohemia, eventually moving to the Kbely and Ruzyne air bases near Prague in late April 1945, where they remained until the end of the war.

No. 2.(F)/122: Unit code F6+, it was formed on 1 April 1936 at Prenzlau. Redesignated as 2./Aufkl.Gr. 22 on 1 October 1937, but it reformed thirteen months later at Goslar as 2.(F)/122. Initially serving on the Western Front, 2.(F)/122 was transferred to Warsaw in May 1941, in anticipation of Operation Barbarossa, the German invasion of the USSR. Following commencement of hostilities, 2.(F)/122 operated on the Eastern Front, being based at Smolensk between September and December 1941. During the final days of 1941, the unit was withdrawn from the Eastern Front, relocating to Munich-Riem for Ju 88D-1 conversion training. In January 1942, 2.(F)/122 transferred to Trapani in Sicily. The unit was to remain in Italy until the end of the war in 1945. In December 1942, the first four Me 210s arrived at Trapani. Nevertheless, 2.(F)/122 retained its Ju 88Ds, as well as some Heinkel He 111H-11s serving alongside the Me 210s until mid-1943. During this time, several reconnaissance sorties were conducted against Allied-controlled harbours along the North African coast. An initial batch of Me 410s arrived in July 1943, replacing the earlier Me 210s. Around this time, two Ar 240s were taken on charge. One of these was written off in a crash at Frosione.

However, the Ju 88Ds were retained for another year, not being completely replaced by Me 410s until June 1944. The final 2.(F)/122 sortie took place on 20 March 1945. The remaining four serviceable Me 410s were ferried back Munich-Riem in early April 1945.

No. 5.(F)/122: Unit code F6+, it was formed at Goslar in October 1939. In October 1944, 5.(F)/122 was based at Riga-Spilve in Latvia. With Russian forces approaching, the unit transferred to Jesau later the same month. In October 1944, a small number of Me 410s arrived. However, Ju 88D-1s and Ju 188D-2s continued to serve with the unit. Another move was made in December 1944, this time to Finow. Here 5.(F)/122 remained until March 1945, when the unit moved to Neuruppin. The following month, 5.(F)/122 transferred to Beldringe in Denmark. Some of the seven Me 410s surrendered at Beldringe may have belonged to 5.(F)/122. During December 1944, two Me 410A-1s, two Me 410A-3s, two Me 410B-2s and nine Me 410B-3s were serving with 5.(F)/122. On 1 April 1945, 5.(F)/122 had seven Me 410s (six serviceable) as well as ten Ju 188s and one Ju 88. Of the twenty crews, sixteen were cleared for operations.

Stab Fernaufklärungsgruppe 1: Formed in May 1942 at Luga. A total of seven reconnaissance *Staffeln* would subordinated to *Stab* FAGr. 1. Four of these were Me 410 units: 3.(F)/22 (between 1943 and March 1945), 1.(F)/33 (between February and May 1945), 3.(F)/122 (between 1943 and 1945), and 5.(F)/122 (between 1942 and February 1945). By February 1944, *Stab* FAGr. 1 had taken up residence at Riga-Spilve in Latvia. The first Me 410B-3 arrived in July, supplementing a solitary Ju 88D. The following month, a Me 410B-3 was lost. However, three Me 410s were on charge on 31 August. In October 1944, a move was made to Prowehren. Unit strength on 31 December 1944 was three Me 410B-3s and one Ju 188D-2. Shortly afterwards, *Stab* FAGr. 1 transferred to Jüterbog-Waldlager. The unit remained at Jüterbog until 7 February, when a further transfer was made, this time to Quakenbrück. Here *Stab* FAGr. 1 remained until the end of the war.

Stab Fernaufklärungsgruppe 3: Formed on 20 August 1944 at Stubendorf. Interestingly, of the four reconnaissance *Staffeln* subordinated to *Stab* FAGr. 3, none were equipped with Me 410s. Nevertheless, *Stab* FAGr 3 received three Me 410A-3s in November 1944. The following month, a move was made to Sprottau.

II./*Zerstörergeschwader* 1: By early 1942, plans to equip this unit with Me 210s were abandoned.

III./*Zerstörergeschwader* 1: Unit code 2N+, it was formed at Lechfeld in Janury 1942, consisting of *Stab* ZG 1 and three *Staffeln*: 7., 8., and 9./ZG 1. The first *Gruppenkommendeur* was Major Roland Bohrt. The first aircraft, 22 Bf 109E-7/U1s, did not arrive until April 1942. Transferring to the Eastern Front in May 1942, III./ZG 1 was initially based at Belgorod, moving to Kuteinikowo two months later. In August 1942, III./ZG 1 transferred to Bir el Abd in Libya, being attached to *Fliegerführer Afrika*. A few Bf 110s arrived shortly afterwards. However, by October 1942, a total of seventeen Me 210s had also been delivered.

Shortly afterwards, III./ZG 1 moved to Trapani on Sicily, becoming part of II. Fliegerkorps. A new *Gruppenkommendeur*, Hptm Fritz Hobein, arrived on 10 September 1942. Hobein would remain with III./ZG 1 until mid-February 1943. During the final months of the North African campaign, III./ZG 1 would experience a quick succession of *Gruppenkommendeurs*: Hptm Reinhard Hubel (16 February–March 1943), Hptm Heinz Roeber (March 1943), and Hptm Drescher (March 1943). At an undetermined date, Drescher was succeeded by Major Wilhelm Berlin, who left his post on 10 October 1943.

Between November 1942 and May 1943, III./ZG 1 would see a considerable amount of action over North Africa and Sicily. The highest number of Me 210s available to III./ZG 1 during this time was forty-one Me 210A-1s and one Me 210C-1 in February 1943. With the Axis defeat in North Africa on 13 May 1943, and increasing Allied raids against Sicily and southern Italy, III./ZG 1 moved to Castel Vetrano. The unit did not remain here for long, relocating to Brest-Süd in France in July 1943. On 30 June, III./ZG 1 counted seven Me 210A-1s, one Me 210C-1, and two Me 410As. The Me 410 would eventually supercede the unit's Me 210s. Between November 1942 and September 1943, III./ZG 1 lost fifty-five Me 210s and seven Me 410s in combat, with an additional seventy-four Me 210s and four Me 410s being written off in accidents, etc.

The twenty-four Me 410s available in July were distributed among *Stab* III./ZG 1 (one), 7./ZG 1 (eleven), and 8./ZG 1 (twelve), with only the third Staffel—9./ZG 1—retaining its Me 210s. In September 1943, III./ZG 1 was withdrawn to Vörden near Neunkirchen for re-equipment with the Ju 88C-6. The following month, III./ZG 1 was reformed at Bordeaux-Merignac as II./ZG 26.

Ergänzungsstaffel Zerstörergeschwader 1: Formed on 4 January 1942 at Merville, France, from *Ergänzungsstaffel* SKG 210. At the time, Bf 109s and Bf 110s were used. At the end of January 1942, Erg.St./ZG 1 transferred to Lechfeld, where it remained until 17 April 1942. The following day, the unit was redesignated as 1./*Ergänzungs-Zerstörergruppe*. On 6 April 1944, Erg.St./ZG 1 was reformed at Illesheim from 3./*Ergänzungs-Zerstörergruppe*, being equipped with Bf 110s and Me 410s. Hptm Johannes Kaufmann was appointed as *Staffelkapitän*. Following a move to Salzwedel on 16 July 1944, the Erg.St./ZG 1 was redesignated as 9./JG 4 the following month.

Stab/Zerstörergeschwader 26 Horst Wessel: Unit code 3U+. Formed on 1 May 1939 at Dortmund from *Stab*/ZG 142. Initially, Bf 109Ds were operated, being replaced by Bf 110s in early January 1940. It was redesignated as *Stab*/NJG 3 on 29 September 1941 and reformed on 13 October 1943 at Wunsdorf from *Stab* I./ZG 1. *Stab*/ZG 26 received a few Me 410s in March 1944, when based at Königsberg-Devau. Two Me 410s were lost in non-operational accidents in June. The following month, *Stab*/ZG 26 was redesignated as *Stab* I./JG 6.

I./*Zerstörergeschwader* 26 Horst Wessel: Unit code E8+, it was formed on 1 May 1939 at Dortmund from I./ZG 142. It was initially equipped with Messerschmitt Bf 109Ds, which had been fully replaced by Bf 110s in January 1940. I./ZG 26 subsequently saw action during the Battle of Britain before transferring to Memmingen in Germany in November 1940. Here, I./ZG 26 remained until late March 1941, when the unit moved to Szeged in Hungary. I./ZG 26 saw action during the invasion of Yugoslavia, Greece, and Crete before moving to Vilnius in Lithuania on 28 June for operations against the USSR. In April 1942, I./ZG 26 was disbanded, with its personnel and aircraft being absorbed by ZG 1 and ZG 2.

However, I./ZG 26 was reformed on 13 October 1943 at Bad Lippspringe from 1./ZG 1, 2./ZG 1 and 3./ZG 1 respectively. On 1 April 1944, I./ZG 26 had fully converted to the Me 410 from the Bf 110, having a strength of 28 Me 410s (including the Me 410 V15). By 30 April, unit strength had risen to forty-eight Me 410s.

Between 1 April and 29 April, I./ZG 26 was based at Fassberg before briefly transferring to Gabbert, remaining there until 17 May. On that day, I./ZG 26 moved to Königsberg-Devau on 17 May. This move was made to get out of range for the USAAF escort fighters. When based at Königsberg-Devau, the Me 410s had the range to intercept USAAF bombers attacking targets along the German Baltic Sea coast and eastern Germany and Poland. Another advantage was that the USAAF fighter escorts did not have enough range to reach Königsberg.

In July 1944, I./ZG 26 was redesignated as I./JG 6, remaining based at Königsberg. Between April and September 1944, I./ZG 26 lost 37 Me 410s in combat and another twenty-five Me 410s in accidents. The final thirty-two Me 410A-1s and sixteen Me 410B-2s were transferred to other units in October 1944.

II./*Zerstörergeschwader* 26 Horst Wessel: Unit code 3U+, it was formed on 1 May 1939 at Werl from II./ZG 142, flying Bf 109Ds. The first Bf 110s began to arrive already in September 1939. The following year, II./ZG 26 saw action over France and Britain and the invasion of Yugoslavia and Greece in April 1941. The unit served on the Eastern Front until March 1942, being disbanded the following month, with its personnel and aircraft being absorbed by ZG 1 and ZG 2.

On 11 October 1943, II./ZG 26 was reformed at Hildesheim from *Stab* III./ZG 1 and 7., 8., and 9./ZG 1. The first Me 410s (as well as a solitary Me 210) began to arrive the same month. On 31 October, no fewer than thirty-nine Me 410s were on charge, with Hptm Eduard Tratt serving as *Gruppenkommendeur*. At this time, II./ZG 26 was based at Hildesheim. Tratt remained with II./ZG 26 until he was shot down and killed on 22 February 1944.

II./ZG 26 remained until February 1944, when a move to Pfaffenhofen was made. Although 4./ZG 26 and 5./ZG 26 moved to Königsberg-Devau on 24 March 1944, 6./ZG 26 remained at Pfaffenhofen until 10 April 1944 before joining the other two *Staffeln* at Königsberg-Devau. Between October 1943 and August 1944, II./ZG 26 lost no fewer than 110 Me 410s in combat, including eighteen in July 1944. The vast majority of these losses occurred during USAAF raids. Another sixty-one aircraft were written off in operational accidents. In July 1944, II./ZG 26 was redesignated as II./JG 6.

III./*Zerstörergeschwader* 26 Horst Wessel: Unit code 3U+, it was formed on 1 May 1939 at Lippstadt from III./ZG 142. Similar to the other two ZG 26 *Gruppen*, Bf 109Ds formed the first equipment of III./ZG 26. However, the Bf 109s were not replaced with Bf 110s until February 1940. Between 25 September 1939 and 4 February 1940, III./ZG 26 was also known as *Jagdgruppe* 126.

After seeing action during the Battle of Britain, III./ZG 26 transferred to southern Italy. By mid-1942, III./ZG 26 had moved to Libya. Following the Allied victory in North Africa in May 1943, III./ZG 26 transferred to Rome-Ciampino, where the unit remained for a short while before moving back to Germany. On 24 March 1944, III./ZG 26 moved to Königsberg-Devau, remaining there until 11 May. On that date, the unit transferred to Leipheim, eventually moving to Lechfeld less than two weeks later. However, only 8./ZG 26 was based at Leipheim, remaining there until 18 August 1944 when it was transferred to Rechlin-Lärz. The other two *Staffeln*, 7./ZG 26 and 9./ZG 26, were based at Fels-am-Wagram and Schwäbisch Hall, before moving to Seyring and Erfurt-Bindersleben respectively.

On 26 September 1944, III./ZG 26 was redesignated as *Kommando* Nowotny, with 8./ZG 26 and 9./ZG 26 becoming 2./ and 1./*Kommando* Nowotny. The third *Staffel*, 7./ZG 26, was absorbed by JG 76.

IV./*Zerstörergeschwader* 26 Horst Wessel: Unit code A4+, it was formed in July 1944. This *Gruppe* consisted of three *Staffeln*: 10./ZG 26 (formed from 13./(Z) JG 5 based in Norway), 11./ZG 26 (formed from 11./ZG 26 based in Greece), and 12./ZG 26 (formed from Küstenstaffel

Krim, based on the Crimean peninsula). Only 11./ZG 26 would eventually receive Me 410s. The unit was transferred to Ørland, Norway, in September 1944, bringing twenty-three Ju 88C-6s with them. Seven of the Ju 88s were transferred to other units in later the same month. On 18 November 1944, 11./ZG 26 moved to Gardermoen outside Oslo, where the unit was to convert to the Me 410. Thirteen Me 410s (consisting of three Me 410A-1s, five Me 410A-1/U2s, and five Me 410B-2/U2s) had been taken on charge by 1 January 1945. One Me 410s had been lost in an operational accident in December 1944. Barely four weeks later, on 25 January 1945, 11./ZG 26 returned to Ørland. However, operational activities appear to have been limited. On 23 February 1945, IV./ZG 26 received orders to disband, with its personnel being transferred to II./JG 5. Before disbanding, additional Me 410s were received by 11./ZG 26, increasing its strength to seventeen aircraft. According to the census of Luftwaffe aircraft remaining in Norway, dated 10 May 1945, fourteen Me 410s of 11./ZG 26 were located at Ørland, with another three at Oslo-Gardermoen. All of these aircraft were scrapped.

Ergänzungsstaffel Zerstörergeschwader 26 Horst Wessel: Unit code 3U+, it was formed on 9 April 1944 at Illesheim from 2./*Ergänzungs-Zerstörergruppe*. Oblt Werner Glomb served as *Staffelkapitän* until 11 May, when he was replaced by Oblt Berhardt Paffrath. In April 1944, the *Ergänzungsstaffel* had thirteen Me 210s and fourteen Me 410A-1s, with one of the former and four of the latter being transferred for overhaul or refurbishment by 30 April. On 9 July, Oblt Willi Radel became *Staffelkapitän*. At an undetermined date in July, Erg.St./ZG 26 moved to Brandis. It did not stay at Brandis very long, moving to Sagan-Küpper later the same month. Unit strength in August 1944 included three Me 210s and 29 Me 410s, all of which had been transferred to other units by 31 August. The following day, Erg.St./ZG 26 was redesignated as 2./*Jagdgruppe* Nord.

Stab/Zerstörergeschwader 76: Unit code M8+, it was formed on 15 April 1940 at Cologne-Wahn, equipped with Bf 110s. Moved to Laval in July 1940, and then to Stavanger-Sola in Norway three months later. It was redesignated on 1 August 1941 as *Stab/Jagdfliegerführer* Norwegen and reformed in August 1943 at Ansbach. The unit moved to Prague-Kbely and Prague-Rusyne on 25 April 1944. Two Me 410A-1s had already arrived during the month, replacing two Bf 110Gs. On 1 June 1944, *Stab*/ZG 76 had six Me 410B-2s on charge. By the end of the month, unit strength had been reduced by 50 per cent, with three Me 410s being lost to enemy action. On 13 June, the unit moved to Vienna-Seyring, transferring to Malacky in the Reichsportektorat (present-day Czech Republic) a month later. On 24 July 1944, *Stab*/ZG 76 was redesignated as *Stab*/JG 76.

I./*Zerstörergeschwader* 76: Unit code M8+, it was formed on 1 May 1939 at Olmütz (present-day Olomuc in the Czech Republic) from II./ZG 141, with Hptm Günther Reinecke as *Gruppenkommandeur*. Initially equipped with Bf 109Ds, these soon gave way to Bf 110s. I./ZG 76 was heavily involved in Operation Weserübung, the invasion of Denmark and Norway, providing air cover for the fleet of Junkers Ju 52/3m transports. The unit remained based in Norway until early September 1940. On 7 September, I./ZG 76 was redesignated as II./NJG 1. In August 1943, I./ZG 76 was reformed at Ansbach. On 25 April 1944, I./ZG 76 transferred to Prague-Kbely and Prague-Ruzyne. At the same time, Me 410s began to arrive, eventually replacing the Bf 110Gs. No fewer than sixty-five Me 410s, including thirty-eight Me 410A-1s and nineteen Me 410B-1s, arrived during April. Eight aircraft were lost during the month, all in non-operational accidents. Another eleven aircraft were written off in May, with six more being transferred to other units. This left thirty-three Me 410A-1s and fourteen Me 410Bs on 31 May. I./ZG 76 first saw combat in early June 1944. Another move was made on 13 June 1944, this time to Vienna-Seyring. During a USAAF raid against Budapest on 2 July 1944, eight four-engined bombers were claimed as destroyed. No Me 410s were lost. Six days later, I./ZG 76 was severely mauled by P-38 Lightnings of the USAAF's 82nd FG. Eight Me 410s were lost during a one-sided combat. This disaster spelled the end of I./ZG 76. The stay at Vienna-Seyring was shortlived, with I./ZG 76 moving to Malacky on 12 July. The same month, I./ZG 76 was redesignated as I./JG 76, with the Me 410s being replaced with Bf 109s. In all, I./ZG 76 lost forty-five Me 410s in combat, and forty-nine to non-operational causes between April and July 1944.

II./*Zerstörergeschwader* 76: Unit code M8+, it was formed on 1 May 1939 at Gablingen from I./ZG 144. The first *Gruppenkommendeur* was Hptm Walter Schmidt Coste. Bf 109Ds remained with II./ZG 76 for nine months, with the first Bf 110s not arriving until early February 1940. At this time, II./ZG 76 was based at Garz auf Usedom on the German Baltic Sea coast. Following the French surrender, II./ZG 76 moved to Abbeville. As with other *Zerstörer* units, II./ZG 76 was highly active during the Battle of Britain. In September 1940, II./ZG 76 returned to Germany.On 1 November 1941, II./ZG 76 was redesignated as III./NJG 3. However, II./ZG 76 was resurrected in August 1943 at Wertheim. Further moves followed, with II./ZG 76 arriving at Prague-Kbely on 25 April 1944. By this time, Me 410s had begun to arrive. However, only three Me 410A-1s were received in April 1944. Re-equipment with Me 410s began in earnest in May, with 33 being on charge on 31 May. Four aircraft, three Me 410A-1s, and one Me 410B-1 had been lost in non-operational accidents during the month. During June and July, II./ZG 76 lost twenty Me 410s in combat. Far more aircraft were lost to non-operational causes, though, with no fewer than fifty-three Me 410s being written off between May and December 1944. On 27 February 1945, II./ZG 76 was redesignated as III./JG 54, with Fw 190s and Bf 109Gs replacing the Me 410s.

Ergänzungsstaffel Zerstörergeschwader 76: Unit code M8+, it was formed on 6 April 1944 at Unterschlauersbach from 4./*Ergänzungs-Zerstörergruppe*. Hptm Hubertus Huy served as *Staffelkapitän* between 6 April and 14 June, being replaced by Olt Herbert Schob on 15 June. On 1 September 1944, Erg.Staffel/ZG 76 was redesignated as 1./*Jagdgruppe* Ost. The initial equipment of Erg.Staffel/ZG 76 consisted of a dozen Me 210A-1s and seven Me 410A-1s. In May 1944, no fewer than twenty-nine Me 410A-1s were on charge, as well as twelve Bf 110Gs and twelve Me 210A-1s. By the end of the month, the number of Me 410s had been reduced to twenty. Two aircraft had been lost in accidents, with the remaining seven having been transferred to other units. Unit strength in July 1944 (no such information exists for August 1944) consisted of twenty Me 410A-1s, five Me 210s, and fourteen Bf 110Gs.

Ergänzungs-Zerstörergruppe: Unit code 4H+, it was formed on 1 April 1940 at Magdeburg-Ost as *Ergänzungs-Zerstörergruppe* with Bf 109s and Bf 110s. Initially consisting of *Stab* and two *Staffeln*, the unit supplied replacement aircraft for regular *Zerstörergruppen*. From June 1940, the unit became known as *Ergänzungs-Zerstörergruppe* Værløse. Between the summer of 1940 and late 1943, the unit was reformed and/or redesignated a number of times. On 1 September 1943, it was reformed at Braunschweig-Broitzem (Brunswick) as *Ergänzungs-Zerstörergruppe*, with *Stab* and four *Staffeln*. Three Me 210A-1s had been taken on charge already in August 1943. Three Me 410s came and went the following month, with eight Me 210A-1s (six being under repair) and three Me 210C-1s being on charge on 30 September 1943. On 3 March 1944, a move was made to Illesheim, where the unit remained until disbandment little over three months later. In April 1944, twenty-three Me 210s (including the Me 210 V24) and eighteen Me 410A-1s were formally on charge with the *Ergänzungs-Zerstörergruppe*. By 30 April, all of these aircraft had been transferred to other units. On 6 June 1944, *Ergänzungs-Zerstörergruppe* was disbanded, with the second, third, and fourth *Staffeln* becoming *Ergänzungsstaffel* ZG 26, ZG 1, and ZG 76 respectively.

I./NJG 1: Unit code G9+, it was formed on 22 June 1940 at Mönchengladbach. The first *Gruppenkommendeur* was Hptm Günther Radusch. Initially flying Messerschmitt Bf 110s, I./NJG 1 became a highly successful night fighter unit, operating from bases in the Netherlands and western Germany. The purpose-designed night fighter Heinkel 219 began to arrive in April 1943. The He 219 did not completely replace the Bf 110 until early 1944. In March and April 1944, four Me 410A-1s were recorded as being on charge with I./NJG 1. However, it seems likely that these were not used on operations. In May 1945, I./NJG 1 was based at Westerland on the island of Sylt and at Husum.

I./NJG 5: Unit code C9+, it was formed at Stendal from II./ZG 2 in September 1942. The Messerschmitt Bf 110 remained the unit's main type of aircraft until August 1944, when replacement with Ju 88Gs began. Only one Me 410A-1, coded C9+EK, was taken on charge in April 1944. The reason behind this was to attempt to counter the DH.98 Mosquito, which was causing Luftwaffe severe headaches. The following month, this Me 410 had been transferred to another unit. I./NJG 1 ended the war in May 1945 at Redlin.

V./KG 2: Unit code U5+, it was formed in June 1943 at Lechfeld from II./KG 40 as part of IX.Fliegerkorps. V./KG 2 consisted of *Stab* V./KG 2 and four *Staffeln*: 13./KG 2 (newly established), 14./KG 2 (from 4./KG 40), 15./KG 2 (from 5./KG 40), and 16./KG 2 (from 5./KG 2). V./KG 2 became the first unit to convert to the Me 410. On 20 June 1943, V./KG 2 moved to Merville in France. Apart from a brief spell in late 1943, when the unit was based at Amsterdam-Schiphol, V./KG 2 would remain in France during its entire existence. In July 1943, V./KG 2 had a total of forty-eight Me 410s on charge, as well as a solitary Do 217K-1. On 29 December 1943, V./KG 2 transferred from Amsterdam-Schiphol to Athies. It was not to remain at Athies for long, moving to Vitry on 22 January 1944. The unit flew a large number of night intruder sorties over Britain, suffering heavily against RAF Mosquito night fighters. V./KG 2 also saw service during the initial stages of Operation Steinbock. In February, V./KG 2 had four Me 410A-1s and eighteen Me 410A-1/U2s. On 6 February 1944, V./KG 2 was redesignated as II./KG 51.

No. 16./KG 6: Unit code 2H+, it was formed on 1 September 1942 at Soesterberg, the Netherlands, from *Erprobungskommando* 210. Nine Me 210A-1s were on charge in September. Four aircraft were lost during the month, three in combat and one in an accident, leaving five serviceable Me 210s on 30 September. Already in October 1942, 16./KG 6 was redesignated as 11./ZG 1. Moving to Sicily with fifteen Me 210s, 11./ZG 1 was redesignated as *Erprobungsstaffel* 410 in December 1942. *Erprobungsstaffel* 410 was responsible for clearing the Me 410 for combat.

Stab/Kampfgeschwader 51 Edelweiss: Unit code 9K+, it was formed on 1 May 1939 at Landsberg-Lech from *Stab*/KG 255. One Me 410 arrived in September 1943. The unit was then based at Evreux, France, moving to Saint-Georges-Motel on 15 February 1944. Three months later, on 23 May, *Stab*/KG 51 transferred to Lechfeld. During its existence, *Stab*/KG 51 never had more than three Me 410s on charge. Two aircraft were lost in action, in April and September 1944 respectively. The final Me 410A-1/U2s were transferred to other units in September 1944, when KG 51 began to receive Messerschmitt Me 262s. On 24 April 1945, orders were received to disband *Stab*/KG 51.

I./*Kampfgeschwader* 51: Unit code 9K+, it was formed on 1 May 1939 at Landsberg-Lech from I./KG 255. The Dornier Do 17Ms was soon replaced by Heinkel He 111Hs. However, I./KG 51 was to operate the Junkers Ju 88A from April 1940 until May 1943. During this period, I./KG 51 was active during the Battle of Britain and the invasion of Yugoslavia and Greece in April 1941, as well as on the Eastern Front.

On 7 September 1943, I./KG 51 moved from Kirovgrad to Illesheim, becoming subordinated to *Luftwaffenbefehlshaber Mitte*. At the same time, conversion from the Ju 88A to the Me 410 took place, with twenty-three of the latter being listed in the unit strength returns for August 1943. On 6 December 1943, I./KG 51 transferred to Evreux in preparation for Operation Steinbock, a major Luftwaffe bombing campaign against Britain. A total of 32 Me 410s were then on charge. In March and April 1944, seven Me 410s were lost in combat. Another fourteen aircraft were lost in accidents between November 1943 and May 1944.

A further move was made on 25 April 1944, to Dreux. The following month, I./KG 51 returned to Germany. By July 1944, only a single Me 410 remained with I./KG 51. Remarkably, this solitary Me 410 was not transferred to another unit until September. By the summer of 1944, Me 262 conversion training began at Lechfeld. However, a severe setback occurred on 19 July 1944, when ten Me 262s were destroyed or severely damaged in an Allied bomb raid. I./KG 51 ended the war at Saaz.

II./*Kampfgeschwader* 51: Unit code 9K+, it was originally formed on 1 April 1940 at Munich-Riem. The unit had a similar combat history to that of I./KG 51, seeing service during the Battle of Britain, the invasion of Yugoslavia and Greece as well as Operation Barbarossa. Between 18 September and 28 November 1943, II./KG 51 was based at Saloniki in Greece. Shortly afterwards, on 4 January 1944, the unit moved to Vinnitza. Up until this juncture, II./KG 51 had flown Junkers Ju 88As. While at Vinnitza, the unit was redesignated as III./KG 3.

However, II./KG 51 was reformed in February 1944 at Lublin from V./KG 2, consisting of the following units: *Stab* II./KG 51 (from *Stab* V./KG 2), 4./KG 51 (from 14./KG 2), 5./KG 51 (from 15./KG 2), and 6./KG 51 (from 16./KG 2).

Me 410s began to arrive in early 1944 as replacements for the Ju 88As. During February, twenty-seven Me 410s were taken on charge, although only eleven remained with the unit on 29 February. Four aircraft had been lost on operations, with another dozen Me 410s being subjected to overhaul.

In April 1944, II./KG 51 moved from Lublin to Gilze-Rijen in the Netherlands. Possibly the most notable combat sortie of II./KG 51 took place on 22 April 1944. Having shadowed USAAF B-24s over the North Sea, six Me 410s attacked the bombers during the landing phase. A total of thirteen B-24s were destroyed. However, the *Gruppenkommendeur* Hptm Dietrich Puttfarken was lost during this raid. II./KG 51 was also active during the final stages of Operation Steinbock, as well as over Normandy following D-Day. Between February and August 1944, a total of twenty-eight Me 410s were lost on operations, with another nine aircraft being written off in accidents. The worst month for II./KG 51 was June 1944, when no fewer than eleven aircraft were lost, with ten of these being shot down. On 15 August 1944, II./KG 51 relocated to Schwäbisch Hall for Me 262 conversion training. On 24 April 1945, orders were received to disband II./KG 51.

IV./*Kampfgeschwader* 51: Unit code 9K+, it was formed on 30 July 1940 at Schwäbisch Hall as *Ergänzungsstaffel* KG 51. On 22 March 1941, Erg.St./KG 51 was expanded to *Gruppe* strength. Initially, IV./KG 51 flew Junkers Ju 88s, the first Me 410s not arriving until November 1943. At the time, IV./KG 51 was based at Hildesheim, moving to Munich-Riem on 2 April 1944. The Me 410 was the main combat aircraft of IV./KG 51 until late 1944, when Me 262s began to arrive. Although only one Me 410 lost in combat, fourteen others were written off in non-operational accidents between February and July 1944. II./KG 51 was finally absorbed by I./KG 51 on 28 December 1944, when based at Neuburg.

Erprobungskommando 25: Formed on 17 April 1943 at Wittmundhaven, it initially commanded by Legion Condor veteran Major Heinz Nacke, who was replaced after a couple of weeks by Hptm Eduard Tratt, who organised the establishment of a Jagdstaffel (equipped with Bf 109s and Fw 190s), a Kampfstaffel (equipped with Do 217s, Ju 88s, a He 177, and a few Bf 109s for escort purposes) and a *Zerstörerstaffel* (designated (Z)/E.Kdo 25), which was initially equipped with about ten Bf 110s, a Me 210, and a pair of Me 410s. However, already in May 1943, the *General der Jagdflieger* (Commander General of the Fighter Forces) Adolf Galland ordered Hptm Horst Geyer to take command of E.Kdo 25. The role of (Z)/E.Kdo 25 was to test heavy cannon armament under operational conditions. Among the weapons tested were the 37-mm Flak 18 and Flak 43 guns, as well as the 50-mm Flak 41. The *Wurfgranate* 21 (W.Gr. 21) mortar was also tested by the (Z)/E.Kdo 25.

Seenotstaffel 80: Unit code F4+, it was formed on 19 August 1944 at Norderney from *Seenotstaffel* 4 and subordinated to *Seenotgruppe* 80 at Norderney. In December 1944, *Seenotstaffel* 80 had a total of twelve Me 410s, including one fresh from overhaul. The unit remained based at Norderney until March 1945, when a move was made to List on the island of Sylt. As mentioned elsewhere, few details of the operational activities of *Seenotstaffel* 80 are known.

Seenotstaffel 81: Unit code unknown, it was formed in August 1944 at Parow from *Seenotstaffel* 2. Subordinated to *Seenotgruppe* 81. In December 1944, eight Me 410s were on charge, including one unserviceable aircraft. These Me 410s had been transferred from the intended, but not formed, *Seenotstaffel* 100. Due to the lack of fuel, the Me 410s were rarely used. Prior to the arrival of Russian forces, the Me 410s at Parow were intentionally destroyed to prevent their capture. Interestingly, the *Seenotgruppe* 81 did fly a casualty evacuation sortie on 18 June 1945 from Guldborg in Denmark to Schleswig, transporting 450 wounded German troops in fifteen Dornier Do 24 flying boats. The flight south was made under heavy escort from RAF Hawker Typhoons.

Flugzeugüberführungsgeschwader 1 (Fl.üG1): Unit code unknown, it was formed on 21 March 1943 and consisted of six *Gruppen* with a *Stab* and five *Staffeln* each. The Fl.ÜG 1 was responsible for ferrying aircraft from factories and modification centres to frontline units—not unlike that of the RAF's Air Transport Auxiliary (ATA) and Ferry Command. A fairly large number of Me 410s are listed as having sustained damage in landing accidents while flown by Fl.ÜG 1 pilots, this being an indication of the aircraft's handling difficulties during the landing phase.

Additionally, Me 210s and/or Me 410s also served with the following units: *Luftbeobachtungsstaffel* 2 (Me 210s), *Luftbeobachtungsstaffel* 3 (Me 210s), NJG 101 (unit code 9W+), ZG 101 (unit code 6U+), and KG 101 (unit code 5T+). A photograph exists of a Me 410 carrying the code 5T+DN. Unfortunately, further details are lacking.

A Me 410 coded 5T+DN of KG 101. Its original *Stammkennzeichen*, GH+YL, can be discerned. Interestingly, the engine cowlings, part of the fuselage (including the gun barbette), and the rudder are unpainted. Unfortunately, the 'where and when' details are lacking. (*NMUSAF*)

19

Messerschmitt Me 410 Technical Description

The following text is inspired by the Me 410 entry in *Jane's All the World's Aircraft* (1945–46 edition).

The Messerschmitt Me 410 is a twin-engined, low-wing cantilever monoplane with a crew of two (pilot and radio operator/gunner) sitting in tandem in an enclosed cockpit. The wing is divided into three main sections, comprising a one-piece centre section to which two tapering outer sections are mounted. The semi-circular wingtips are detachable. The wing structure comprises a single I-section main spar, a secondary false spar carrying the aileron, flap hinges and control brackets, and a number of lateral former ribs with narrow turned-over flanges, with a series of top-hat section stringers to which the outer stressed skin is attached through flush riveting. The forward leading-edge slats are reinforced through a large-diameter tube within both the centre section and outer wings. The main spar is built up from extruded light alloy angles riveted to a single plate flange with additional riveted cap strips and vertical web stiffeners. The secondary spar consists of a flanged plate with an additional angle riveted to the top and bottom opposite the bent-over flange. The wing joints outboard of the engine nacelles consists of self-aligning joints at the main spar with lugs at the top and bottom flanges, and a Junkers-type spherical joint on the ends of the leading edge tubes. The all-metal camber-changing flaps are hydraulically operated, and fitted between the fuselage and the respective outer wings. The metal-framed ailerons are covered with a D-shaped nose section, and fabric-covered trailing edges. Hydraulically operated dive brakes are fitted to the upper and lower surfaces of the wings. The dive brakes comprise a series of angle slats fitted onto a parallel link bars, which are hinged to the flanges of the main spar in order to provide sideways motion. When the dive brakes are retracted, the slats nest together flush with the wing surfaces. The lower dive brakes have four slats, and the upper dive brakes have two slats. Automaticically operated slats are fitted to the forward leading edges of the outer wings. Six self-sealing fuel tanks (total capacity 2,090 litres) constructed of rubberised flexible materials are carried inside the wings.

Fuselage

The fuselage is built-up from an all-metal structure consisting of two vertical halves, which are joined together at the top and bottom. The flush-riveted outer skin is carried by a series of continuous top-hat section stringers supported by widely spaced frames, some of which are formed by flanging the edges of the vertical skin panels. At these points, the outer skin joints are joggled in order to give a flush external finish. The two fuselage halves are joined at the top and bottom by being riveted to wide channel longerons with lipped flanges.

Tail Section

The tail section is of the cantilever monoplane type. It consists of two spars built-up from light alloy angles and plate webs, pressed-sheet ribs and stressed outer skin. The upper and lower surfaces are joined together at the leading edge through flanges on webs of spars. The tips of the rudders are detachable. The elevators are metal-framed, metal D-leading edges, metal tips with the remainder being fabric-covered. The fin is entirely built-up from metal, with the trim rudder being metal-framed and fabric-covered. The tailplane is adjustable on the ground only. Trim tabs are fitted to the elevators and rudder.

Undercarriage

The undercarriage is retractable, with the main undercarriage retracting hydraulically into the rear section of the engine nacelles. The main wheels turns through 90 degrees to lie horizontally into wells that are closed by fairing doors. The tail wheel is retractable.

Power Plants

The Me 410 is powered by two Daimler-Benz DB 603 twelve-cylinder inverted Vee liquid-cooled engines, each rated at 1,720 hp at an altitude of 5,800 metres, on hollow welded semi-cantilever mounting beams supported at their mid-points by steel tube struts. A GM-1 emergency power-boost system is occasionally fitted. The pair of VDM constant-speed propellers has an armoured plate disc fitted behind the spinner. Armour protection is also fitted to the undersurfaces of the engine nacelles and radiatiors.

Accommodation

The crew of two, pilot/bomb aimer and rear gunner/radio operator are seated in the forward fuselage, underneath an enclosed transparent fairing. Flat transparent glass panels for bomb aiming are fitted in the extreme lower nose section.

Armament

The normal bomber variant carries an armament consisting of two fixed forward-firing 7.9-mm MG 17 machine guns and two fixed forward-firing 20-mm MG 151/20 cannons in the forward fuselage. These guns are operated by the pilot. Two 13-mm MG 131 machine guns mounted in faired blisters, one on each side of the rear fuselage, are remotely aimed and fired by the rear gunner. These blisters are mounted on the ends of a barrel set across the fuselage and carried on annular ball bearings on the inner walls of the fuselage. This barrel may be revolved to elevate or depress the guns, or further gearing within the barrel may traverse the guns through a torque multiplier, driven by a small electric motor and trains of gears. All movements of the guns is controlled by a pistol grip in the gunner's compartment. The guns may be elevated or depressed through a range of about 70 degrees and traversed independently of each other through about 40 degrees from the sides of the fuselage. The guns may also be fired together rearwards. A contact-breaker device interrupts firing when the guns, which are electrically fired, are pointing at any part of the aeroplane structure. The heavy fighter variants have an additional 20-mm MG 151/20 cannons, or one 50-mm BK 5 cannon carried in the nose section.

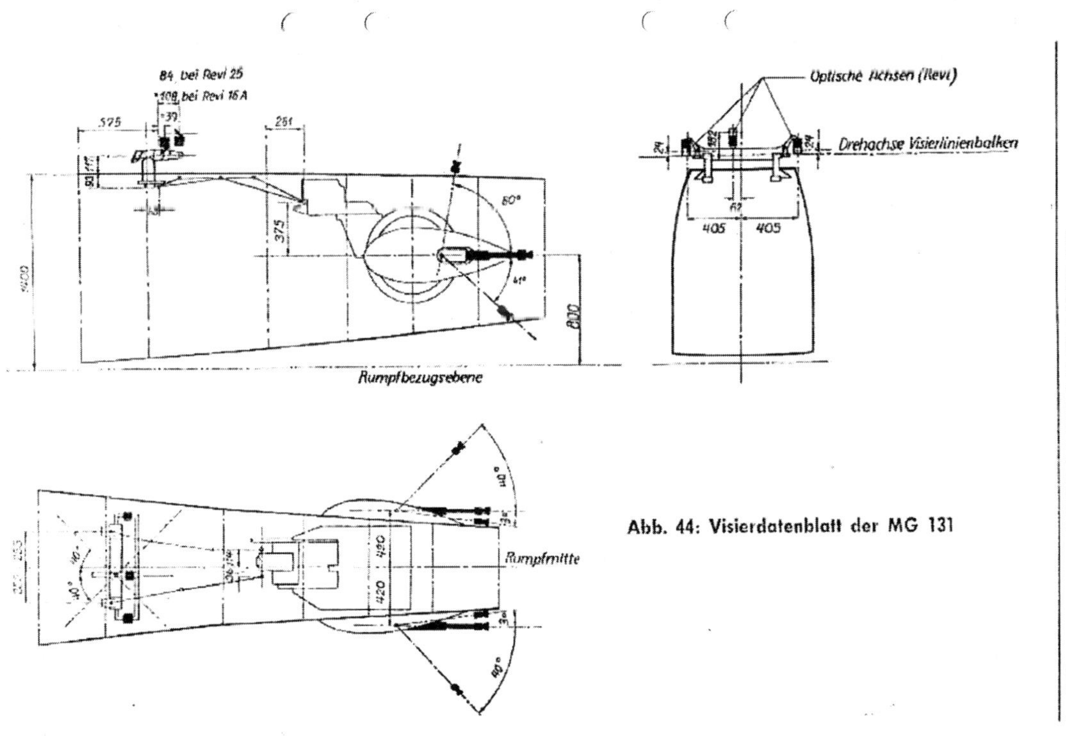

A drawing from the handbook showing the MG 131 barbettes. (*Miro Patocka*)

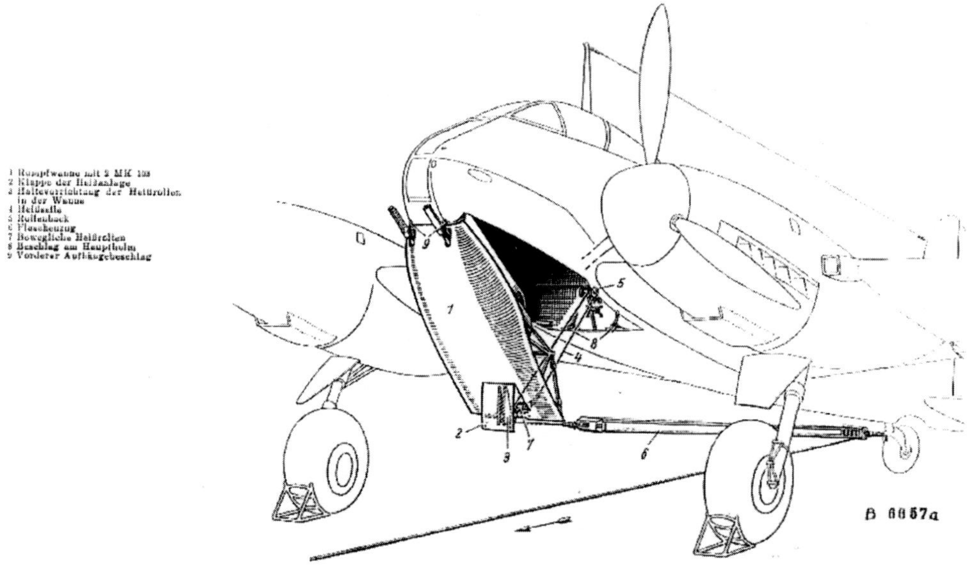

Abb. 10: Gesamtübersicht Heißlanlage MK 103

A drawing from the handbook showing the opening and closing sequence of the hatch for the MK 103 cannons. (*Miro Patocka*)

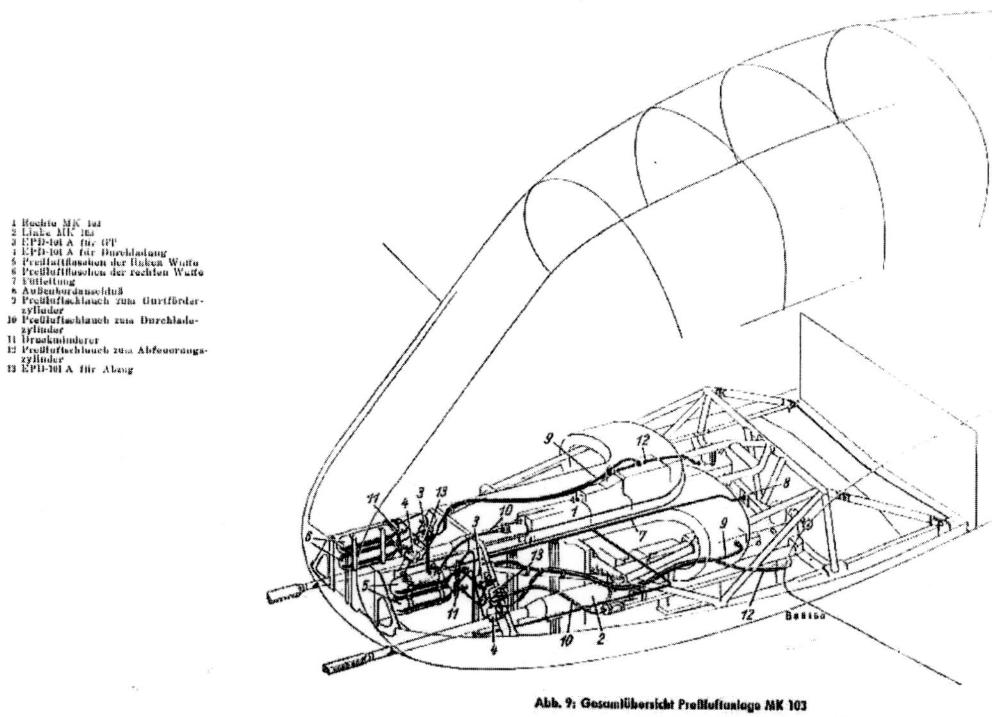

Abb. 9: Gesamtübersicht Preßluftanlage MK 103

A drawing from the handbook showing the pneumatic firing system of the MK 103 cannons. (*Miro Patocka*)

Bomb Load

The bomb compartment is in the extreme forward fuselage beneath the pilot's cockpit, having provision for carrying either two 250-kg bombs or one 500-kg bomb. A 1,000-kg bomb may be stowed, but bomb loads of over 500-kg count as overloads. For photographic reconnaissance duties, cameras are carried in the bomb compartment.

Armour

Armour protection to a weight of approximately 477 kg (7.75 per cent of the airframe's empty weight) is fitted, protecting the pilot's seat, cabin roof, the gunner's position, engines, radiators, coolant pipes, etc.

Equipment

The radio gear consists of the FuG 10 (*Funkgerät*, Radio Apparatus) ground/air set, complete with direction finding and blind approach facilities, and the FuG 16 air/air set, with remote tuning.

Messerschmitt Me 410A-1 Technical Data and Performance Characteristics

Engines: two 1,750-hp DB 603 A
Wingspan: 16.35 m
Length: 12.48 m
Height: 4.28 m
Wing area: 36.20 m^2
Empty weight: 6,700 kg
Maximum weight: 11,300 kg
Maximum speed: 575 kph at an altitude of 6,300 m
Range: 1,350 km
Service ceiling: 8,400 m at maximum weight
Armament: two 7.9-mm MG 17 machine guns, two 20-mm MG 151/20 cannons, and two 13-mm MG 131 rearward firing machine guns in remote-controlled barbettes (500 rounds each)

Messerschmitt Me 410 Variants

Eighteen prototypes, all converted from Me 210 airframes.

Me 410A-1: Fast bomber variant. Armament consisted of two MG 17 machine guns, two MG 151/20 cannons, and two remote-controlled MG 131s. Two SD 500 bombs could be carried internally. If two SC 500 bombs were carried, only one of the bomb bay doors could be closed. Lacked bomb sight suitable for level bombing. First production variant, and also the numerically most important Me 410 variant with 394 delivered, of which 260 converted from Me 210 airframes.

Me 410A-1/U1: Photographic reconnaissance variant. Cameras carried in bomb bay, with armament reduced to two MG 151/20 cannons. Unconfirmed reports speak of this variant also being able to carry cameras in the rear fuselage. Six built.

Me 410A-1/U2: Auxiliary destroyer variant. The *Waffenbehälter* (Weapons Container) WB 151 A, which, incidentally, was built out of wood, is fitted in lower forward fuselage, containing two 20-mm MG 151/20 cannons. The gunsight was either a Revi 12C or a Revi 12D. Pilot protection increased by fitting an armoured windscreen. 277 delivered, of which 200 converted from Me 210 airframes.

Me 410A-1/U3: Single seat heavy fighter variant. Featured GM-1 engine boost and reduced weight, with the rearward firing armament removed. Tested by II./ZG 26 with little success. Did not enter production.

Me 410A-1/U4: Heavy destroyer variant. Fitted with 5-cm BK 5 cannon, and Revi 12C/D or ZFR 4A gunsight. Forward-firing MG 17s often deleted. About sixty built/converted.

Me 410A-2: Fast destroyer variant. Initially planned as a single seater, then as a two seater. Was to have been fitted with ZFR 4 gunsight. Cancelled due to the 30-mm MK 103 cannon not having been cleared for service.

Me 410A-2/U4: Heavy destroyer variant. Was to have been armed with the 5-cm BK cannon. Remained a project.

Me 410A-3: Photographic reconnaissance variant. A camera pod was fitted in the lower forward fuselage. On some aircraft, the armament was removed. Remained in use until the end of the war. Seventy-seven built.

Me 410A-3/U1: Photographic reconnaissance variant. Carried cameras in rear fuselage. GM-1 engine boost fitted. A few may have been converted from Me 410A-3s.

Me 410B: In contrast to the earlier Me 410As, all Me 410Bs were newly built. The Me 410B was optimised for high-altitude operations. The undercarriage was strengthened. Originally, DB 603 G engines were to power the Me 410B. However, due to various problems, DB 603 A engines were fitted instead.

Me 410B-1: Fast bomber variant. Doubtful if any Me 410B-1s saw service in their intended role. Many Me 410B-1s were modified as Me 410B-1/U2 destroyers. Seventy-four built.

Me 410B-1/U2: Destroyer variant. Similar in most respects to the Me 410A-1/U2.

Me 410B-1/U4: Destroyer variant. Similar in most respects to the Me 410A-1/U4.

Me 410B-2: Destroyer variant. Carried a *Waffenbehälter* WB 151 A with two MG 151s, two MG 151/20s, and two MG 131s. Originally planned to fit 30-mm MK 103 cannons, but these were not introduced until June 1944. An armoured windscreen was fitted, with the gunsight being either a Revi 16B or a ZFR 4. Some 165 built.

Me 410B-2/U2: Destroyer variant. Fitted with a *Waffenbehälter* WB 151 A, with two MG 151/20 cannons. Planned to fit two MK 103 cannons. According to one source, this variant had FuG 200 radar fitted. Some forty-eight built.

Me 410B-2/U4: Destroyer variant. Fitted with the 5-cm BK 5 cannon. Some 111 built.

Me 410B-3: Photographic reconnaissance variant. Thirty-five built.

Me 410B-3/U1: Photographic reconnaissance variant. Fitted with GM-1 boost, and cameras in rear fuselage.

Me 410B-5: Torpedo bomber variant. Ability to carry one LT 5b or two BT torpedoes. Rear-firing MG 131s removed, and FuG 200 Hohentwiel anti-shipping radar fitted. Had increased range. Not proceeded with.

Me 410B-6: Anti-shipping variant. Armament consisted of two MG 131 and two 30-mm MK 108¸ the latter in an under-fuselage *Waffenbehälter* 103 (Weapons Container 103).

Me 410B-7: Photographic reconnaissance variant, based on the Me 410B-3. Prototype only.

Me 410B-8: Photographic night reconnaissance variant, based on Me 410B-7. Flare illuminators fitted in bomb bay and behind wing main spar. Prototype only.

Me 410C: High-altitude fighter/reconnaissance variant. Was to have been powered by two 2,000-hp DB 603 JZ engines in annular cowlings. High aspect ratio wing fitted to the Me 310 considered. None completed.

Me 410D: High-altitude night fighter/reconnaissance variant. Was to have been powered by two turbo supercharged 1,810-hp BMW 801 TJ or two 1,800-hp Junkers Jumo 213 E/JZ engines. Outer wing panels constructed from wood. Apparently, these wooden wing sections were designed at Oberammergau by a team of Latvian aircraft designer, including Karlis Iribitis. Lichtenstein C-1 or SN-2 radar was to have been fitted.

Me 410H: Was to have been powered by two 1,900-hp DB 603 G engines. Proposed armament consisted of two 30-mm MK 103 cannons, two 30-mm MK 108 cannons, two 20-mm MG 151/20 cannons, and two rear firing 13-mm MG 131 machine guns. Increased wing span of 23 metres. None completed.

20
Preservation

Although at least one intact Me 210 was found following the German surrender in May 1945, no Me 210s were included among the multitude of Luftwaffe aircraft selected for evaluation by the Allied nations. Various small Me 210Ca-1 components still survive in Hungary. These include a pilot's seat, an engine nacelle, and part of a wing main spar. The latter comes from Me 210Ca-1 serial number Z003, with the attached data plate identifying it as having been constructed by the Gothaer *Waggonfabrik* AG in 1941.

Of the fairly limited numbers of Me 410s found in Germany, Denmark (four at Kastrup, ten at Værløse, seven at Beldringe, and five at Aalborg West for a total of twenty-six) and Norway (twenty-two) in May 1945, only three—all surrendered at Værløse, Denmark—were brought to Britain for evaluation and exhibition. The remaining aircraft were all scrapped, with the materials being reused in the reconstruction of the civilian infrastructure and industries of Western Europe. However, it is interesting to note that several Me 410s (devoid of propellers but otherwise intact) were on public display at an airshow held at Beldringe, Denmark, during the summer of 1945.

Only two complete Me 410s have survived, one each in Britain and one in the USA, as detailed below. Since the early 1990s, a fairly large number of former Luftwaffe aircraft have been recovered from crash sites in Russia. However, it seems extremely unlikely that any Me 210 or 410 will emerge from this part of the world.

Nevertheless, apart from the pair of complete Me 410s, numerous small components survive with various aviation museums and private collectors around the world, including a cockpit canopy frame at the Wings to Victory Museum in the Netherlands, and a *Waffenbehälter* (type unknown) at the New Omaha Beach Museum in Vierville, France. At least a dozen DB 603 engines are preserved at aviation museums in Austria (one), Great Britain (one), France (two, including one fitted with Me 410 cowlings), Germany (five), Lithuania (one), and the USA (two). Not all of these engines may have originally been fitted to Me 410s, though. Since the 1970s, a number of Me 210 and Me 410 crash sites have been excavated, particularly in Britain, Germany, and the Czech Republic, with some of the recovered components being on display at various aviation museums.

Me 410A-1/U2
W Nr 420430
RAF Museum, Cosford
PD+VO
3U+CC
3U+AK
Air Min V-1
AM 72
8483M

Having been built at Augsburg during the autumn of 1943, the wartime service of this Me 410 remains largely unknown. Upon completion, the aircraft was allocated the factory call sign PD+VO. However, it most likely served with 2./ZG 26 (coded as 3U+CC) at some point. By 1944, it was probably operated by 11./ZG 26 in Norway. Along with several other Me 410s, it was surrendered at Værløse, Denmark in May 1945. Selected for transfer to the UK and evaluation by the RAE on 9 June, the temporary serial number Air Min V-1 was applied (V being short for Værløse). Contemporay records erroneously states the W Nr as being '410.478'. On 20 August, Sqn Ldr Ian 'Curly' Sommerville ferried the Me 410 to Kastrup; other sources mention Group Captain Hards being at the controls. Prior to landing, an oil tank burst, with one engine catching fire as a result. Repairs effected, the Me 410 took to the air once again on 25 August. More than a month later, on 3 October, Sqn Ldr McCarthy ferried the Me 410 to Schleswig in Northern Germany, finally arriving at RAE Farnborough on 13 October. However, the aircraft remained grounded until flown to 6 MU at Brize Norton on 28 December for storage.

In May 1946, the Me 410 was selected for preservation by the Air Historical Branch. However, it remained in storage and in a disassembled state, being shuffled between 76 MU at Wroughton, where it arrived on 14 August 1946, 47 MU at Sealand (following the closure of 76 MU), 3 MU at Stanmore (where the aircraft arrived ca. 1949), 15 MU Wroughton (arrived during the final months of 1955), and RAF Fulbeck (possibly arrived in 1958) before arriving at RAF Cosford and 60 MU in the spring of 1960. At Cosford, the Me 410 was finally assembled and repainted, with the code 'CC' being applied. In September 1961, it was on static display at RAF Finningley during the Battle of Britain weekend. Moving on to RAF Gaydon, the Me 410 appeared at the annual Battle of Britain weekend between 1966 and 1969. However, the RAF Museum's data sheet on the Me 410 does not state that the aircraft was on display during the 1968 event. Between November 1975 and June 1976, it was exhibited outside the RAF Museum, Hendon during the 'Wings of the Eagle' display. The aircraft was then returned to RAF Cosford. Before this took place, the RAF Maintenance serial number 8483M was assigned on 16 February 1976. Due to necessary refurbishment work on the display hangar, the Me 410 was on placed on outside display during the summer of 1985.

On 20 November 1985, the Me 410 was roaded to RAF St Athan, where the DB 603 engines were restored to working order. In October 1986, the DB 603 engines were ground run for the first time. The engines were subsequently ground run on several occasions, including the 1988 Battle of Britain display. With the wind-down of the St Athan historical

The only Me 410 in the world on public display can be seen at the RAF Museum at Cosford. This photo was taken by Per Björkner in 1976. (*The Arlanda Civil Aviation Collection*)

aircraft collection, the Me 410 was returned RAF Cosford on 20 December 1989. This unique survivor is currently on display at the RAF Museum, Cosford. It remains the sole Me 410 on public display anywhere in the world.

Me 410A-2/U1
W/Nr 10018
National Air & Space Museum (NASM), Washington DC, USA
DI+NN
F6+WK
EB-103
FE-499
T2-499

This particular Me 410 was captured at Trapani, Sicily, in early August 1943. Built by Messerschmitt at Augsburg, the Stammkennzeichen DI+NN had been assigned for test and delivery flights. Prior to its capture, the Me 410 had served with 2.(F)/122, with the unit code F6+WK. Following capture, the aircraft was shipped to the USA. The Me 410 arrived at Wright Field in January 1944. The fact that some six months passed before the aircraft finally arrived in the USA may possibly be due to several factors, such as lack of necessary transport facilities as well as low priority for evaluation. The Me 410 was still present at Wright Field on 7 October 1944. Initially, the serial number EB-103 was assigned, with EB being short for the Evaluation Branch of the Technical Data Laboratory. However, it seems that the aircraft remained grounded, with an 'Airplane Flight Report' for EB-103 stating 'Gas tank removed Props damaged', with '00:00' hours having been flown. The DB 603 A-2 engines were noted as being serial numbers 500258 and 500016 respectively. After a short while, the serial number EB-103 was changed to FE-499, (FE standing for Foreign Equipment). This was later amended to T2-499, with T2 indicating the T-2 Office of Air Force Intelligence.

By 17 May 1946, the Me 410 was at Freeman Field until subsequently selected for preservation by the Smithsonian Institute. For many years, the Me 410 was stored at Park Ridge, Illinois, until transferred to the NASM in 1965 for further storage at Silver Hill, Maryland. In the meantime, some of the flight instruments had apparently gone missing. In 1979, the NASM corresponded with a private collector in the USA regarding flight instruments suitable for the Fw 190 and Me 410. The aircraft remained at Silver Hill until 1994. The Me 410 is currently awaiting its queue for restoration and display. Interestingly, many reference works on Luftwaffe aircraft usually include a photo of this particular Me 410, showing the aircraft after it had arrived in America.

Me 410 F6+WK in profile. (*NMUSAF*)

Another view of F6+WK in the USA. (*NMUSAF*)

The Me 410 owned by the NASM remains in storage. (*NASM*)

APPENDIX I

Arado Ar 240 Production List

Although this book concerns itself with the Messerschmitt Me 210 and Me 410, it may be of some interest to include information on the limited number of Arado Ar 240 produced. As detailed in the main text, the Ar 240 was the main competitor of the Me 210. A few Ar 240s were used operationally, albeit with little success. The table below include details assembled from several different sources. Although most of the Ar 240s completed were built by Arado, a few were built by AGO. This company had submitted the highly advanced AGO Ao 225 in response to RLM's *Zerstörer* specification. No Ao 225s were completed, though. An order for forty Ar 240Bs was subsequently placed with AGO, but this was cancelled before any aircraft had been completed.

Prototype	W Nr	Code/s	Date of first known flight	Remarks
Ar 240 V1	240001	DD+QL	5 June 1940	Powered by DB 601 engines. W/o 18 April 1941.
Ar 240 V2	240002	DD+CE *	15 September 1940	Used for engine (DB 601, DB 601 E and DB 603 E) and armament (MG 17 and MG 151) tests. Presumed withdrawn from use by early 1942.
Ar 240 V3	240003	KK+CD	9 May 1941	Used for engine (DB 601 E and possibly Jumo 213) pressure cabin and FA-13 and FA-3 armament trials. Used in 1941 for reconnaissance flights over Britain. Last known flight occurred on 18 April 1944..
Ar 240 V4	240004		19 June 1941	Used for engine (DB 601 E and DB 603 A) and dive bombing trials. W/o on 7 August 1941

Ar 240 V5	240005	GL+QA * T5+MH	11 September 1941	Built by AGO. Used for FA-13 armament trials. To Aufklärungsgruppe Oberbefehlshaber der Luftwaffe (Luftwaffe Commander-in-Chief Reconnaissance unit, Aufkl.Ob.d.L.) on 25 March 1942. To E-Stelle Rechlin in late 1942.
Ar 240 V6	240006	GL+QB * T5+KH	18 January 1942	Built by AGO. Used by the 3.(F)/100 reconnaissance unit in Charkov, USSR, area in 1942–43. Damaged at unknown date.
Ar 240 V7	240007	DM+ZU	October 1942 *	Powered by DB 605 A engines fitted with MW-50 methanol-water injection. Prototype for projected Ar 240B series. Probably not completed.
Ar 240 V8	240008		December 1942 *	Probably not completed.
Ar 240 V7	240009	DH+ZU	1 February 1942	Delivered to Luftwaffe in 1943.
Ar 240 V8	240010		8 January 1943	Used by the 1.(F)/100 reconnaissance unit on Eastern Front. Sustained 15 per cent damage in a forced landing on 3 August 1943 at Orscha-Süd. Repaired. Damaged in belly landing near Prenzlau, 24 January 1944.
Ar 240 V9/C-01	240017	BO+RC	March 1943 *	Prototype for the Ar 240C Zerstörer variant. W/o at unknown date.
Ar 240 V10/C-02	240018	BO+RC	27 September 1943	Ar 240C Zerstörer prototype. Powered by Jumo 213 engines. Still undergoing trials in June 1944.
Ar 240 V11/C-03	240019			Ar 240C Zerstörer prototype. Believed not completed.
Ar 240 V12/C-04	240020			Ar 240C Zerstörer prototype.
Ar 240 V13				Prototype for the projected Ar 240D. Believed not completed. Was to have been powered by DB 614 engines.
Ar 240 V14				Prototype for the projected Ar 240E. Believed not completed. Was to have been powered by DB 603 and Jumo 004 engines.
Ar 240 V15				Believed not completed, although one source states it was fitted with FuG 202 radar and used for reconnaissance over the Eastern Front.

Ar 240A-01	240011	GL+QA * T5+YP	28 June 1942	To 3.(F)/100 reconnaissance unit. W/o on 16 February 1943 at Poltava-Sechinskaya, USSR. Crew killed.
Ar 240A-02	240012	GL+QB	13 September 1942	Used for high-altitude tests.
Ar 240A-03	240013	DI+CY	September 1942 *	To 2.(F)/122 reconnaissance unit. Sustained 70 per cent damage in forced landing at Frosimone, Italy, on 14 July 1943. Wreck discovered by Allies.
Ar 240A-04	240014	DI+CZ	Late 1942	To 2.(F)/122 reconnaissance unit. Damaged in crash in Poland, mid-1944. Repaired and returned to Arado.
Ar 240A-05	240015			Powered by DB 603 or BMW 801 engines. Reportedly used by Aufklärungsgruppe 10 and Aufkl.Ob.d.L. on the Eastern Front.

* Indicates unconfirmed.

APPENDIX II

Messerschmitt Me 210/Me 410 Production List

Introduction

The following production list has been compiled using a large number of sources. The basic list is to a large extent based on the one found in Peter Petrick and Werner Stocker's excellent book *Messerschmitt Me 210/Me 410 Hornet*, published in 2007 by Midland Publishing. Other sources include Luftwaffe loss lists, available on microfilm at the Imperial War Museum.

Establishing exact production quantities for any type of German aircraft between 1939 and 1945 is notoriously difficult. This is due to several different circumstances. First of all, much contemporary documentation—including various aircraft manufacturer, Luftwaffe, and RLM records—was lost during the war. Additionally, many Luftwaffe units intentionally destroyed their administrative records as the war came to an end. Much information on the Luftwaffe can still be found at German archives, as well as the British National Archives at Kew and the US National Archives in Washington, DC. However, some of these primary archival resources occasionally provide contradictory information.

Assembling a production list for any type of German aircraft must take into consideration that completed or near-completed aircraft can be modified or rebuilt as other variants (as indeed was the case with a large number of Me 210s reemerging as Me 410s instead). Other aircraft can be diverted for test purposes, not reaching frontline units or being written off before delivery. The latter may include aircraft destroyed in air raids, pre-delivery crashes, or aircraft that for various reasons did not pass acceptance trials. Also, different statistics can appear in contemporary, official documentation.

Thus, establishing a 100 per cent accurate production list for the Me 210 and Me 410 is an impossible task. Future research into surviving Luftwaffe and RLM archives will in all likelihood provide more information.

The first production orders for Me 210s were placed prior to the first flight of the Me 210 V1. Me 210 production was centred at Augsburg and Regensburg. Additionally, a small production batch was completed by the *Lutherwerke* (part of the MIAG conglomerate) at Braunschweig. A large licence production programme for the Me 210 also involved MIAG (W Nr to begin at 210.4001), Fieseler *Flugzeugwerke* at Kassel (W Nr to begin at 210.3001),

Gothaer *Waggonfabrik* at Gotha (W Nr to begin at 210.5001), and by Erla at Leipzig-Mockau (W Nr unknown). However, nothing came of these ambitious plans.

Due to the unforeseen problems with flight and handling characteristics, followed by the difficulties experienced during operational trials and initial frontline experience, orders for the Me 210 were reduced, with production eventually being ordered to stop in March 1942. Exactly how many Me 210s were completed remains unclear, with quantities from a low of 356 to 706 aircraft being quoted in various printed sources.

According to the lowest figure, ninety-six aircraft were built in 1941, ninety-seven in 1942, eighty-nine in 1943, and seventy-four in 1944. This obviously also include the Hungarian production. However, another source states that a total of 483 Me 210s being completed, with 259 (53.6 per cent) being accepted by Luftwaffe. The table below provides details on the various Me 210 production variants.

Messerschmitt Me 210 Production

Variant	Quantity	Use	Remarks
Me 210 V1 – V16	16	Prototypes	
Me 210A-0, A-1	257	Destroyer	Short fuselage. A total of 148 Me 210A-1s were rebuilt with a longer fuselage.
Me 210A-1	36	Destroyer	Long fuselage.
Me 210B-1	4	Reconnaissance	Short fuselage.
Me 210C-1	16	Reconnaissance	Long fuselage.
Me 210Ca-1	105	Destroyer	Hungarian-built aircraft supplied to Luftwaffe.
Me 210Ca-1	272 #	Destroyer	Hungarian-built aircraft supplied to MKHL.
	706		Total production, of which 329 in Germany and 377 (or 288) in Hungary.

The above table is based on German sources. However, the total quantity of 706 is obviously in error, as only 159 (or 160) Me 210Ca-1s were actually delivered to the MKHL, with another 128 Hungarian-built aircraft serving with the Luftwaffe. Subtracting 288 from 706 gives a total of 418 German-built Me 210s.

Following the shutdown of Me 210 production and subsequent reinstatement of the improved Me 410, examples of the latter began to reach frontline units in the summer of 1943. Messerschmitt Me 410 production was centred at Augsburg-Haunstetten (Messerschmitt) and at Munich-Oberspfaffenhofen (Dornier).

Messerschmitt completed 376 Me 410As and 158 Me 410Bs for a total of 634 aircraft. Dornier completed 107 Me 410A-1s and 165 Me 410Bs for a total of 272 aircraft. Additionally, a batch of thirty Me 410B-2/B-3s from an unidentified manufacturer was delivered. This makes a total of 836 aircraft, far below the total of 1,160 (or 1,189) usually quoted in secondary, printed sources. However, apart from these 836 Me 410s, an additional 460 aircraft were rebuilt from Me 210 airframes. This brings the total number of Me 410s completed—including those rebuilt from Me 210s—to 1,296, which, in all probability, is closer to the truth.

What is known, though, is that 1943 production totals included one Me 410A-1 (built by Dornier), 203 Me 410A-1/U2, and thirty-four Me 410A-3s, with the vast majority (237 out of 238) being built by Messerschmitt.

Production plans for January 1944 included seventy-four Me 410s, broken down as thirty-nine Me 410A-1s (thirty-two from Messerschmitt Augsburg and seven from Dornier Munich), twenty-five Me 410A-1/U2s (all from Messerschmitt Augsburg), and ten Me 410A-3s (all from Messerschmitt Augsburg). A total of seventy Me 410s were built, including fifty-six Me 410A-1/U2s and fourteen Me 410A-3s, all by Messerschmitt.

The following month, Messerschmitt planned to build forty-two Me 410A-1s (sixteen delivered), fifteen Me 410A-1/U2 (five delivered), and ten Me 410A-3s (four delivered). Dornier planned to build nine Me 410A-1s (seven delivered), for a total of thirty-two aircraft delivered against plans for sixty-seven aircraft.

March 1944 saw a marked increase in Me 410 production. Messerschmitt planned to build forty-two Me 410A-1s (but managed to complete sixty aircraft), fifteen Me 410A-1/U2s (sixteen delivered), and ten Me 410A-3s (only one completed). Dornier production figures included no Me 410A-1s (eleven built) and ten Me 410B-1s (of which none were completed). Thus, 88 Me 410s were built in March 1944. From 1943 until 31 March 1944, a total of 428 Me 410s were completed.

A number of Me 410A-1s were converted by Erla as Me 410A-1/U2 *Zerstörers*, with twenty-nine out of a planned thirty being completed between January and March 1944. At the same timeframe, Dornier converted sixty aircraft as Me 410A-1/U4s. This involved fitting the powerful BK 5 cannon.

In May 1944, a total of eighty-nine Me 410s were accepted by the Luftwaffe. However, the Me 410 was already being phased out of production. Although the *Zerstörer* class of aeroplanes, including the Me 410, were classified in the No. 2 (the second-most important category; the type of aircraft most required by the Luftwaffe at that time were single seat fighters).

As a result, by mid-1944, emphasis was on the production of single-seat fighters (Bf 109s and Fw 190s) and jet aircraft (such as the Messerschmitt Me 262 and Arado Ar 234). The manufacturing resources of the crumbling Third Reich could no longer afford to retain the Me 410 in production. Me 410 production came to an end in August 1944, with forty aircraft being taken on charge the following month.

A close-up of a Me 410B. The pair of MG 151 cannons are in clear evidence. (*Wolfgang Mühlbauer/ DEHLA Archives*)

Messerschmitt Me 410 Production

Variant	Quantity	Use	Remarks
Me 410 V1 – V18	18	Prototypes	All converted from Me 210s.
Me 410A-1	394	Fast Destroyer	260 converted on the production line from Me 210s, with 134 newly built aircraft.
Me 410A-1/U1	6	Reconnaissance	
Me 410A-1/U2	277	Auxiliary destroyer	200 converted on the production line from Me 210s, with seventy-seven newly built aircraft.
Me 410A-3	74	Reconnaissance	
Me 410B-1	61	Fast destroyer	
Me 410B-2	165	Destroyer	
Me 410B-2/U2	48	Destroyer	
Me 410B-2/U4	111	Destroyer	
Me 410B-3	35	Reconnaissance	
	1,189		

NB: the above table has been assembled from various sources. However, it is believed that the actual total was somewhat higher—1,296 aircraft. This discrepancy can possibly be explained though aircraft written off prior to delivery (ie destroyed in pre-delivery crashes or Allied air raids).

Production List

Messerschmitt Me 210

Sixteen Me 210 prototypes—W Nrs 2100001 to 2100016

210.0001: V1 D-AABF, Stkz CE+BY. First flown on 2 September 1939. Initially fitted with twin fins/rudders, but later modified with single fin/rudder.

210.0002: V2 WL+ABEO, Stkz CE+BZ. First flown on 10 October 1939. Built initially with twin fins/rudders, but modified with single fin/rudder prior to first flight. Outer wings of Me 210 V3 fitted. Used for dive brake tests. W/o near Augsburg on 5 September 1940. Fritz Wendel baled out safely.

210.0003: V3 Stkz CF+BA. Used for static tests, and transferred to E-Stelle Rechlin by 30 March 1940.

210.0004: V4 Stkz CF+BB. Fitted with single fin/rudder from the outset. Performed 29 flights for dive brake tests. The dive brakes were subsequently removed, and the aircraft was transferred to E-Stelle Rechlin in late 1940.

210.0005: V5 Stkz ND+VX. Fitted with DB 601 BF engines. To E-Stelle Rechlin on 21 November 1940.

210.0110.08: V8 Stkz NF+LA. Rebuilt with longer fuselage, and subsequently used for undercarriage tests.

210.0110.09: V9 Stkz NF+LB. Used for tail section tests, including internally balanced elevators. Featured smaller wing fillets than the Me 210 V2. Completed forty-one flights before transfer to E-Stelle Rechlin on 28 November 1940.

210.0110.10: V10 Stkz GI+SN. First flown in late 1940, with flight tests beginning on 6 December 1940.

210.0110.011: V11 Stkz GI+SO. First flown on 1 November 1940, with flight tests beginning on 24 November 1940.

210.0110.012: V12 Stkz GI+SP. Used for automatic dive brake tests.

210.0110.013: V13 Stkz GI+SQ. First flown on 17 April 1941. Used for automatic cooling flaps and electrical de-icing tests. Later fitted with four-blade propellers.

2100110.014: V14 Stkz GI+SR. Used for spin handling tests, being fitted with anti-spin and brake parachute in tail section. Also used for ejection seat trials.

2100110.015: V15 Stkz GI+SS. First flown on 31 May 1941. Powered by DB 601 F engines, and used for radio gear tests.

2100110.016: V16 Stkz GI+ST. Retained short fuselage. Initially used for de-icing tests, followed by comparative stall behaviour tests against the Me 210 V17.

Eighty-four pre-production Me 210A-0/-1: First Production Contract

All aircraft built at Augsburg. Deliveries took place between January and April 1941. Many of these aircraft were delivered to operational units, III./ZG 1 in particular. Others were rebuilt as Me 410s.

210.0110.005: Stkz ? To 11./KG 51 9K+EV W/o near Riedesheim on 28 March 1944.

210.0110.017–210.0110.021: Stkz DI+NM to DI+NQ. Rebuilt as Me 410 in 1943.

210.0110.022: Stkz DI+NR. Rebuilt as Me 410A-1 in 1943. Possibly to 14./KG 2, which lost a Me 410 with W Nr 022 on 1 September 1943.

210.0110.028: Stkz DI+NX. To I./NJG 1. Sustained 10 per cent damage in taxiing accident at Deelen, the Netherlands, 26 November 1943.

210.0110.029: Stkz DI+NY. To III./ZG 1 2N+CD. Intentionally destroyed by German troops, Tunisia, 6 April 1943.

210.0110.031: Stkz DU+IA. To 11./ZG 1 2N+MV. S/d by USAAF P-38 Lightning 20 km S Tunis, Tunisia, 29 November 1942. Hptm Friedrich Plank (*Staffelkapitän*) and Fw Heinz Pastoors MiA.

210.0110.033: Stkz DU+IC. Modified by Blohm & Voss as dual control conversion trainer, November 1943.

210.0110.034: Stkz DU+ID. To III./ZG 1. W/o in take-off accident, Iraklion, Crete, 30 October 1942.

210.0110.036: Stkz DU+IF. To 8./ZG 1 2N+GS. S/d by flak NE Apollonia, Libya, 18 November 1942. Oblt Heinz Redlich and Fw Friedrich Hamburger killed.

210.0110.038: Stkz DU+IH. To 7./ZG 1. Sustained 35 per cent damage in landing accident, Trapani, Sicily, 27 November 1942. Repaired.

210.0110.042: Stkz DU+IL. To *Erprobungsstaffel* 210. To III./ZG 1. Sustained 30 per cent damage at Cabul, 19 March 1943. Repaired. Modified by Blohm & Voss as dual control conversion trainer.

210.0110.044: Stkz DU+IN. Modified by Blohm & Voss as dual control conversion trainer.

210.0110.051: Stkz DU+IU. To 9./ZG 1. Damaged by flak near Tunis, Tunisia, 25 November 1942. Wreck located at El Aquina, Tunisia, 1943. Crew (names unknown) found dead.

210.0110.052: Stkz DU+IV. To 2./(F)122 F6+UK. Captured in wrecked condition at Trapani, Sicily, August 1943.

210.0110.053: Stkz DU+IW. To III./ZG 1 W/o at Trapani, Sicily, 11 December 1942. Crew safe.

210.0110.056: Stkz DU+IZ To III./ZG 1. Sustained 10 per cent damage due to engine trouble at Lecce, Italy, 11 February 1943. Captured in wrecked condition at Gerbini, Sicily, August 1943.

210.0110.057: Stkz NT+CA. To III./ZG 1 2N+DT. Sustained 10 per cent damage when hit by Allied fighter, NE Apollonia, Libya, 18 November 1942. Pilot (name unknown) safe, Uffz Hans Ziesch wounded.

210.0110.060: Stkz NT+CD. To 11./ZG 1. Sustained 80 per cent damage in forced landing following aerial combat near Tunis, Tunisia, 25 November 1942. Crew safe.

210.0110.062: Stkz NT+CF. To III./ZG 1 2N+DA. Sustained 10 per cent damage in forced landing at Trapani, Sicily, 26 December 1942. Repaired. To I./NJG 1 Sustained 20 per cent damage in forced landing at Achmer, 5 December 1943. Repaired. To I./ZG 101. Sustained 10 per cent damage in landing accident at Memmingen, 15 June 1944. The latter incident possibly involved W Nr 150062.

210.0110.064: Stkz NT+CH. To III./ZG 1. Sustained 10 per cent damage in landing accident, Tunisia, 27 February 1943. Repaired. Sustained 15 per cent damage, Tunisia, 16 April 1943. Rebuilt by Blohm & Voss as dual control conversion trainer.

210.0110.065: Stkz NT+CI. To III./ZG 1 S/d by RAF fighters near Tunis, Tunisia, 3 December 1942. Crew safe.

210.0110.066: Stkz NT+CJ. To III./ZG 1. Sustained 10 per cent damage due to engine trouble, Santa Ilagio, Italy, 14 March 1943. Rebuilt by Blohm & Voss as dual control conversion trainer. To ZG 101. Sustained 15 per cent damage in taxiing accident, 24 May 1944. The latter incident possibly involved W Nr 150066.

210.0110.067: Stkz NT+CK. To III./ZG 1 2N+BV S/d by RAF Spitfire, 15 km NE Sousse, Tunisia, 23 December 1942. Uffz Klaus Leibrandt and Gefr. Heinz Zobel MiA.

210.0110.068: Stkz NT+CL. To 9./ZG 1. Sustained 60 per cent damage, Trapani, Sicily, 25 November 1942. Rebuilt by Blohm & Voss as dual control conversion trainer.

210.0110.070: Stkz NT+CN. To 1./Üb.u.Einfl.Kdo Jüterbog W/o 22 September 1942.

210.0110.071: Stkz NT+CO. To 9./ZG 1 2N+AT S/d by USAAF P-38 Lightning, force landed 50 km E Faid, Tunisia, 4 December 1942. Lt Alwin Meyer and Uffz Karl Morgenröther both wounded.

210.0110.073: Stkz NT+CQ. To 7./ZG 1 2N+DR. S/d by flak W Medjez el Bab, Tunisia, 25 November 1942. Lt Walter Hanke and Gefr. Heinrich Auer both killed.

210.0110.075: Stkz NT+CS. To 11./ZG 1 3E+NQ. S/d by RAF Spitfire 30 km E Algiers, Algeria, 13 November 1942. Uffz Hans Krüger and Uffz Rudolf Faisst both MiA.

210.0110.078: Stkz NT+CV. To III./ZG 1. Sustained 95 per cent damage at Bronte, 1 February 1943.

210.0110.080: Stkz NT+CX. To I./ZG 1. Seriously damaged when overturned on landing at Landsberg, 31 January 1942.

210.0110.083: Stkz GT+VA. Modified for 'Kutonase' tests. To III./ZG 1. Sustained 80 per cent damage due to engine trouble, Gerbini, Sicily, 1 June 1943. Captured at Gerbini in wrecked condition by Allied forces, August 1943.

210.0110.085: Stkz GT+VC. Rebuilt as Me 410 V22. To 5./ZG 26 coded Black 10. W/o near Wesermünde on 24 December 1943. Also reported as surrendered at Tulln, Austria, on 8 May 1945.

210.0110.087: Stkz GT+VE. Modified as 'Kutonase' prototype. To III./ZG 1 2N+OT Destroyed in Allied bomb raid against Castel Vetrano, Italy, 11 June 1943.

210.0110.088: Stkz GT+VF. To 8./ZG 1. Collided with another Me 210 on take-off from Trapani, Sicily, 22 December 1942. Hptm Heinrich Sass (*Staffelkapitän*) and Fw Rudolf Blandowski both killed.

210.0110.090: Stkz GT+VH. To I./ZG 1 Seriously damaged when overturned on landing at Landsberg, 31 January 1942.

210.0110.092: Stkz GT+VJ. To 9./ZG 1 2N+JT S/d 30 km NW Gabes, Tunisia, 6 April 1943. Uffz Gerhard Lemke and Uffz Emil Deleh both killed.

210.0110.094: Stkz GT+VL. To I./ZG 2. Sustained 35 per cent damage at Wiener-Neustadt, Austria, 30 September 1942.

210.0110.099: Stkz GT+VQ. To III./ZG 1. Destroyed on ground in Allied bomb raid at El Aouina, Tunisia, 4 December 1942. This aircraft is also reported as sustaining 10 per cent damage on 10 February 1943 at Galatone, Italy, due to engine trouble. Most likely, this concerned Me 410 W Nr 089. Additonally, an Me 410 of the *Ergänzung-Zerstörergruppe* that sustained 70 per cent damage in a forced landing at Völkenrode on 13 October 1943 has been attributed to this aircraft.

Some 204 (or 216) Me 210As delivered between May 1941 and May 1942. Most of the late production aircraft were subsequently rebuilt as Me 410s.

210.0110.101: Stkz GT+VS. To Daimler-Benz at Echterdingen for engine tests on 3 April 1941. Returned to Augsburg on 14 March 1942, and modified with lengthened fuselage. Redesignated Me 210C-1 Stkz NE+BH. Modified as Me 210D-1 prototype on 11 November 1942. Still used for aerial reconnaissance tests by Messerschmitt on 27 August 1943.

210.0110.105: Stkz PN+PD. Used for dive bombing tests. Me 210C/V18 prototype, fitted with DB 605 B engines. W/o on 15 July 1942. Also reported to have been supplied to Hungary as a pattern aircraft.

210.0110.110: Stkz PN+PI. To E-Stelle Rechlin on 2 September 1941. To 2./(F)122 F6+ZK S/d by RAF Spitfire (possibly Flg Off D.C. Deuntzer of 43 Sqn, flying Spitfire Vc JG769) 75 km NE Cap Bon, Tunisia, 18 April 1943. Lt Norbert Schliefhauer and Obfw Wilhelm Giesea both killed.

210.0110.116: Stkz SJ+GF. To E-Stelle Rechlin on 25 September 1941. To *Erprobungsstaffel* 210. W/o at Rechlin, 27 October 1941.

210.0110.117: Stkz SJ+GG. To E-Stelle Rechlin on 17 September 1941. To *Erprobungsstaffel* 210. W/o on 23 September 1941.

210.0110.119: Stkz SJ+GI. To E-Stelle Rechlin on 17 September 1941. W/o in landing accident on 12 October 1941.

210.0110.125: Stkz SJ+GO. To I./SKG 210 on 9 November 1941. To I./ZG 1. Sustained 20 per cent damage (undercarriage) in landing accident at Lechfeld, 27 January 1942.

210.0110.128: Stkz SJ+GR. To I./SKG 210 on 11 November 1941. To 3./ZG 1. Sustained 25 per cent damage in landing accident at Tours, France, 3 March 1942.

210.0110.130: Stkz SJ+GT. To 2./(F)122 F6+YK. Lost (presumed s/d by flak) during reconnaissance sortie in the Tripoli-Misrata-Zuara area, Libya, 8 February 1943 Uffz Kurt Schulz and Gefr. Johannes Franks MiA.

210.0110.131: Stkz SJ+GU. To I./SKG 210 on 9 November 1941. To I./ZG 1 Sustained 35 per cent damage at Lechfeld, 28 January 1942.

210.0110.141: Stkz VC+SE. To I./SKG 210 on 9 November 1941. To I./ZG 1 S9+EH. W/o at Lechfeld, 15 January 1942.

210.0110.143: Stkz VC+SG. To I./SKG 210 on 12 November 1941. To I./ZG 1 W/o at Lechfeld, 28 January 1942 due to pilot error.

210.0110.151: Stkz VC+SO. To E-Stelle Tarnewitz on 11 March 1942. To III./ZG 1 Sustained 80 per cent damage at Lecce, Italy, 22 January 1943.

210.0110.152: Stkz VC+SP. To 2./SKG 210. Sustained 45 per cent damage at Landsberg due to engine trouble, 2 January 1942. Modified by Blohm & Voss as dual control conversion trainer, November 1943.

210.0110.155: Stkz VC+SS. To 7./ZG 1 2N+BR. S/d by RAF Spitfire SW Medjez el Bab, Tunisia, on 26 November 1942. Hptm Kurt Loos killed with Obfw Heinz Schrodt becoming a PoW.

210.0110.156: Stkz VC+ST. To III./ZG 1 2N+AT. Sustained 70 per cent damage in Allied bomb raid at Castel Vetrano, Italy, on 20 June 1943.

210.0110.157: Stkz VC+SU. Modified as Me 210S-1 for long-range flight tests. To 2./(F)122 F6+XK W/o S Cap Passero, Italy, on 24 June 1943.

210.0110.159: Stkz VC+SW. To 7./ZG 1. Sustained 95 per cent damage at Wiener Neustadt, Austria, on 23 October 1942.

210.0110.162: Stkz VC+SZ. Used for comparative landing flaps tests with Me 210 W Nr 2344, June 1941. To 2./Üb.u.Einfl.Kdo Jüterbog. W/o near Augsburg, 7 October 1942.

210.0110.163: Stkz VN+AA. To III./ZG 1. Force landed following combat with RAF fighters near Bougie, Algeria, 13 November 1942. Aircraft intentionally destroyed by German troops.

210.0110.164: Stkz VN+AB. To 11./ZG 1. Sustained 30 per cent damage in landing accident at Trapani, Sicily, 28 November 1942 Modified by Blohm & Voss as dual control conversion trainer, November 1943.

210.0110.165: Stkz VN+AC. Modified by Blohm & Voss as dual control conversion trainer, November 1943.

210.0110.167: Stkz VN+AE. Modified by Blohm & Voss as dual control conversion trainer, November 1943.

210.0110.170: Stkz VN+AH. To 9./ZG 1 2N+BR. Presumed s/d over Mediterranean, 5 April 1943. Uffz Walter Luttka and radio operator (name unknown) MiA.

210.0110.172: Stkz VN+AJ. To III./ZG 1. Sustained 20 per cent damage in take-off accident at Wiener Neustadt due to pilot error, 15 October 1942. Repaired. W/o 8 July 1943 due to engine trouble.

210.0110.173: Stkz VN+AK. To 16./KG 6 2H+LA. Lost on 5 September 1942. N.B.: This Me 210 was possibly one of the two of its kind s/d over Britain by RAF Typhoons on 6 September 1942.

210.0110.174: Stkz VN+AL. To III./ZG 1. Sustained 30 per cent damage in take-off accident at Trapani, Sicily, 7 December 1942.

210.0110.177: Stkz VN+AO. To III./ZG 1. W/o due to engine trouble at Araxos, Greece, 5 November 1942.

210.0110.179: Stkz VN+AQ. Fitted with Me 310 outer wing panels for flight tests lasting between 24 August and 7 September 1943. To Gen. Q Abt. Sustained 20 per cent damage in Allied bomb raid at Lechfeld on 18 March 1944. Repaired. Modified as tug for Me 163 rocket fighter in June 1944. W/o on 24 July 1944.

210.0110.180: Stkz VN+AR. Sustained 50 per cent damage in North Africa, 5 February 1943. Scrapped.

210.0110.182: Stkz VN+AT. To *Erprobungsstaffel* 210, Soesterberg, the Netherlands, June 1942. 2H+AA. W/o near Schweinfurt, 7 February 1943.

210.0110.183: Stkz VN+AU. To III./ZG 1 2N+RT. W/o in forced landing due to engine trouble, Gerbini, Sicily, 15 April 1943.

210.0110.184: Stkz VN+AV. To 16./KG 6 2H+VA. S/d by Flt Lt Tony Johnston of 266 Sqn, 13 August 1942. A/c crashed into sea off Great Yarmouth. Lt Heinz Menger was killed and Uffz Erich Rudolph rescued on 19 August ‘somewhat the worse for wear’.

210.0110.186: Stkz VN+AX. To 11./ZG 1. Sustained 30 per cent damage when attacked by Allied fighters near Trapani, Sicily, on 25 November 1942. Crew safe.

210.0110.187: Stkz VN+AY. To *Erprobungsstaffel* 210, Soesterberg, the Netherlands, June 1942 2H+xA. To *Luftbeobachtungsstaffel* 3. S/d by USAAF fighters, 11 February 1944.

210.0110.188: Stkz VN+AZ. To III./ZG 1. Sustained 20 per cent damage at Trapani, Sicily, 12 November 1942. Repaired. Sustained 15 per cent damage at Märk, 31 August 1943.

210.0110.189: Stkz DI+NA. To III./ZG 1. Sustained 90 per cent damage in landing accident at Catania, Sicily, 10 December 1942.

210.0110.190: Stkz DI+NB. To 7./ZG 1. Sustained 20 per cent damage in landing accident at Trapani, Sicily, on 18 December 1942. Repaired. Returned to Messerschmitt for BK 5 gun tests on 13 September 1943. Surrendered at Tulln, Austria, on 8 May 1945.

210.0110.192: Stkz DI+ND. To 11./ZG 1 2N+QV. S/d by USAAF P-38 Lightning 60 km S Kairouan, Tunisia, on 4 December 1942. Fl.St.ing Heinz Pfister safe and Obgfr Günther Weber wounded.

210.0110.196: Stkz DI+NH. To III./ZG 1. Sustained 70 per cent in taxiing accident at Trapani, Sicily, 2 June 1943. Possibly not w/o, as reported with 2./(F)122 when sustaining 25 per cent damage in landing accident at Perugia, Italy, 16 December 1943. Also reported as w/o on 31 March 1944, when serving with the *Ergänzung-Zerstörergruppe* (coded 1E+QC).

210.0110.198: Stkz DI+NJ. Used for variable pitch propellers and camera installation tests, March 1942. To *Erprobungsstaffel* 210. Sustained 70 per cent damage in landing accident, 24 March 1942.

210.0110.203: Stkz GT+VU. Rebuilt as Me 410A-2 in 1943. To *Erprobungsstaffel* 410. W/o at Ruderatshofen on 12 July 1943.

210.0110.204: Stkz GT+VV. Rebuilt as Me 410 in 1943. To *Erprobungsstaffel* 410. Sustained 65 per cent damage in accident at Lechfeld on 5 April 1943.

210.0110.205: Stkz GT+VW. To 9./ZG 1 2N+LT. Sustained 40 per cent damage in take-off accident at Gerbini, Sicily, 4 March 1943. Repaired, and still in service by 27 May 1944.

210.0110.206: Stkz GT+VX. Rebuilt as Me 410A-3 in 1943. To 2.(F)/122 F6+YK W/o near Bari, Italy, on 4 December 1943.

210.0110.207: Stkz GT+VY. Rebuilt as Me 410A-2 in 1943. To *Erprobungsstaffel* 410. W/o on 12 July 1943.

210.0110.208: Stkz GT+VZ. Rebuilt as Me 410A-1 in 1943. To 3./ZG 26 W/o at Gabbert on 14 May 1944 due to engine trouble.

210.0110.210: Stkz KD+JB. To 2./(F)122 F6+ZK. Lost on 22 February 1943 over Mediterranean. Fw Walter Spizner and Uffz Waldemar Küch both MiA.

210.0110.211: Stkz KD+JC. Rebuilt as Me 410 V16 in 1943. Used for MG 131 and external bomb rack tests at E-Stelle Tarnewitz.

210.0110.212: Stkz KD+JD. Rebuilt as Me 410A-3 in 1943. To 2.(F)/122 F6+XK W/o near Bari, Italy, on 15 October 1943.

210.0110.213: Stkz KD+JE. Rebuilt as Me 410A-1 in 1943. Presumably issued to 2.(F)122 or III./ZG 1, as reportedly captured at Gerbini in August 1943. Also reported as serving with *Ergänzungsgruppe* Fl.ÜG 1 on 27 April 1944.

210.0110.214: Stkz KD+JF. Rebuilt as Me 410A-1 in 1943. Reported to have sustained 50 per cent damage due to engine trouble on 6 April 1943 while serving with III./ZG 1. Also reported as issued to 15./KG 2 U5+CF and lost near Dunkirk, France, on 23 August 1943.

210.0110.215: Stkz KD+JG. Rebuilt as Me 410A-1 in 1943. To 14./KG 2 Sustained 45 per cent damage in take-off accident at Schiphol, the Netherlands, on 5 November 1943.

210.0110.216: Stkz KD+JH. To E-Stelle Tarnewitz, 11 February 1943. To III./ZG 1 Sustained 20 per cent damage in Tunisia on 25 March 1943.

210.0110.219: Stkz KD+JK. To III./ZG 1. Sustained 30 per cent damage due to pilot error, Lecce, Italy on 15 January 1943. Returned to Messerschmitt for repairs. To *Ergänzungs-Zerstörergruppe*. W/o in take-off accident at Waggum on 30 November 1943.

210.0110.220: Stkz KD+JL. To III./ZG 1. Sustained 30 per cent damage in landing accident, Tunisia, on 12 April 1943. Repaired, and rebuilt as Me 410A-1 in 1943.

210.0110.221: Stkz KD+JM. To 2./(F)122 F6+ZK S/d by Flt Lt A.M. Thom, 87 Sqn RAF (flying Spitfire Vc JK193) N Algiers, Algeria, 19 April 1943. Uffz Erich Förster and Gefr. Adolf Hahn both killed.

210.0110.223: Stkz KD+JO. To III./ZG 1. Sustained 10 per cent damage due to engine trouble at Lecce, Italy, on 11 February 1943. Repaired. Sustained 55 per cent damage in landing accident, Tunisia, on 13 February 1943.

210.0110.224: Stkz KD+JP. To 2./(F)122. Sustained 15 per cent damage in landing accident, Munich-Riem, on 17 January 1943.

210.0110.225: Stkz KD+JQ. To III./ZG 1 2N+KT S/d near Baglio Rizzo, Italy, on 30 May 1943.

210.0110.226: Stkz KD+JR. To 1./SKG 210. Sustained 20 per cent damage (undercarriage) at Landsberg on 16 December 1941. Repaired, and rebuilt as Me 410A-1 in 1943 To V./KG 2 W/o at Le Mans, France, on 12 August 1943.

210.0110.228: Stkz KD+JT. Rebuilt as a Me 410A-1 in 1943. To V./KG 2 U5+EE S/d on 23 August 1943.

210.0110.230: Stkz KD+JV. Rebuilt as a Me 410A-1 in 1943. Used for *Waffenbehälter* WB 151 tests at Anklam in July 1943. To 15./KG 2 Sustained 25 per cent damage in Allied bomb raid at Vitry Artois, France, on 9 September 1943.

210.0110.231: Stkz KD+JW. Rebuilt as a Me 410 in 1943. To 7./ZG 1 2N+LR. Lost in Bremen area on 8 October 1943. Also reported as s/d near Halberstadt on 17 January 1944 while serving with 6./ZG 26.

210.0110.232: Stkz KD+JX. Rebuilt as a Me 410A-1 in 1943. To 15./KG 2. Sustained 35 per cent damage due to engine fire at Schiphol, the Netherlands, on 23 September 1943. Repaired, and issued in October 1943 to 7./ZG 1 2N+HR To *Ergänzung Fernaufklärungsgruppe*. W/o near Bromberg on 28 June 1944.

210.0110.233: Stkz KD+JY. Rebuilt as a Me 410A-1 in 1943. To III./ZG 1. Sustained 10 per cent damage near Förden on 11 September 1943. Repaired. S/d near Apeldoorn, the Netherlands, on 10 October 1943. Oblt J. Hallerbach killed.

210.0110.235: Stkz SI+IA. Rebuilt as a Me 410A-1 in 1943 To 14./KG 2. Sustained 60 per cent damage in take-off accident at Lechfeld on 3 August 1943.

210.0110.236: Stkz SI+IB. Rebuilt as a Me 410A-1 in 1943 To 16./KG 2. Sustained 15 per cent damage at Evreux, France, due to pilot error on 16 August 1943. Repaired. Sustained 30 per cent damage at Schiphol, the Netherlands, in Allied bomb raid on 3 October 1943. To 13./KG 2 9K+OX W/o on 4 March 1944.

210.0110.237: Stkz SI+IC. Rebuilt as a Me 410A-1 in 1943. To *Stab* V./KG 2 U5+CJ. Lost near Dunkirk, France, on 16 July 1943.

210.0110.238: Stkz SI+ID. Rebuilt as a Me 410A-1 in 1943. To 16./KG 2 U5+KG. S/d near Felixstowe, UK, on 3 July 1943.

210.0110.239: Stkz SI+IE. Rebuilt as a Me 410A-1 in 1943. To 9./ZG 1 2N+KT. S/d near Melle on 13 October 1943.

210.0110.241: Stkz SI+IG. To 9./ZG 1 2N+MS. Sustained 80 per cent damage due to engine trouble, Palermo, Italy, on 2 June 1943.

210.0110.244: Stkz SI+IJ. To III./ZG 1. Lost in accident at San Pancrazia, Italy, on 10 February 1943.

210.0110.245: Stkz SI+IK. Possibly to III./ZG 1. Ferried Tunis-Oberwiesenfeld, on 10 March 1943.

210.0110.246: Stkz SI+IL. To 8./ZG 1 2N+LS S/d by USAAF P-38 Lightning 100 km W Sfax, Tunisia, on 6 December 1942. Lt Fritz Malt and Uffz Fritz Meiser both killed.

210.0110.250: Stkz SI+IP. To III./ZG 1. Damaged in Allied bomb raid against Chinisia on 5 April 1943. Repaired, and issued to LdKdo 61/62. Sustained 50 per cent damage in taxiing accident at Zwischenhahn on 30 September 1943.

210.0110.251: Stkz SI+IQ. To 2./(F)122. Sustained 15 per cent damage in take-off accident, Tunisia, on 15 March 1943. Repaired, and issued to *Ergänzung Zerstörergruppe* coded 1E+WC. W/o near Gifhorn on 19 February 1944.

210.0110.252: Stkz SI+IR. To III./ZG 1. Sustained 35 per cent damage (undercarriage) at Oberwiesenfeld on 11 May 1943. Repaired, and issued to I./ZG 101 Sustained 80 per cent damage at Memmingen on 21 July 1944.

210.0110.254: Stkz SI+IT. To Kdo FlBer 5/XII. Sustained 80 per cent damage in landing accident at Bordeaux Merignac, France, on 21 June 1944. Captured by Allies in wrecked condition.

210.0110.255: Stkz SI+IU. Used for Me 410B-1 de-icing tests. To III./ZG 1. Sustained 30 per cent damage through flak at Sfax, Tunisia, on 20 March 1943.

210.0110.258: Stkz SI+IX. To III./ZG 26. S/d on 18 April 1943.

210.0110.260: Stkz SI+IZ. To E-Stelle Tarnewitz. W/o on 4 June 1942.

210.0110.261: Stkz SO+MA. Rebuilt as a Me 410 in 1943. To III./ZG 1 coded 2N+BT (or 2N+HS). Captured at Gerbini, Sicily, in August 1943.

210.0110.263: SO+MC. To 9./ZG 1 2N+HT. Captured at Gerbini, Sicily, on 25 August 1943. Taken on charge by 601 Sqn, RAF, and subsequently transferred to 12th BG, USAAF. Crashed on take-off on 1 October 1943, Lt-Col. G. E. Hall killed.

210.0110.265: Stkz SO+ME. To 8./ZG 1 2N+MS. S/d on 9 April 1943.

210.0110.272: Stkz SO+ML. Rebuilt as a Me 410A-1 in 1943. To E-Stelle Tarnewitz for BK 5 cannon ground target tests on 26 June 1943. To *Erprobungskommando* 25. Sustained 25 per cent damage in forced landing at Stade on 4 January 1944.

210.0110.274: Stkz SO+MN. Rebuilt as Me 410A-1 in 1943. To 16./KG 2 U5+DG. Lost on 24 August 1943.

210.0110.275: Stkz SO+MO. Rebuilt as Me 410A-1 in 1943. To 16./KG 2 U5+IG. Destroyed in Allied strafing raid at Avord, France, on 27 June 1942.

210.0110.277: Stkz SO+MQ. Rebuilt as Me 410A-1 in 1943. To Flg.Pl.So.Kdo Ob.d.L. W/o near Straubling on 12 July 1943.

210.0110.278: Stkz SO+MR. Rebuilt as Me 410A-1 in 1943. To 16./KG 2. Sustained 30 per cent damage due to engine fire at Schiphol, the Netherlands, on 23 September 1943.

210.0110.279: Stkz SO+MS. To 7./ZG 1. Sustained 30 per cent damage in landing accident at Antwerp, Belgium, 15 July 1943.

210.0110.281: Stkz SO+MU. Sustained 65 per cent damage at Augsburg-Haunstetten on 23 March 1943.

210.0110.282: Stkz SO+MV. Rebuilt as Me 410A-1 in 1943 To 14./KG 2. W/o at Lechfeld on 1 July 1943.

210.0110.284: Stkz SO+MX. Rebuilt as Me 410A-1 in 1943. To 13./KG 2 on 12 July 1943. Transferred to 14./KG 2 as U5+HE and w/o at Königsbrunn on 31 July 1943. Unconfirmed reports state this aircraft served with 13./KG 200 at unknown date.

210.0110.286: Stkz SO+MZ. Rebuilt as Me 410A-1 in 1943. To 17./KG 2. Sustained 60 per cent damage at Reuth due to engine trouble on 22 July 1943.

210.0110.287: Stkz SI+KA. Rebuilt as Me 410A-1 in 1943. To 16./KG 2 U5+EG. Lost on 24 August 1943.

210.0110.288: Stkz SI+KB. Rebuilt as Me 410A-1 in 1943. To 5./KG 2 U5+EX. Sustained 15 per cent damage at Soesterberg, the Netherlands, due to engine trouble on 24 May 1943. Repaired. To 13./KG 2 Sustained 30 per cent damage due to pilot error at Coulommiers, France, on 18 September 1943.

210.0110.290: Stkz SI+KD. To 9./ZG 1 2N+IT Lost 6 April 1943. Also reported as sustaining 40 per cent damage on 18 August 1943 while serving with V./KG 2.

210.0110.291: Stkz SI+KE. Rebuilt as Me 410A-1 in 1943. To V./KG 2 U5+GF. W/o at Epinoy, France, on 18 August 1943.

210.0110.293: Stkz SI+KG. To *Ergänzungsstaffel* ZG 76 1E+IE. W/o at Oels on 15 July 1944.

210.0110.295: Stkz SI+KI. Rebuilt as Me 410A-1 in 1943. To 13./KG 2 U5+DX. W/o in ground collision at St Dizier, France, on 23 September 1943.

210.0110.296: Stkz SI+KJ. Rebuilt as Me 410A-1 in 1943. To V./KG 2. Sustained 30 per cent damage in taxiing accident at Evreux on 3 September 1943.

210.0110.298: Stkz SI+KL. Rebuilt as Me 410A-1 in 1943. To 13./KG 2 U5+BX. W/o at Montegny, France, on 15 December 1943.

210.0110.300: Stkz SI+KN. Rebuilt as Me 410A-1 in 1943. To 15./KG 2. Sustained 20 per cent damage at Lechfeld on 22 July 1943. Repaired. To FTS 6 and surrendered at Bayreuth-Bindlach on 8 May 1945.

210.0110.303: Stkz SI+KQ. Rebuilt as Me 410A-1 in 1943. To 16./KG 2. Sustained 40 per cent damage in Allied bomb raid at Romilly, France, on 3 September 1943. Repaired. To Bachmann & Blumenthal. Sustained 15 per cent damage in Allied bomb raid on 9 August 1944.

210.0110.304: Stkz SI+KR. Rebuilt as Me 410A-1 in 1943. To Fl.ÜG 1. Sustained 60 per cent damage on 28 August 1944.

Messerschmitt, Regensburg: Second Me 210 production batch

Some 100 Me 210A-1s were delivered between September 1942 and March 1943. A few were converted as Me 210C-1 variants, with others being rebuilt as Me 410s as indicated below. Several aircraft were delivered to operational units, III./ZG 1 in particular, with one aircraft from this batch, W Nr 2350, being delivered to Japan for evaluation. There was only one W Nr batch: 2251 to 2350.

2260: Stkz VC+GJ. To 1./SKG 210. Sustained 70 per cent damage due to pilot error, Landsberg on 5 December 1941.

2261: Stkz VC+GK. To 3./ZG 1 S9+IL. Sustained 65 per cent damage in taxiing accident at Tours, France, on 9 March 1942.

2265: Stkz VC+GO. Converted as Me 210C-1. To I./ZG 1 S9+HL. W/o at Tours, France, on 9 March 1942.

2266: Stkz VC+GP. To I./SKG 210 S9+CK. W/o near Hörsching on 10 December 1941.

2276: Stkz BN+CA. Converted as Me 210C-1. To 9./ZG 1 S/d over Sousse, Tunisia, on 10 April 1943.

2281: Stkz BN+CF. To III./ZG 1. Sustained 35 per cent damage in taxiing accident at Sfax, Tunisia, on 24 March 1943.

2289: Stkz BN+CN. To III./ZG 1. Lost due to engine trouble over the Mediterranean on 17 April 1943.

2293: Stkz BN+CR. To 8./ZG 1 2N+CR. S/d by 154 Sqn Spitfire near Bougie, Algeria, on 13 November 1942. Uffz Hans Krüger and Uffz Rudolf Faißt both MiA.

2296: Stkz BN+CU. To 9./ZG 1. Noted by Petrick as s/d on 10 April 1943 over Sousse, Tunisia. Possible confusion with W Nr 2276.

2297: Stkz BN+CV. To III./ZG 1 S/d by USAAF Spitfires in Kairouan area, Tunisia, on 9 April 1943.

2298: Stkz BN+CW. To III./ZG 1. S/d over Marettimo, Italy, on 30 May 1943.

2299: Stkz BN+CX. Coded +HT, and captured at Gerbini, Sicily, in August 1943.

2308: Stkz DF+EG. Captured at Gerbini, Sicily, in August 1943.

2309: Stkz DF+EH. To *Stab* IV./NJG 1 G9+AE. S/d in error by Luftwaffe fighter over Kimbrück on 9 October 1943.

2310: Stkz DF+EI. To III./ZG 1. Sustained 80 per cent damage due to engine trouble at Vicenza, Italy, on 23 June 1943.

2312: Stkz DF+EK. Modified by Blohm & Voss as dual control conversion trainer in November 1943.

2313: Stkz DF+EL. To 9./ZG 1 2N+LS. Lost over Sicily on 21 May 1943.

2314: Stkz DF+EM. To 7./ZG 1 2N+BD. S/d by RAF fighter 50 km N Gabes, Tunisia, on 7 March 1943. Uffz Johannes Häring wounded and Uffz Ernst Bonnrath killed.

2315: Stkz DF+EN. To III./ZG 1. Sustained 10 per cent damage in Allied bomb raid against Chinisia, 5 April 1943. Repaired, and modified by Blohm & Voss as dual control conversion trainer in November 1943.

2316: Stkz DF+EO. To 7./ZG 1. S/d by USAAF 82 FG P-38 Lightning on 11 March 1943. Ditched 1 km NW Marettimo, Italy, with Fw Karl-Heinz Thiemann being rescued and Uffz Alfred Telizki being killed.

2317: Stkz DF+EP. Modified by Blohm & Voss as dual control conversion trainer in November 1943.

2319: Stkz DF+ER. To 1./(F)121. Sustained 20 per cent damage in landing accident, Chartres, France, on 10 September 1943.

2321: Stkz GF+CA. To 16./KG 6 2H+HA. S/d by P/O Bridges of 1 Sqn over Sunnyside Farm, Sledgate, Yorks., UK, on 6 September 1942. Oblt Walter Mauer and Rudolf Jansen baled out successfully, becoming PoWs.

2322: Stkz GF+CB. To 16./KG 6. S/d by 266 Sqn Typhoons over North Sea on 9 August 1942. Oblt Ernst Haberland anad Uffz Heinz Dingel were both killed.

2325: Stkz GF+CE. To 9./ZG 1 2N+HT sustained 90 per cent damage after running out of fuel, Gerbini, Sicily, on 12 March 1943.

2326: Stkz GF+CF. To 9./ZG. 1 S/d by USAAF 52 FG Spitfires in Kariouba area, Tunisia, on 10 April 1943.

2329: Stkz GF+CI. To *Ergänzung Zerstörergruppe* sustained 60 per cent damage in forced landing at Broitzem on 22 December 1943.

2334: Stkz GF+CN. To *Erprobungsstaffel* 210. To 16./KG 6 2H+CA, S/d by 1 Sqn Typhoon on 6 September 1942. Crashed near Redcar reservoir, New Marske. Fw Heinrich Mösges & Obgfr Eduard Czerny both baled out, but were killed on impact with the ground when their parachutes failed to deploy.

2335: Stkz GF+CO. To 16./KG 6. Sustained 90 per cent damage due to engine trouble, Beauvais, France, on 16 September 1942.

2336: Stkz GF+CP. To II./ZG 1. Sustained 60 per cent damage in forced landing at Gabes, Tunisia, on 17 March 1943.

2343: Stkz GF+CW. To *Erprobungsstaffel* 210. Sustained 45 per cent damage in landing accident at Stade on 31 May 1942. Repaired, to *Ergänzung Fernaufklärungsgruppe*. W/o near Posen (Poznan), on 28 November 1943.

2350: Stkz GE+KV. To E-Stelle Rechlin for DB 605 engine tests. Delivered to Japan, January/February 1943. Evaluated by Imperial Japanese Army Air Force.

Messerschmitt, Augsburg: Final Me 210 Production Batch

There were twenty-six Me 210A-1s. Some were converted as Me 210C-1s as noted below. Aircraft converted by using 'short' Me 210 fuselages originally built by the Luther Werke (part of the MIAG concern) at Braunschweig. There was only one W Nr batch: 8151 to 8176 (twenty-six), delivered between December 1942–January 1943.

8153: Stkz GA+YC. To 8./ZG 1 2N+HS. Sustained 45 per cent damage in Allied bomb raid on 20 March 1943. Repaired. Captured at Gerbini, Sicily, in August 1943.

8154: Stkz GA+YD. Converted as C-1. Sustained 90 per cent damage due to engine failure on 4 November 1943.

8156: Stkz GA+YF. To 2./(F)122. Sustained 80 per cent damage at Trapani, Sicily, on 22 March 1943.

8157: Stkz GA+YG. To III./ZG 1. Destroyed at Sfax, Tunisia, in Allied bomb raid, on 29 March 1943.

8161: Stkz GA+YK. To III./ZG 1. Sustained 90 per cent damage at Sfax, Tunisia, in Allied bomb raid on 29 March 1943.

8162: Stkz GA+YL. To III./ZG 1. Sustained 85 per cent damage at Sfax, Tunisia, in Allied bomb raid on 29 March 1943.

8165: Stkz GA+YO. To 8./SG 103. To 2 *Ergänzungs-Zerstörergruppe* 1E+UC Captured in burnt state at Metz, February 1945.

8167: Stkz GA+YQ. To III./ZG 1. Sustained 80 per cent damage at Sfax, Tunisia, in Allied bomb raid on 29 March 1943.

8169: Stkz GA+YS. To 7./ZG 1 2N+GR. S/d near Bon Thadi, Tunisia, on 10 April 1943.

8170: Stkz GA+YT. To 7./ZG 1. S/d over Tunisia on 10 April 1943.

8171: Stkz GA+YU. To 7./ZG 1 2N+PR. Lost near Aetna on 12 March 1943.

8172: Stkz GA+YV. To III./ZG 1. Sustained 15 per cent damage at Sfax, Tunisia, in Allied bomb raid on 29 March 1943.

8173: Stkz GA+YW. Converted as C-1. To III./ZG 1. Sustained 10 per cent damage at Gerbini, Sicily, in mid-June 1943. Captured at Gerbini in damaged state in August 1943.

8174: Stkz GA+YX. To 9./ZG 1 2N+NT. Sustained 10 per cent damage in taxiing accident in Tunisia on 30 March 1943. Repaired. Sustained 55 per cent damage over Catania, Sicily, on 10 May 1943. Captured at Catania in damaged state in August 1943.

8175: Stkz GA+YY. To III./ZG 1. Sustained 10 per cent damage in taxiing accident, Tunisia, on 30 March 1943.

8176: Stkz GA+YZ. To III./ZG 1. Sustained 25 per cent damage in Allied bomb raid, Tunisia, on 5 April 1943.

Messerschmitt Me 410

Messerschmitt, Augsburg: First Me 410 Production Batch

Some 147 Me 410A-1s were delivered between July and September 1943. There were five W Nr batches: 10011 to 10050 (forty) delivered in July 1943; 10101 to 10120 (twenty) delivered in July–August 1943; 10171 to 10200 (thirty) delivered in August 1943; 10230 to 10270 (forty-one) delivered in August–September 1943; and 10300 to 10315 (sixteen) delivered in September 1943.

10011: Stkz SI+KS. To V./KG 2. S/d 30 July 1943.

10013: Stkz SI+KU. To 1./KG 51 9K+AH. S/d over Freudenstadt, 11 September 1943.

10015: Stkz SI+KW. To FÜG 1. Sustained 70 per cent damage due to engine trouble, 24 June 1943. Also reported to have sustained 25 per cent damage in landing accident at Memmingen, 17 August 1943, while serving with I./ZG 101.

10016: Stkz SI+KX. To I./KG 51. Sustained 20 per cent damage in taxiing accident at Wels, 4 October 1943. Repaired. To *Seenotgruppe* 80 F4+EC Still in service at Westerland, 25 April 1945.

10018: SI+KZ. Converted as A-2/U1, F6+WK of 2.(F)/122. Captured in Sicily. Shipped to USA for evaluation, serial number FE-499/T2-499. Preserved.

10022: Stkz GF+TM. To II./ZG 26. Sustained 70 per cent damage in landing accident near Limburg, 20 December 1943.

10024: Stkz GF+TO. To 4./ZG 26 3U+NM. S/d near Wittmundshaven, 14 December 1943.

10025: Stkz GF+TP. To 5./ZG 26 2N+CS. Sustained 25 per cent damage in landing accident near Hesepe, 26 August 1943. Repaired. To 1./ZG 26 3U+AK Sustained 10 per cent damage in forced landing near Demmin, 12 July 1944. Repaired. To 3./ZG 26 Crashed into Schweriner See, 22 July 1944.

10026: Stkz GF+TQ. To *Ergänzungsstaffel* /ZG 76. Lost near Ohlau, 12 July 1944.

10027: Stkz GF+TR. To *Seenotgruppe* 80. Still in service at Westerland, 25 April 1944.

10030: Stkz GF+TU. To 4./ZG 26. Lost near Celle, 18 February 1944.

10031: Stkz GF+TV. To 2./(F)122 F6+PK. S/d near Avellino, Italy, 24 September 1943.

10034: Stkz GF+TY. To *Seenotgruppe* 80. Surrendered at Westerland, 8 May 1945.

10037: Stkz GH+YB. To 6./ZG 26. Coded Yellow 4. S/d near Assen, 27 September 1943.

10038: Stkz GH+YC. To II./ZG 26. Sustained 40 per cent damage due to engine trouble near Vechta, 11 December 1943.

10040: Stkz GH+YE. To III./ZG 1. S/d near Friedberg, 16 October 1943.

10043: Stkz GH+YH. To 3./KG 51 9K+DL. Lost near Passau, 18 October 1943.

10044: Stkz GH+YI. To II./ZG 26 3U+BM. Sustained 20 per cent damage due to engine trouble, 23 November 1943.

10045: Stkz GH+YJ. To II./ZG 26. Sustained 70 per cent damage on 22 December 1943.

10046: Stkz GH+YK. To 1./KG 51 9K+HH. Sustained 10 per cent damage in landing accident at Lechfeld, 21 October 1943. Repaired. Lost near Augsburg, 3 November 1943.

10049: Stkz GH+YN. To I.KG 51 9K+SH. Crashed at Königsbrunn, 20 August 1943.

10050: Stkz GH+YO. Used for W Gr 21 revolving drum magazine tests. To 12./KG 51 9K+EW. Lost near Riedesheim, 28 March 1944.

10106: Stkz GH+YU. To I./KG 51 9K+AK. W/o in landing accident, Illesheim, 20 September 1943.

10107: Stkz GH+YV. To I./ZG 76 M8+ White 9. Crashed into Plattensee, 30 June 1944.

10108: Stkz GH+YW. To I./KG 51. Sustained 40 per cent damage after hitting Me 410s W Nr 10042 and 10242 during take-off from Hörsching, 6 October 1943.

10110: Stkz GH+YY. To 2./(F)122 F6+UK. Lost near Perugia, Italy, 24 February 1944.

10111: Stkz GH+YZ. To 2./(F)122 F6+MK. Lost near Corsica, France, 29 September 1943.

10112: Stkz TF+EA. Used for spinner-mounted landing lights tests. Sustained 15 per cent damage at Berlin-Schönefeld, 18 November 1943.

10116: Stkz TF+EE. To III./ZG 1 2N+HT. Sustained 20 per cent damage in taxiing accident at Vörden, 19 September 1943. Repaired. S/d over Apeldoorn, the Netherlands, 10 October 1943.

10119: Stkz TF+EH. To *Ergänzungsstaffel*/ZG 26. Lost near Teuplitz, 27 April 1944.

10120: Stkz TF+EI. To V./KG 2 U5+AF. S/d near Ipswitch, UK, 23 August 1943.

10171: Stkz TF+EJ. To 15./KG 2 U5+AF. S/d near Bradwell, UK, 15 September 1943.

10172: Stkz TF+EK. To 16./KG 6. Lost 4 September 1943. Hptm G Näder.

10174: Stkz TF+EM. To V./KG 2. Sustained 15 per cent damage when fuel tank blew up, Venneville, France, 24 August 1943.

10175: Stkz TF+EN. To 15./KG 2. Sustained 25 per cent damage in Allied bomb raid, Vitry, France, 9 September 1943. Repaired. To 13./KG 2 U5+MX W/o near Romilly, France, 29 November 1943.

10176: Stkz TF+EO. To 15./KG 2 U5+LF. S/d near Brentwood, UK, 18 October 1943.

10177: Stkz TF+EP. To 15./KG 2 U5+xF. Sustained 45 per cent damage in forced landing, Brussels, Belgium, 23 September 1943.

10178: Stkz TF+EQ. To 13./KG 2 U5+AX. Crashed near Sens, France, due to engine trouble, 17 October 1943.

10183: Stkz TF+EV. To *Stab Fliegerführer* England. Destroyed in Allied bomb raid at Beauvais, France, 9 September 1943.

10184: Stkz TF+EW. To 2./(F)122. S/d in error by German flak, 28 October 1943. Crashed near Falinora, Italy.

10185: Stkz TF+EX. To 16./KG 2 U5+KG. S/d off Dungeness, UK, 7 October 1943.

10186: Stkz TF+EY. To 2./(F)122 F6+MK. Lost near Rimini, Italy, 12 April 1944.

10188: Stkz TF+TJ. To 15./KG 2. Sustained 15 per cent damage at Vitry, France, 27 September 1943. Repaired. Sustained 15 per cent damage at Chartres, France, 14 November 1943. Repaired. To 12./KG 51 9K+EW Lost in crash near Munchen-Riem, 24 June 1944.

10189: Stkz TF+TK. To 16./KG 2. Sustained 60 per cent damage at Schiphol, the Netherlands, 4 October 1943.

10191: Stkz TF+TM. To *Seenotgruppe* 81. In service at Parow, 25 April 1945.

10192: Stkz TF+TN. Used for Dornier flame dampener tests. Captured at Göttingen, 18 April 1945.

10193: Stkz TF+TO. To Fl.Ü.G 1. Sustained 85 per cent damage at Melsbroek, Belgium, 8 September 1943.

10194: Stkz TF+TP A-1 14./KG 6 Dbr at Schiphol, Netherlands on 4 October 1943 in Allied bomb raid.

10196: Stkz TF+TR. To *Ergänzungsstaffel*/ZG 76 1E+YE. W/o near Märzförffel, 2 July 1944.

10198: Stkz SI+TB. To 1./ZG 26. W/o near Zerbst, 22 July 1944.

10200: Stkz SI+TD. To 16./KG 2. Sustained 70 per cent damage after striking obstacle, Juvincourt, France, 1 November 1943.

10230: Stkz SI+TE. To 15./KG 2. Sustained 25 per cent damage in Allied bomb raid at Vitry, France, 9 September 43. Repaired. Sustained 35 per cent damage in landing accident at Hesepe, 5 December 1943. Repaired. To 11./ZG 26 Surrendered at Ørland, Norway, 10 May 1945. Scrapped.

10235: Stkz SI+TJ. To 2./(F)122 F6+PK. S/d near Sulmona, Italy, 8 January 1944.

10236: Stkz SI+TK. To 13./KG 2 U5+WX. W/o near Munich, 24 February 1944.

10237: Stkz SI+TL. To V./KG 2. Sustained 20 per cent damage in landing accident at Schiphol, the Netherlands, 26 November 1943. Repaired. To FÜG 1 Sustained 30 per cent damage in landing accident, 28 May 1944.

10238: Stkz SI+TM To 16./KG 2 U5+KG S/d 5 miles E of Felixstowe, UK, at 11.59 a.m. on 13 July 1943 by F/L E.N. Bunting and P/O F.G. French, RAF 85 Sqn. Fw Franz Zwissler and Ofw Leo Raida killed.

10240: Stkz SI+TO. To Überkommando /KG Luftwaffe Italien. To 14./KG 2 Sustained 30 per cent damage in accident due to pilot error, Schiphol, the Netherlands, 22 October 1943.

10241: Stkz SI+TP. To E-Stelle Travemünde. Used for BK 5 cannon trials. To (Z)./EKdo 25 in April 1944. Coded Black 13. S/d 12 May 1944 near Plauen. Lt Paul Kaschuba and Fw Karl Bredemeier killed.

10242: Stkz SI+TQ. To I./KG 51. Sustained 20 per cent damage when struck by Me 410 W Nr 10108 at Hörsching, 6 October 1943.

10244: Stkz SI+TS. To 15./KG 2 U5+BF. S/d near Eastbourne, UK, 8 November 1943.

10245: Stkz SI+TT. To 15./KG 2 U5+HF. S/d by flak over Surrey, UK, 31 October 1943.

10246: Stkz SI+TU. To V./KG 2. Sustained 35 per cent damage in landing accident, 21 December 1943.

10250 Stkz SI+TY. To 1./ZG 26 3U+JH. S/d near Brühl, 27 July 1944.

10251 Stkz SI+TZ. To 3./KG 51 9K+EL. W/o near Marienbad, 3 November 1943.

10252 Stkz SN+HA. To 16./KG 2. Sustained 50 per cent damage at Rennes, France, 19 November 1943. Repaired. To *Ergänzungsstaffel* /ZG 76.

10253: Stkz SN+HB. To 2./(F)122 F6+QK crashed near River Sangro, Italy, 11 November 1943.

10254: Stkz SN+HC. To 16./KG 2. Sustained 10 per cent damage in take-off accident at Epinoy, France, 20 December 1943.

10255: Stkz SN+HD. To 14./KG 2 U5+FE. S/d in error by Luftwaffe fighters near Mönchengladbach, 5 November 1943.

10259: Stkz SN+HH. Converted as A-3. To 2(F)/122 F6+OK. Landed by mistake at Monte Corvino, Italy, 27 November 1943. Evaluated by RAF as TF209.

10261: Stkz SN+HJ. To 16./KG 2. Sustained 40 per cent damage in Allied bomb raid at Epinoy, France, 1 December 1943.

10263: Stkz SN+HL. To 1./KG 51. Sustained 50 per cent damage in landing accident at Bindersleben, 1 October 1943.

10264: Stkz SN+HM. To 15./KG 2. Sustained 35 per cent damage in landing accident at Vitry, France, 21 December 1943.

10265: Stkz SN+HN. To I./KG 51. Sustained 30 per cent damage in taxiing accident at Illesheim, 17 October 1943.

10266: Stkz SN+HO. To 2./KG 51 9K+NK. Crashed near Caen, France, 15 May 1944.

10268: Stkz SN+HQ. To 9./KG 51 9K+BR. W/o at Burgbernheim, 9 January 1944.

10269: Stkz SN+HR. To 14./KG 2. Sustained 70 per cent damage at Epinoy, France, 30 December 1943.

10301: Stkz SN+HU. To 14./KG 2 U5+BE. S/d near Reydt, 5 November 1943.

10302: Stkz SN+HV. To 12./KG 51 9K+DV. W/o near Ismaning, 20 May 1944.

10303: Stkz SN+HW. To II./KG 2. Sustained 40 per cent damage in Allied bomb raid at Romilly, France, 3 September 1943. Repaired. To 3./KG 51 9K+FL. W/o near Augsburg, 13 November 1943.

10304: Stkz SN+HX. To 2./KG 51 9K+MK. W/o near Chauvigny, France, 24 March 1944.

10306: Stkz SN+HZ. To I./KG 51. Sustained 20 per cent damage at Illesheim, 11 November 1943. Repaired. To 11./ZG 26. Surrendered at Ørland, Norway, 10 May 1945. Scrapped.

10309: Stkz RK+XC. To I./KG 51. Sustained 40 per cent damage in forced landing near Lechfeld, 22 December 1943. Repaired. To FÜG 1 Sustained 50 per cent damage in forced landing due to engine failure, 28 April 1944. Repaired. To II./KG 51.

10311: Stkz RK+XE. To 14./KG 2 U5+HE. S/d near Manston, UK, 8 November 1943.

10312: Stkz RK+XF. To I./KG 51 9K+FH. W/o near Bobingen, 27 October 1943.

10315: Stkz RK+XI. To 15./KG 2 U5+FF. Lost 31 October 1943.

10398: To 14./KG 2. Sustained 10 per cent damage in forced landing at Gilze-Rijen, the Netherlands, 16 October 1943.

Dornier, München: Second Me 410 Production Batch

Some 107 Me 410A-1s were delivered between January and April 1944. There were two W Nr batches: 120001 to 120027 (twenty-seven) delivered between January and March 1944 and 120092 to 120172 (eighty) delivered between February and April 1944. Discrepancies include aircraft with W Nr 120075, 120079, and 120236.

120.003: Stkz SN+HV 2./KG 51 9K+CK. Damaged in forced landing near Epaignes, France, on 14 April 1944.

120.004: Stkz SN+HW. Delivered on 1 February 1944. To Fl.Ü.G.1. Sustained 10 per cent damage on 25 February 1944, repaired. To EKdo 25. Sustained 25 per cent damage in Allied strafing raid at Parchim on 21 May 1944. Repaired. To 2./ZG 26 Suffered damage on 22 July 1944 at Deutsch-Krone. Repaired. To 11./ZG 26 With O. Qu. Reserve at Vaernes, Norway. Surrendered on 10 May 1945. Scrapped.

120.005: A-1 Stkz SN+HX. To 1./KG 51 9K+JH. MiA on intruder raid against London on 19 April 1944.

120.006: Stkz SN+HY. To 6./KG 51 9K+KP. Lost on 29 May 1944.

120.007: A-1 Stkz SN+HZ. To EKdo 25. Sustained 15 per cent damage on 21 May 1944 at Parchim. Repaired. To 11./ZG 26 SN+HZ Surrendered at Ørland, Norway on 10 May 1945. Scrapped.

120.008: Stkz RK+XA. To 5./KG 51 9K+EN. W/o in take-off accident at Gilze-Rijen, the Netherlands, on 29 May 1944. Pilot Uffz A Döhler. Possibly collided with W Nr 420431, pilot Oblt H. Niebler.

120.014: Stkz RK+XG. To 1./Fl.ÜG 1. Lost near Nancy, France on 25 February 1944.

120.015: Stkz RK+XH. To EKdo 25. Sustained 10 per cent damage during raid against Parchim on 21 May 1944. Repaired. To 1./ZG 76 M8+ White 15 Lost at Kralowe on 5 July 1944.

120.016: Stkz RK+XI 2./ZG 26. S/d on 21 June 1944 over Ihlenfeldersumpf, NE Neubrandenburg, Germany. Obfrh Augustin Kaiser and Uffz Fritz Anders killed.

120.017: Stkz BR+JX. To 1./KG 51 9K+CH. Lost during attack on London, UK, on 12 April 1944.

120.018: Stkz BR+JY 6./KG 51 9K+DP. FTR from sortie over England on 7 June 1944. Possibly crashed into North Sea. Fw Hans Seemann and Uffz Karl-Heinz Steffen MiA.

120.019: Stkz BR+JZ. To 2./ZG 76 M8+ Black 8. Lost near Sare on 23 June 1944.

120.021: Stkz BR+KB. To *Ergänzungsstaffel*/ZG 26. Lost near Sagan on 19 May 1944.

120.023: Stkz BR+KD. To 3./ZG 26. Lost near Magdeburg on 30 May 1944.

120.024: Stkz BR+KE. To 3./ZG 26. Sustained 35 per cent damaged in forced landing near Lütgenhagen on 5 June 1944.

120.025: Stkz BR+KF: To 2./ZG 26. Coded 5. Damaged in crash near Andernach, presumed repaired. To 3./ZG 26. Crashed near Arnswalde on 29 May 1944.

120.027: Stkz BR+KH. To 1./ZG 76 M8+ White 11. W/o near Vienna-Seyring, Austria, on 29 June 1944.

120.093: Stkz BR+KJ. To 2./ZG 26 3U+CK. S/d near Löcknitz on 21 June 1944.

120.095: Stkz BR+KL. To I./ZG 76 M8+ Black 10. W/o near Plattensee on 8 July 1944.

120.096: Stkz BR+KM. To *Seenotgruppe* 81. Grounded at Parow on 25 April 1945.

120.099: Stkz BR+KP. To *Seenotgruppe* 80. In service at Westerland on 25 April 1945.

120.101: Stkz BR+KR. To 2.ZG 26 3U+GK. Lost at Parchim on 1 August 1944.

120.102: Stkz BR+KS. To II./ZG 26. Crashed into hill near Uncín, near the city of Teplice (present-day Czech Republic), on 2 November 1944. Three crew killed, with the third person presumed to be a mechanic.

120.105: Stkz BR+KV. To 2./ZG 26. W/o at Rügen Island on 27 June 1944.

120.108: Stkz BR+KY 11./ZG 26. Surrendered at Ørland, Norway on 10 May 1945. Scrapped.

120.109: Stkz BR+KZ. To 3./ZG 26. Lost near Greifswald on 27 June 1944.

120.110: Stkz BR+LA. To 3./KG 51 9K+BL. Lost near Saint André, France on 5 April 1944. Also reported as lost on 19 June 1944 when serving with *Stab* I./ZG 76 (code M8+ < +).

120.119: Stkz ? To *Seenotgruppe* 60. Sustained 90 per cent damage after inadvertently striking the ground at Heiligenberg on 24 January 1945.

120.120: Stkz ? To 1./ZG 26. Lost near Burg on 30 May 1944.

120.122: Stkz ? To 3./ZG 26. Lost near Lübeck, 28 June 1944.

120.123: Stkz PE+TK. To 1./ZG 26. Lost at Königsberg in May 1944.

120.124: A-1/U2 Stkz PE+TL. To 1./ZG 76 M8+ White 12. Lost near Tulln, Austria, on 8 July 1944.

120.125: Stkz PE+TM. To 2./ZG 26 3U+EK. S/d near Parchim on 21 July 1944.

120.126: Stkz PE+TN del 9 March 44. To 11./ZG 26 Surrendered at Ørland, Norway, on 10 May 1945. Scrapped.

120.127: Stkz PE+TO. To *Seenotgruppe* 80. Grounded at Westerland on 25 April 1945.

120.128: Stkz PE+TP. To 1./ZG 26 3U+DH. Lost near Brühl on 26 July 1944.

120.130: Stkz PE+TR. To 4./ZG 76 M8+ White 16. Lost near Seerappen on 3 August 1944.

120.131: Stkz PE+TS. To *Stab* I./ZG 76. Lost near Neuburg on 19 June 1944.

120.134: Stkz PE+TV. To 2./ZG 26. S/d near Greifenberg on 5 June 1944.

120.138: Stkz PE+TZ 11./ZG 26. Surrendered at Ørland, Norway, on 10 May 45. Scrapped.

120.141: Stkz PL+PN. To 2./Fl.ÜG. To 1./ZG 26 PL+PX. W/o near Prenzlau on 25 June 1944.

120.156: A-1/U2 Stkz PS+UV. To 1./ZG 76 M8+ White 2. W/o near Grafenwörth on 8 July 1944.

120.157: A-3 Stkz PS+UW. To 2./(F)122. Destroyed on ground at Ghedi, Italy on 12 March 1945.

120.158: Stkz PS+UX. To 3./ZG 26. S/d near Regentin on 29 May 1944.

120.159: A-1/U2 Stkz ? To 1./ZG 76 White 14. Lost near Landshut, date unknown.

120.161: Stkz PT+BL. To 2./ZG 76 M8+ Black 17. Lost near Unterkemenau on 5 July 1944.

120.163: Stkz PT+BN 11./ZG 26. Surrendered at Ørland, Norway, on 10 May 45. Scrapped.

120.166: Stkz PT+BQ. To 1./ZG 76. Lost near Sare on 23 June 1944.

120.236: Sustained 20 per cent damage in forced landing due to engine trouble on 9 March 1944.

Unknown Manufacturer: Third Me 410 Production Batch

Thirty Me 410B-2 and B-3s were delivered in July 1944, making one W Nr batch only: 130351 to 130379. There are several notable discrepancies, including a Me 410B-2/U4 with W Nr 130330 surrendered in Norway in May 1945.

130.102: B-2 6./Fl.ÜG 1 CG+ZJ. W/o in landing accident at Roth on 5 November 1944.

130.325: B-2. To 5./(F)122. Sustained 20 per cent damage in landing accident near Wittstock on 24 March 1945.

130.330: B-2/U4 11./ZG 26. Surrendered at Oslo-Gardermoen, Norway, on 10 May 1945. BK 5 cannon possibly not fitted. Scrapped.

130.363: TI+WM. Lost over Parchim on 11 February 1945.

130.379: B-2/U4. Captured by Soviet forces at Prowehren, East Prussia in March 1945. Evaluated by the NII-VVS.

Messerschmitt, Augsburg: Fourth Me 410 Production Batch

Fifty-four Me 410B-1, B-2, and B-3s were delivered in July 1944, making only one W Nr batch: 150083 to 150136. As usual, there are several discrepancies. Only nineteen aircraft from this production batch have been identified. Me 410Bs with W Nr 150139, 150165, and 150250 are also known.

150.083: To 6./ZG 76 M8+ Yellow 7. Lost near Prague-Reuth on 30 May 1944.

150.094: To 1./ZG 76. Sustained 80 per cent damage near Prague-Kbely on 27 June 1944.

150.095: B-2. To 3./ZG 76. Sustained 30 per cent damage due to unknown cause on 22 August 1944.

150.096: B-3. To 2./(F)122 F6+KK. S/d near Mirano, Italy on 8 February 1945.

150.097: B-2 To 3./ZG 76 M8+ Yellow 15. Lost over Hungary on 5 July 1944. Also reported as having been sold to Hungary in early 1945.

150.104: To 5./ZG 76 M8+ Black 4. Lost near Königswusterhausen on 25 June 1944.

150.105: B-1/U2. To 1./ZG 76 M8+ White 5. Lost near Tulln, Austria, on 8 July 1944.

150.110: To *Stab* I./ZG 76 Coded > Blue 2. Lost near Mainburg on 13 June 1944.

150.117: To 5./ZG 76 M8+ Black 6. Lost near Dubora, Slovakia, on 5 July 1944.

150.118: B-3. To 5./(F)122 F6+SN. W/o near Jesau on 16 January 1945.

150.120: FÜG 1. Sustained 40 per cent damage in landing accident, Prague-Kbely on 8 May 1944.

150.121: B-1 FÜG 1. Sustained 10 per cent damage in forced landing near Chemnitz on 12 September 1944.

150.124: To 5./ZG 76 M8+ Black 7. Lost near Budapest, Hungary, on 27 June 1944.

150.126: To 4./KG 51 9K+FM. W/o in take-off accident, Clastres, France, on 25 July 1944.

150.136: To 5./ZG 76 M8+ > 3. Lost near Luckau on 21 June 1944.

150.165: To 5./(F)122 F6+RH. Lost 12 February 1945.

150.250: B-1 FÜG 1. Sustained 15 per cent damage in forced landing due to engine trouble on 12 September 1944.

Messerschmitt, Augsburg: Fifth Me 410 Production Batch

Some 109 Me 410A-3s were delivered between October 1943 and May 1944. There were two W Nr batches: 170001 to 170043 (forty-three) delivered in October–November 1943 and 170087 to 170152 (sixty-six) delivered between February and May 1944.

However, no evidence appear to exist of W Nr 170010 to 170024 (fifteen aircraft), W Nr 170099 to 170108 (ten aircraft) and W Nr 170123 to 170132 (ten aircraft) having actually been built. Thus, it seems likely that only twenty-eight aircraft from the first batch and forty-six aircraft from the second batch were actually completed, for a total of seventy-four Me 410A-3s.

170.002: Stkz DG+XI. To 2./(F)122 F6+QK. S/d near Corsica, France, 7 February 1944. Also reported as having crashed near Birnbaum on 5 March 1944 while attached to the *Ergänzungsstaffel Aufklärungsgruppe*, coded F2+CX.

170.003: Stkz DG+XJ. Captured at Les Chanoines in wrecked condition on 15 September 1944.

170.005: Stkz DG+XL. To 2./(F)122 F6+RK. Lost near Elba, Italy, 18 December 1943.

170.009: Stkz DG+XP. To 1.(F)/121. Fitted with FuG 216 tail warning radar. S/d by USAAF P-51 Mustangs near Paris, France, on 20 April 1944. Wreck destroyed by fire.

170.026: Stkz DG+XR. To 1./(F)121. Sustained 15 per cent damage due to pilot error at Guyancourt, France, 9 November 1943. S/d over Le Havre, France, on 25 April 1944 by F/L Rogers, 85 Sqn. Fw Kurt Stoll, Fw Herbert Kraupatz and Uffz Hans Ziegler were all killed.

170.028: Stkz DG+XT. To 2./(F)122 in December 1943. Sustained 20 per cent damage in landing accident at Munich-Riem, 13 April 1944 while attached to ÜKdo KG dLW Italien. Repaired. To I./(F)122 W/o near Berlin-Frohnau on 7 October 1944.

170.031: Stkz DG+XW. To 1.(F)/121 S/d by USAAF P-51 Mustangs near Paris, France, on 20 April 1944. Wreck destroyed by fire.

170.032: Stkz DG+XX. To 1./(F)121/ Sustained 10 per cent damage in landing accident at Paris, France, 12 December 1943. Repaired. S/d off Portsmouth, UK, by F/L Burbridge, 85 Sqn, on 26 April 1944. Oblt (*Staffelkapitän*) Hermann Kroll was killed with Ofhr Werner Meyer becoming a PoW.

170.033: Stkz DG+XY. To 1./(F)33. Captured at Les Chanoines in wrecked condition on 15 September 1944.

170.035: Stkz KR+UO. To 1./(F)121. Sustained 80 per cent damage in accident due to pilot error near Orly, France on 13 December 1943.

170.040: Stkz KR+UT. To 2./(F)122 F6+NK. Lost near Lago di Bolsena, Italy, on 18 April 1944.

170.087: Stkz KR+UX. To ÜKdo KG dLW Italien on 6 April 1944. To 2.(F)/122 F6+IK S/d on 10 August 1944 over Tyrrhenian Sea by 241 Sqn Spitfires. Lt Dietrich Stämmler and Uffz Arthur Karsch killed.

170.088: Stkz KR+UY. To 1.(F)/121. S/d by USAAF P-51 Mustangs near Paris, France, on 20 April 1944.

170.089: Stkz KR+UZ. To 2./(F)122 F6+ K. Destroyed at Perugia, Italy, May 1944. Captured in burnt condition on 11 June 1944.

170.090: Stkz BR+JA. To 2.(F)/122 F6+QK. Lost near Cetina, Italy, 24 July 1944.

170.091: Stkz BR+JB. To ÜKdo KG dLW Italien. To 2./(F)122 F6+NK. Lost near Termoli, Italy, on 14 March 1944.

170.098: Stkz BR+JI. To ÜKdo KG dLW Italien. To 2./(F)122 F6+KK. Lost near Vasto, Italy, on 15 May 1944.

170.114: Stkz PS+TF. To 2./(F)122 F6+DK. Captured at Perugia, Italy, in burnt condition.

170.133: Stkz NE+QA. Sustained 10 per cent damage due to engine trouble, 28 April 1944.

170.134: Stkz NE+QB. To 1(F)./121 7A+EH. Destroyed in Allied bomb raid, Villacoublay, France in 1944. NB: one source states that this aircraft was destroyed on 25 October 1944, which most certainly is erroneous, as a photo was released to the US press on 14 October 1944.

170.135: Stkz NE+QC. To 1(F)./121 7A+HH. Destroyed in Allied bomb raid, Florennes, Belgium, early September 1944.

170.140: Stkz NE+QH. To 1(F)./122 F6+AH. Lost on 16 August 1944.

170.148: Stkz NE+QP. To ZG 26 3U+ZL. W/o near Fruenwelche on 6 August 1944.

170.150: Stkz NE+QR. To Ükdo. KG dLW Italien To 2./(F)122 F6+GK S/d near La Spezia, Italy, on 13 August 1944.

170.151: Stkz NE+QS. To *Stab* /FAGr. 3. W/o at Parchim on 25 February 1945.

Messerschmitt, Augsburg: Sixth Me 410 Production Batch

Thirty-four Me 410B-3s were delivered in June–July 1944. There were two W Nr batches: 190.121 to 190.132 (eleven) delivered in June 1944 and 190.157 to 190.179 (twenty-three) delivered in June–July 1944.

190.124: Stkz GG+WN. To 2./(F)122. W/o at Mantua, Italy, 15 August 1944.

190.127: B-3 Stkz 2.(F)/122 F6+HK. Found at Ghedi airfield, Italy, on 2 May 1945 in wrecked condition.

190.128: B-3 Stkz GG+WR. Captured at Hanau-Langendiebach, 5 April 1945.

190.130: Stkz GG+WT. To *Erprobungskommando* 16. W/o near Schweinfurt, 24 April 1944.

190.131: B-3 Stkz GG+WU. To 1./(F)122. Sustained 40 per cent damage in landing accident at Neubrandenburg, 23 March 1945.

190.160: Stkz GG+WZ. To 2./(F)122 F6+KK. W/o near Ghedi, Italy, 3 September 1944.

190.161: Stkz GO+MW. To 2./(F)122 F6+ZK. S/d near Villafranca, Italy, on 10 December 1944.

190.163: B-3 Stkz GO+MY. To 2.(F)/122 F6+MK. Fuselage found at Villafranca di Verona airfield, Italy, 2 May 1945.

190.165: Stkz SO+NH. To 2.(F)/122 F6+GK. W/o near Arcona, Italy, 29 December 1944.

190.167: B-3 Stkz SO+NJ. To 2./(F)122 F6+FK. Found at Ghedi airfield, Italy on 2 May 1945 in wrecked condition.

190.169: B-3 Stkz SO+NL. To 2./(F)122. S/d near Grumone, Italy, 23 February 1945.

190.171: B-3 Stkz SO+NN. To 5./(F)122 F6+RN. W/o at Seerappen, 25 January 1945.

190.172: B-3 Stkz SO+NO. To 5./(F)122. Sustained 12 per cent damage in take-off accident at Pillau, 18 January 1945.

Messerschmitt, Augsburg: Seventh Me 410 Production Batch

Seventy-five Me 410B-2s were delivered between June and September 1944. There were two W Nr batches: 410.047 to 410.102 (fifty-five) delivered between June and September 1944 and 410.208 to 410.226 (twenty) delivered in September 1944.

410.014: A-1. To 5./ZG 26. Sustained 35 per cent damage in landing accident near Hesepe, 1 November 1943.

410.051: B-2 Stkz GF+YZ. To 2./ZG 76. W/o near Fels am Wagram, 8 July 1944.

410.072: Stkz SU+WL. To 2./ZG 3U+UK. Force-landed near Rossitten, 10 August 1944.

410.076: B-2 Stkz SU+WP. To FÜG 1. Sustained 10 per cent damage in landing accident, 28 July 1944.

410.098: A-1 Stkz SX+DL. Delivered in September 1944. To 3.(F)/22 Surrendered at Lista, Norway, 10 May 1945. Scrapped.

410.099: B-2 Stkz SX+DM. To FÜG 1. Sustained 35 per cent damage in forced landing due to engine failure, 5 September 1944.

410.198: Stkz ? Reported with 4./ZG 26 3U+EM on 24 July 1944, presumed clerical error.

410.208: B-6, surrendered at Værløse, Denmark. To AM74.

410.209: B-2 Stkz SX+DR. To 3.(F)/22. Surrendered at Lista, Norway, 10 May 1945. Scrapped.

410.212: B-2 Stkz SX+DU. To II./ZG 76. W/o near Grossenhain, 26 January 1945.

410.218: B-2 Stkz SU+OA. To 6./ZG 76. Coded Yellow 1. W/o in forced landing at Riesa, 27 January 1945.

410.257: To *Ergänzungsstaffel*/ZG 76. W/o near Neustadt, 28 June 1944.

410.278: B-6 To I./ZG 1. Surrendered at Værøse, Denmark, 8 May 1945. Transferred to RAE Farnborough as s/n AM 74.

410.303: To 3./KG 51 9K+FL. W/o near Augsburg on 13 November 1943.

410.445: B-2. To Flugzeugführerschule (FFS) 38. W/o on 16 September 1944.

410.468: To 4./ZG 26 3U+BM. Damaged in crash near Anklam on 4 July 1944.

410.482: To 4./ZG 26. Damaged in crash near Grabow on 28 June 1944.

Messerschmitt, Augsburg: Eighth Me 410 Production Batch

Some 255 Me 410A-1s were delivered between September 1943 and May 1944. There were seven W Nr batches: 420.001 to 420.041 (forty) delivered in September–October 1943; 420.082 to 420.104 (twenty-five) delivered in September–October 1943; 420.188 to 420.202 (fifteen) delivered in October–November 1943; 420.283 to 420.299 (seventeen) delivered in November 1943; 420.402 to 420.509 (108) delivered between November 1943 and January 1944; 420.622 to 420.640 (nineteen) delivered in January–February 1944; and 420.653 to 420.683 (thirty-one) delivered in May 1944.

420.001: Stkz RK+XJ. To 2./KG 51 9K+EK. Damaged near Mittelstetten, 26 February 1944.

420.002: A-1 Stkz RK+XK. To II./ZG 26. Sustained 35 per cent damage in forced landing near Lübbecke, 13 November 1943.

420.005: A-1 Stkz RK+XN. To 16./KG 2 U5+AJ. S/d on 3 January 1944, crashed into English Channel off Dover. Fw Friedrich Hess and Uffz Max von Poblotzki killed.

420.006: A-1 Stkz RK+XO. To 13./KG 2 U5+XO. To 6./KG 51 9K+KP. FTR from sortie over England on 29 May 1944. Possibly crashed into North Sea. Fw Ernst Dietrich and Uffz Walter Schaknies MiA.

420.007: A-1 Stkz RK+XP. Delivered on 21 September 1943. Converted as A-1/U2 To 11./ZG 26 Surrendered at Oslo-Gardermoen, Norway, on 10 May 45. Scrapped.

420.009: A-1 Stkz RK+XR. To 6./KG 51 9K+BP. W/o at Saint André on 25 October 1944.

420.010: Stkz RK+XS. To 11./KG 51 9K+RV. Lost near Hildesheim on 15 April 1944.

420.012: A-1 Stkz RK+XU. Delivered on 19 October 1943. To 11./ZG 26. Surrendered at Ørland, Norway, on 10 May 1945. Scrapped.

420.013: A-1 Stkz RK+XV. To I./KG 51. Sustained 55 per cent damage in taxiing accident at Lechfeld on 3 December 1943.

420.014: A-1 Stkz RK+XW. To II./ZG 26 2N+HR. S/d near Diepholz on 13 November 1943. Also reported as serving with *Ergänzungsstaffel* ZG 76 on 7 June 1944.

420.016: Stkz RK+XY. To 12./KG 51 9K+BW. W/o near Geislingen on 12 June 1944.

420.017: A-1 Stkz RK+XZ. To 14./KG 2. W/o near Calais, France, on 3 January 1944.

420.018: Stkz RN+ZA. To 6./ZG 26 2N+IP. S/d near Dinkelage on 15 November 1943.

420.019: Stkz RN+ZB. To 3./KG 51 9K+BL. MiA during raid on London, UK, on 17 April 1944.

420.022: A-1 Stkz RN+ZE. To V./KG 2. Destroyed at Epinoy, France, in Allied bomb raid on 26 November 1943.

420.025: Stkz RN+ZH. To III./ZG 1. S/d on 10 October 1943.

420.026: A-1 Stkz RN+ZI. To 14./KG 2. Destroyed at Schiphol, the Netherlands, on 13 December 1943 in Allied bomb raid.

420.027: A-1 Stkz RN+ZJ. Converted as A-1/U2. To 6./KG 51 9K+HP. S/d by flak over London, UK, on 13 June 1944.

420.028: A-1 Stkz RN+ZK. To II./ZG 26. Sustained 10 per cent damage during forced landing near Cologne on 1 December 1943. Repaired. To *Stab* II./ZG 26 Coded Blue 4. W/o near Fallingbostel on 10 February 1944.

420.030: Stkz RN+ZM. To 5./ZG 26 3U+MN. S/d near Plantluenne on 13 November 1943.

420.031: A-1 Stkz RN+ZN. To 7./ZG 1 2N+HR. S/d near Lohne on 14 October 1943.

420.033: Stkz RN+ZP. To 3./ZG 26. Coded 11. W/o near Warburg on 2 March 1944.

420.034: A-1 Stkz RN+ZQ. To II./ZG 26. Sustained 10 per cent damage in forced landing near Vechta due to engine trouble on 11 December 1943.

420.035: A-1 Stkz RN+ZR. To *Ergänzungsstaffel* /ZG 26. S/d near Sprottau on 13 June 1944.

420.036: A-1 Stkz RN+ZS. To II./ZG 26. Sustained 35 per cent damage in forced landing near Langenhagen on 29 November 1943.

420.037: A-1 Stkz RN+ZT. To 6./ZG 26. Coded 1+ S/d on 20 February 44 by USAAF bombers over the island of Fyn, Denmark. Crashed near Faaborg. Obfw Siegfried Haase baled out safely. Uffz Fritz Schröder was killed when his parachute failed to deploy.

420.038: A-1 Stkz RN+ZU. To *Stab* II./ZG 26 3U+EC. S/d near Oldenburg on 15 November 1943.

420.039: Stkz RN+ZV. To *Ergänzungsstaffel* /ZG 26. W/o in Silesia, location unknown, on 10 August 1944.

420.040: Stkz RN+ZW. To 5./ZG 26. Coded Yellow 2. W/o near Hannover on 7 March 1944.

420.041: A-1 Stkz RN+ZX. To II./ZG 26 9K+LW. Converted as A-1/U2. Sustained 30 per cent damage when overturned on landing at Hesepe on 13 November 1943. Repaired. To 12./KG 51. W/o near Hörnle on 26 July 1944.

420.083: A-1 Stkz RN+ZZ. To II./ZG 26. Sustained 80 per cent damage on 22 December 1943 at Ahlhorn. Possibly repaired as reported with 3.(F)/22 and surrendered at Lista, Norway, on 10 May 1945. Scrapped.

420.084: A-1 Stkz PP+VA. To II./ZG 26. Sustained 10 per cent damage in forced landing near St Trond on 1 December 1943. Repaired. To 3./ZG 76. S/d on 22 June 1944, crashed into woods near Trebotov (present-day Czech Republic). The crew baled out safely. The pilot was possibly Fw. Heinrich Huck.

420.085: A-1 Stkz PP+VB. To 14./KG 2. S/d over UK on 19 December 1943.

420.087: A-1 Stkz PP+VD. To II./ZG 26. Sustained 35 per cent damage in taxiing accident at Hesepe on 23 June 1943. Repaired. Lost on 20 December 1943.

420.089: Stkz PP+VF. To 2./ZG 26. S/d near Zabitz-Köthen on 29 June 1944.

420.090: Stkz PP+VG. To E-Stelle Gotenhafen (present-day Gdynia, Poland) in September 1944 for LTA 30A torpedo trials. Crashed at Hexengrund on 4 October 1944.

420.091: A-1 Stkz PP+VH. To 11./ZG 26 Surrendered at Ørland, Norway, on 10 May 1945. Scrapped.

420.092: A-1 Stkz PP+VI. To 14./KG 2 Destroyed at Schiphol, the Netherlands, on 13 December 1943 in Allied bomb raid.

420.095: Stkz PP+VL. To *Ergänzungsstaffel*/ZG 26. W/o near Sprottau, 15 June 1944.

420.096: A-1 Stkz PP+VM. To 14./KG 2. Sustained 75 per cent damage at Schiphol, the Netherlands, on 13 December 1943 in Allied bomb raid.

420.100: Stkz PP+VQ. To 8./KG 51 9K+HS. W/o near Giebelstadton, 4 March 1944.

420.101: A-1 Stkz PP+VR. Converted as A-1/U2. To 6./KG 51. W/o at Saint André on 25 October 1944.

420.104: Stkz PP+VU. To *Seenotgruppe* 80. Still in service at Westerland on 25 April 1945.

420.122: To 3./ZG 26. Lost near Andernach on 28 February 1944.

420.136: B-2. To 4./KG 51 9K+GH. Lost on 25 July 1944.

420.190: Stkz PP+VY. To *Seenotgruppe* 80. Still in service at Westerland on 25 April 1945.

420.191: Stkz PP+VZ. To 5./ZG 26. W/o near Pritzwalk on 24 July 1944.

420.198: A-1 Stkz PT+BG. Sustained 50 per cent damage at Oberpfaffenhofen on 20 January 1944.

420.200: A-1 Stkz PT+BI. To 4./KG 51 9K+IM. FTR from sortie over England on 7 June 1944. Possibly crashed into North Sea. Uffz Karl-Heinz Mond and Uffz Hugo Hagel both MiA.

420.201: A-1 Stkz DQ+XA. To 5./KG 51 9K+DN. S/d by RAF night fighter E. Beauvais, France, on 12 May 1944. Oblt Claus Bieber and Fw Heinz Closken killed.

420.202: Stkz DQ+XB. To (Z)/EKdo 25 on 6 February 1944. To 5./ZG 26 3U+5. S/d near Magdeburg on 12 March 1944.

420.214: A-1 15./KG 2 U5+CF. S/d by RAF night fighter 8 km off Zeebrugge, Belgium, on 24 August 1943 at 0315 hrs by Sqn Ldr Arbon and Fg Off. Ashcroft of 29 Sqn. They subsequently submitted a claim for a 'Me 210' off Knokke. Oblt Wilhelm Schmitter and Ofw Heinz Graeber baled out, being rescued ninety minutes later. Graeber had struck the tail section of the Me 410, resulting in both his legs being broken.

420.284: Stkz DQ+XE. To 8./KG 51 9K+BS. W/o near Kitzingen, 16 February 1944.

420.288: A-1 Stkz DT+PC. Converted as A-1/U4. To 6./ZG 26. W/o at Königsberg on 16 April 1944.

420.289: Stkz DT+PD. To 6./KG51 9K+PB. W/o in take-off accident, Soesterberg, the Netherlands, on 21 April 1944. Hptm D-H. Vester survived.

420290: Stkz DT+PE. To (Z)EKdo 25, 18 November 1943. To 5./ZG 26 code Black 6. S/d over Kehrberg on 6 March 1944.

420.291: A-1 Stkz DT+PF. To 11./ZG 26. Surrendered at Ørland, Norway, on 10 May 1945. Scrapped.

420.293: A-1 Stkz DT+PH. To 1./KG 51 9K+KH. S/d on 19 April 1944 at St Nicholas Churchyard, Brighton, Sussex. Hpt Richard Pahl and Fw Wilhelm Schubert killed.

420.298: Stkz DT+PM. To 1./KG 51 9K+FH. W/o near St André, France, on 14 March 1944.

420.299: Stkz DT+PN. To 3./KG 51 9K+HL.Lost over Vitry-en-Artois, France, on 17 April 1944.

420.314: A-1 5./KG 51 U5+MN. Failed to return from sortie over England on 22 April 1944. Possibly hit by USAAF B-24 return fire during intruder raid over East Anglia. Presumed crashed into the North Sea. Hptm Dietrich Puttfarken and Ofw Willi Lux both MiA.

420.402: Stkz DT+PO. To 15./KG 2 U5+HF. S/d by flak near Felixstowe, UK, on 13 January 1944.

420.406: Stkz DT+PS. To 2./KG 51 9K+DK. S/d in error by German flak near Westringen on 27 February 1944.

420.407: Stkz DT+PT. To 12./KG 51 9K+DW. Crashed near Munich on 13 June 1944.

420.408: A-1 Stkz DT+PU. To 14./KG 2 U5+FE. S/d near Hesepe on 11 January 1944.

420.410: A-1 Stkz DT+PW. To *Stab* II./ZG 26. Coded White 1. S/d near Nordhausen on 22 February 1944. Hptm Eduard Tratt (*Gruppenkommendeur*) and Ofw Gillert both killed.

420.412: Stkz DT+PY. To Fl.Ü.G 1. Sustained 65 per cent damage in landing accident at Gablingen on 22 December 1943.

420.415: Stkz CN+RB. To V./KG 2. Crashed at Vitry, France, 22 January 1944.

420.417: A-1 Stkz CN+RD. To 5./KG 51 9K+GN. FTR from sortie over England on 15 June 1944. Possibly crashed into North Sea. Uffz Heinrich Ramm and Uffz Karl Seeland both MiA.

420.418: Stkz CN+RE. To 4./ZG 26 3U+LM. S/d near Frankfurt an der Oder on 21 May 1944.

420.419: Stkz CN+RF. To 5./KG 51. Lost over Normandy on 25 June 1944.

420.420: Stkz CN+RG. To 2./KG 51. W/o near Beauvais, France, on 15 March 1944.

420.425: A-1 Stkz CN+RL. Sustained 80 per cent damage in Allied bomb raid, Lechfeld, on 18 March 1944.

420.428: A-1 Stkz CN+RO. To 4./KG 51 9K+AM. S/d by RAF night fighter prior to landing, crashed at St André sur l'Eure, France, on 6 June 1944. Ofw Hermann Bolten wounded and Fw Wilhelm Lohe killed.

420.430: A-1/U2, manufactured at Augsburg, Stkz PD+VO. 3U+AK, later 3U+CC of 2./ZG 26. Surrendered at Vaerløse, Denmark, in May 1945. To AM 72. Preserved RAFM Cosford.

420.431: Stkz CN+RR. To 5./KG 51 9K+AN. W/o in landing accident, Gilze-Rijen, the Netherlands, on 29 May 1944. Oblt H. Niebler was killed.

420.434: Stkz CN+RU. To 5./ZG 26 3U+3. S/d near Döberitz on 9 March 1944.

420.435: Stkz CN+RV. To 2./KG 51. S/d near Le Havre, France, on 21 March 1944.

420.436: Stkz CN+RW. To 12./KG 51 9K+AW. W/o near Hohenblick on 1 August 1944.

420.438: Stkz CN+RY. To 4./KG 51. W/o in forced landing in Channy on 3 August 1944.

420.439: A-1/U2 Stkz CN+RZ. Surrendered at Kastrup, Denmark, on 8 May 1945.

420.440: Stkz DW+IA. To 6./ZG 26 3U+BP. S/d near Parchim on 21 July 1944.

420.441: Stkz DW+IB. To 5./ZG 26 3U+KN S/d near Kolberg on 10 May 1944.

420.445: A-1 Stkz DW+IF. To *Stab* II./KG 51 9K+ZP. Mid-air collision with Airspeed Oxford serial LX196 of 18 (P)AFU, near Church Lawford airfield, crashed Frankton near Rugby on 27 April 1944. Lt Wolfgang Wenning and Fw Gustav Delp killed.

420.446: Stkz DW+IG. To 4./ZG 26. Coded White 5. W/o near Osterholz on 17 February 1944.

420.448: A-1 Stkz DW+II 4./KG 51. S/d by RAF night fighter over Nouilly, France, on 2 June 1944. Lt Martin Kneis wounded.

420.451: Stkz DW+IL. To 4./KG 51 U5+DE. W/o in landing accident, Eindhoven, the Netherlands, on 21 April 1944.

420.452: Stkz DW+IM. To 6./ZG 26 3U+JP. W/o near Jena on 13 July 1944.

420.455: Stkz DW+IP. To 5./ZG 26 3U+ Black 2. Destroyed in mid-air collision over Brandenburg on 14 March 1944. Also reported as lost near Anklam when serving with 6./ZG 26 on 20 June 1944 (Coded 3U+NP). Presumed s/d by 355 FG P-51 Mustangs.

420.456: Stkz DW+IQ. To 6./ZG 26 3U+HP. S/d over Crossen on 17 May 1944.

420.458: A-1, Stkz DW+IS. To 6./KG 51 9K+HP. S/d by return fire from USAAF B-24 on 22 April 1944 at Hall farm, Ashby St Mary, near Loddon, Norfolk. Oblt Klaus Kruger and Fw Michael Reichardt both killed.

420.460: Stkz DW+IU. To 5./KG 51 9K+DN. Lost over Normandy on 13 July 1944.

420.461: A-1 Stkz DW+IV. Converted as A-1/U4. Captured at Posen (present-day Poznan), April 1945.

420.463: Stkz DW+IX. To 14./KG 2 U5+CE. S/d by Sqn Ldr Caldwell and Fg Off. Rawling, RAF 96 Sqn, at 12.30 a.m. on 23 February 1944. The aircraft came down at Bentley Farm, Framefield near Uckfield, Sussex, UK. Uffz Reinhard Eggers and Ogfr Stefan Bednorz were both killed.

420.464: A-1 Stkz DW+IY. To 16./KG 2 U5+CG. S/d near Fürstenau on 11 January 1944. Also reported as s/d near Felixstowe by British flak on 13 January 1944. A Me 410 with this W Nr of 4./ZG 26, coded 3U+AM, was reported as being written off near Stettin on 28 June 1944.

420.465: Stkz DW+IZ. To 6./ZG 26 3U+EP. S/d near Reppen on 13 May 1944.

420.466: Stkz DW+KA. To 6./ZG 26 3U+GP. W/o near Königsberg on 19 April 1944.

420.469: Stkz DW+KD. To 4./ZG 26 coded White 3. S/d near Hannover on 10 February 1944. Also reported as s/d near Nienburg on 14 February and over Schwarmstedt on 17 February. Presumably, these all refer to the loss of the same aircraft.

420.470: Stkz DW+KE. To 2./ZG 26. Coded 15. W/o near Fassberg on 8 April 1944.

420.473: Stkz DW+KH. To 4./ZG 26. Coded Black 1 + -. S/d on 20 February 1944.

420.474: Stkz DW+KI. To 4./ZG 26. W/o near Hildburgshausen on 18 May 1944.

420.475: Stkz DW+KJ. To 6./ZG 26 3U+BP. S/d near Frankfurt on 18 May 1944. Presumed repaired, as reportedly s/d near Garz on 25 June 1944.

420.476: Stkz DW+KK. To 4./ZG 26 3U+BM. S/d near Parchim on 21 July 1944.

420.477: Stkz DW+KL. To 4./ZG 26. Coded White 1. Damaged in forced landing near Schwarmstädt on 17 February 1944.

420.478: Stkz DW+KM. To 5./ZG 26 3U+LP. Sustained 80 per cent damage in forced landing near Gotha on 19 May 1944.

420.481: Stkz DW+KP. To 6./ZG 26 3U+LP. S/d near Zielenzig on 18 May 1944.

420.483: B-2 Stkz DW+KR. Surrendered at Lister, Norway, on 10 May 1945. Scrapped.

420.484: A-1 Stkz DW+KS. To Fl.Ü.G 1. Sustained 15 per cent damage in taxiing accident at Oberpfaffenhofen on 5 April 1944.

420.488: Stkz DW+KW. To 5./ZG 26 3U+KN. W/o at Königsberg on 18 July 1944.

420.489: Stkz DW+KX. To 4./ZG 26 3U+NM. S/d near Pyritz on 16 April 1944.

420.490: Stkz DW+KY. To 4./ZG 26 3U+. S/d on 2 June 1944. Also reported as having sustained 20 per cent damage in landing accident at Greifswald on 25 June 1944, when serving with *Stab* II./ZG 26 and coded 3U+C.

420.491: Stkz DW+KZ. To 6./ZG 26. Damaged when overturned on landing at Oberpfaffenhofen on 8 March 1944.

420.492: A-1 Stkz KR+UA. To 1./(F)122. W/o near Werneuchen on 25 February 1944.

420.493: Stkz KR+UB. To 6./ZG 26 3U+EC. W/o near Senneberg on 18 May 1944.

420.496: A-1/U2 KR+UE. Del. Jan. 1944. 11./ZG 26 3U+JV Surrendered at Oslo-Gardermoen, Norway, on 10 May 45. Scrapped.

420.497: Stkz KR+UF. To 5./ZG 26. W/o near Königsberg, 14 April 1944.

420.501: Stkz KR+UJ. To 11./ZG 26. Surrendered at Ørland, Norway, 10 May 1945. Scrapped.

420.502: Stkz KR+UK. To 5./ZG 26 3U+AN. S/d near Kolberg, 11 June 1944.

420.503: Stkz KR+UL. To 6./ZG 26 3U+KP. W/o near Frankfurt an der Oder, 24 May 1944.

420.505: Stkz KR+UN. To 5./ZG 26 3U+8. Sustained 50 per cent damage in forced landing near Bernburg on 12 March 1944.

420.506: Stkz KR+UO. To *Seenotgruppe* 80. W/o at Jever on 3 November 1944.

420.509: Stkz BR+JL. To *Stab* II./ZG 26 3U+MM. S/d near Neubrandenberg on 26 June 1944.

420.622: A-1 Stkz BR+JM. To 4./ZG 76 3U+KM. Converted as A-1/U4 S/d on 11 April 1944 by Swedish anti aircraft artillery at Sövde. Fw Josef Kaularz and Fw Max Werner Schulz were both killed as well as the Swedish soldier Nils Holmberg, who was hit by falling wreckage (N.B.: noted in Swedish records as a Me 410B-1/U4).

420.625: Stkz BR+JP. To 5./ZG 26 3U+BC. Damaged in forced landing near Bad Schönfliess on 11 April 1944. Repaired. To 6./ZG 26 3U+AP. S/d near Jena on 13 July 1944.

420.626: Stkz BR+JQ. To 5./ZG 26 3U+BC. Damaged in crash near Bad Schönfliess on 23 March 1944.

420.627: Stkz BR+JR. To 4./ZG 26 3U+PM. Damaged in forced landing near Königsberg on 25 June 1944.

420.630: A-1 Stkz BR+JU. Converted as A-1/U4. To 6./ZG 26. W/o near Stettin on 13 March 1944.

420.631: Stkz BR+JV. To 5./ZG 26. S/d near Schönbeck on 26 June 1944.

420.633: A-1/U2. To *Stab* /ZG 76 M8+ <2. S/d near Dachau, 13 June 1944.

420.635: A-1 Stkz BF+IH 3.(F)/22 BF+IH. Surrendered at Stavanger-Sola, Norway, on 10 May 1945. Scrapped.

420.637: Stkz BF+IJ. To *Seenotgruppe* 81. Still in service at Parow on 25 April 1945.

420.638: Stkz BF+IK. To 3./ZG 26 3U+GL. Crashed into Schweriner See on 25 July 1944.

420.653: Stkz NE+QU. To Kom.Gen.d.Dt.LW. Sustained 15 per cent damage (undercarriage) at Munich on 8 February 1945.

420.654: A-1 Stkz NE+QV. To 4./KG 51 9K+HM FTR from sortie over England on 7 June 1944. Possibly crashed into North Sea. Hptm Werner Dörr and Fw Walter Heinemann MiA.

420.656: A-1/U2 Stkz NE+QX. To 4./KG 51 9K+DM. Damaged in forced landing at Corneilles, France, on 7 July 1944.

420.660: Stkz NN+GB. To 5./(F) 122. S/d in error by Luftwaffe fighters over Greifenhagen on 21 March 1945.

420.665: Stkz NN+GG. To 4./KG 51 9K+. Lost over Normandy, 8 July 1944.

420.668: Stkz NN+GJ. To 6./ZG 76 M8+ Yellow 10. Lost in Vienna/Pressburg (present-day Kosice, Slovakia) area on 16 June 1944.

420.669: Stkz NN+GK. To 5./ZG 76 M8+ Black 15. W/o near Raab on 16 June 1944.

420.671: Stkz NN+GM. To 4./KG 51 9K+FM. Lost over Normandy on 15 July 1944.

420.677: Stkz NN+GS. To 3./ZG 76 M8+ Yellow 9. W/o near Hainburg on 30 June 1944.

420.678: Stkz BT+TA. To 4./ZG 76 M8+ White 3. Lost near Pressburg (present-day Bratislava, Slovakia) on 5 July 1944.

420.680: A-1/U2 Stkz BT+TC. To 1./ZG 76 M8+ White 3. W/o near Hohenau-Hausbrunn on 7 July 1944.

Messerschmitt, Augsburg Ninth Me 410 Production Batch

Forty-nine Me 410B-2s were delivered in May–June 1944. There was one W Nr batch: 470092 to 470140 (forty-nine).

470.092: Stkz BT+TG 4./ZG 76 M8+ White 11. Lost near Bernburg on 20 June 1944.

470.093: Stkz BT+TH 4./ZG 76 M8+ White 13. Lost near Bernburg on 20 June 1944.

470.094: B-2 Stkz BT+TI 1./ZG 76 M8+ White 12. Damaged in crash at Kralowe on 26 June 1944. Also reported to have crashed near Vienna on 5 July 1944 while serving with 4./ZG 76.

470.099: Stkz GK+KD 6./ZG 76 M8+ >4. W/o near Osmersleben on 20 June 1944.

470.100: Stkz GK+KE 5./ZG 76 M8+ Black 14. W/o near Pressburg (present-day Bratislava, Slovakia), on 5 July 1944.

470.101: Stkz GK+KF 5./ZG 76 M8+ Black 12. W/o near Luckau on 27 June 1944.

470.102: B-2/U2 Stkz GK+KG 5./ZG 76. Lost near Tanabanya on 27 June 1944.

470.103: Stkz GK+KH 5./ZG 76 M8+ Black 11. W/o near Raab on 16 June 1944.

470.104: Stkz GK+KI 2./Fl.ÜG 1, transferred to 4./ZG 76 M8+ White 4.

470.106: 4./ZG 76 M8+ White 15. W/o near Raab on 16 June 1944.

470.108: B-2/U2 Stkz CR+QP 2./ZG 76 M8+ Black 8. W/o near Krems on 8 July 1944.

470.111: Stkz CR+QS 5./ZG 76 M8+ Black 16. W/o near Luckau on 21 June 1944.

470.112: Stkz CR+QT 6./ZG 76 M8+ Yellow 15. W/o near Niederlausitz on 21 June 1944.

470.114: Stkz CR+QV 4./ZG 76 M8+ Black 18. W/o near Hasprunka on 5 July 1944.

470.116: Stkz CR+QX 4./ZG 76 M8+ White 17. W/o near Lukacz on 16 June 1944.

470.123: B-2/U2 Stkz CR+OJ 1./ZG 76 M8+ White 1. W/o near Hollabrunn on 5 July 1944.

470.124: B-2/U2 Stkz CR+OK 3./ZG 76 M8+ Yellow 8. W/o on 8 July 1944. Also see W Nr 10124.

470.125: B-2 Later modified to B-2/U2 Stkz CR+OL 2./ZG 76, 20 per cent damaged near Falnhaly, Hungary, on 22 August 1944.

470.126: B-2/U2 Stkz CR+OM 3./ZG 76 M8+ Yellow 8 (also reported as White 2). W/o near Breclav (present-day Czech Republic), on 26 June 1944. Fw. Helmut Genicke and Uffz Karl-Heinz Schuldt killed.

470.127: B-2/U2 Stkz CR+ON 1./ZG 76 M8+ White 6. Lost near Pressburg (present-day Kosice, Slovakia), on 7 July 1944.

470.130: B-2/U2 Stkz CR+OQ 1./ZG 76 M8+ White 9. W/o near Kuty on 5 July 1944.

470.131: B-2/U2 Stkz CR+OR 1./ZG 76 M8+ White 7. W/o near Grosschützen on 5 July 1944.

470.135: Stkz TG+MJ 5./KG 51 9K+EN. Lost near Rosiéres on 1 August 1944.

470.136: B-2 4./KG 51 9K+GM. FTR from sortie over England on 25 July 1944. Possibly crashed into the North Sea. Uffz Walter Brügel and Uffz Rudolf Sperlich MiA.

470.137: Stkz TG+ML 4./ZG 76 M8+ White 17. S/d near Lukacz on 14 June 1944.

470.138: B-2/U2 Stkz TG+MM *Stab*/ZG 76 M8+>3. W/o near Banhida on 27 June 1944.

470.139: Stkz TG+MN 5./KG 51 9K+LN. W/o near Bruch Bargny on 1 August 1944.

Dornier, München Tenth Me 410 production batch

Some 111 Me 410B-2s were delivered in May and June 1944. There were three W Nr batches: 710310 to 710383 (seventy-four); 710399 to 710406 (seven); and 710444 to 710473 (thirty). However, aircraft identified by W Nr outside of the batches above certainly did exist, as noted below.

710.023: 6./ZG 26. Lost near Pasewalk on 28 June 1944.

710.313: B-2/U4 5./ZG 26 3U+TN. Sustained 65 per cent damage at Gostingen in July 1944 due to engine trouble.

710.319: B-2/U4 4./ZG 26 3U+QM. W/o near Neubrandenburg on 26 June 1944.

710.321: B-2/U4 11./ZG 26. Surrendered at Ørland, Norway, 10 May 1945. BK 5 cannon possibly not fitted. Scrapped.

710.330: B-2/U4 6./ZG 26 3U+HP. W/o near Frankenhausen on 13 July 1944.

710.331: B-2/U4 6./ZG 26 3U+UP. S/d near island of Rügen on 20 June 1944. Crew killed. Presumed s/d by 355 FG P-51 Mustangs.

710.334: B-2/U4 5./ZG 26 3U+MN. W/o near Jena on 13 July 1944.

710.335: B-2/U4 4./ZG 26. W/o near Neubrandenberg on 28 June 1944.

710.337: B-2/U4 4./ZG 26 3U+LM. Lost or damaged over Neubrandenberg on 28 June 1944.

710.339: B-2/U4 4./ZG 26 3U+NM. Lost over Baltic Sea, 20 June 1944. Presumed s/d by 355 FG P-51 Mustangs.

710.340: B-2/U4 11./ZG 26 3U+MV Modified with external fuel tanks. Reportedly surrendered at Ørland, Norway, 10 May 1945.

710.341: B-2/U4 5./ZG 26, 70 per cent damaged in take-off accident at Königsberg on 1 June 1944. Possibly repaired.

710.342: B-2/U4 6./ZG 26. Lost over Baltic Sea on 28 June 1944. Cause unknown.

710.354: B-2/U4 6./ZG 26, 30 per cent damaged in forced landing near Dessau in June 1944.

710.457: B-2/U4 4./ZG 26 3U+UM. W/o near Prenzlau on 25 June 1944.

710.458: B-2/U4 6./ZG 26 3U+BP. Lost near Pasewalk on 20 June 1944. Crew baled out, wounded. Presumed s/d by 355 FG P-51 Mustangs.

710.361: B-2/U4 11./ZG 26. Surrendered at Ørland, Norway, 10 May 1945. BK 5 cannon possibly not fitted. Scrapped.

710.362: B-2/U4 4./ZG 26. 70 per cent damaged during combat sortie over Neubrandenburg.

710.364: B-2/U4 5./ZG 26 3U+YP. W/o near island of Rügen on 25 June 1944.

710.369: B-2/U4 Fl.Sd.Kdo. Ob.d.L. BP+BK. W/o near Pullach on 2 June 1944.

710.371: B-2/U4 6./ZG 26 3U+SP. W/o near Königsberg on 25 June 1944.

710.374: 4./KG 51 9K+AM. Lost over Normandy on 5 August 1944.

710.388: B-2 5./ZG 76 M8+4. Crashed near village of Zábori (in present-day Czech Republic) on 4 July 1944, possibly due to a technical malfunction. The pilot, Lt Adolf Briedl was killed, with Uffz Herbert Dahnken baling out safely.

710.399: 5./ZG 76 M8+ Black 4. Lost near Melnick.

710.445: Stkz BW+HD 2./FüG 1 by 2 July 1944.

710.457: Stkz BW+HP. Found at Neubiberg, May 1945.

710.458: Stkz BW+HQ. Found by US forces at stretch of *Autobahn* near Munich, May 1945.

710.488: 5./ZG 26. W/o near Königsberg, 24 July 1944.

Hungarian Me 210 Production List

A total of 159 DAF-built Me 210s—(serials Z001 to Z159) including five prototypes, three tactical reconnaissance aircraft, three long-range reconnaissance aircraft (serials Z006 to Z011), sixteen night fighters, six conversion trainers, and 127 heavy fighters/bombers—were officially taken on charge by the MKHL. One additional aircraft, serial Z160, was completed. This aircraft went into storage, later being collected and handed over to the 102. FBG. It was lost on operations on 23 December 1944.

However, the list below only contains 144 aircraft, with gaps between Z126–130 (five), Z132–134 (three), Z136, Z138–139 (two), and 141–145 (five). Incidentally, some renumbering appears to have taken place, such as serial Z104 becoming Z118. The reason behind this is unclear.

Lack of contemporary official documentation—such as delivery schedules, MKHL acceptance information, unit assignments, and loss lists—makes it very difficult to compile a production list. Nevertheless, through the efforts of Hungarian aviation historian Csaba B. Stenge, the production list presented below includes some previously unpublished information. The *Werk Nummern* can be broken down to give further information—using 210.007.003 as an example, this can be broken down as 210 (type of aircraft), 007 (seventh aircraft built) and 003 (the third aircraft delivered to the MKHL). The second series of numerals is problematical, and possibly includes aircraft delivered to the Luftwaffe.

210.002.001: Z001. Delivered to MKHL in July 1943.

210.004.002: Z002. Delivered to MKHL in July 1943.

210.007.003: Z003. Used for weapons tests, including WGr. 21 mortar (March and July 1944) and 40-mm Bofors cannon (October 1944). Fitted with ventral gondola for reconnaissance tests.

210.008.004: Z004. Delivered to MKHL in 1943. Intentionally destroyed at Lesvár on 28 March 1945.

210.012.005: Z005. Used for night fighter tests.

210.013.006: Z006. Delivered to MKHL in July 1943.
210.014.007: Z007. Delivered to MKHL in July 1943.
210.020.008: Z008. Delivered to MKHL in September 1943.
210.021.009: Z009. Delivered to MKHL in September 1943.
210.022.010: Z010. Delivered to MKHL in September 1943.
210.023.011: Z011. Delivered to MKHL in September 1943.
210.024.012: Z012. Delivered to MKHL. To 5/1 NFS.
210.033.013: Z013. Delivered to MKHL. To 5/1 NFS.
210.034.014: Z014. Delivered to MKHL. To 5/1 NFS.
210.035.015: Z015. Delivered to MKHL in October 1943.
210.036.016: Z016. Delivered to MKHL in September 1943.
210.037.017: Z017. Delivered to MKHL in September 1943.
210.038.018: Z018. Delivered to MKHL. To 5/1 NFS.
210.039.019: Z019. Delivered to MKHL.
210.040.020: Z020. Delivered to MKHL. To 5/1 NFS.

210.051.021: Z021. Delivered to MKHL in November 1943. Intentionally destroyed at Lesvár on 28 March 1945 (Possible misidentification with serial Z027).

210.052.022: Z022. Delivered to MKHL in November 1943.
210.053.023: Z023. Delivered to MKHL in November 1943.
210.054.024: Z024. Delivered to MKHL in November 1943.
210.055.025: Z025. Delivered to MKHL in November 1943.
210.056.026: Z026. Delivered to MKHL on 8 October 1944.

210.057.027: Z027. Delivered to MKHL in December 1943. Intentionally destroyed at Lesvár on 28 March 1945. Possible misidentification with serial Z021.

210.058.028: Z028. Delivered to MKHL in December 1943.
210.059.029: Z029. Delivered to MKHL in December 1943.
210.060.030: Z030. Delivered to MKHL in December 1943.
210.073.031: Z031. Delivered to MKHL on 23 December 1943. To 5/1 NFS.
210.074.032: Z032. Delivered to MKHL on 12 January 1944. To 5/1 NFS.
210.075.033: Z033. Delivered to MKHL on 20 January 1944.
210.076.034: Z034. Delivered to MKHL on 31 January 1944.
210.077.035: Z035. Delivered to MKHL on 20 January 1944. To 5/1 NFS.
210.078.036: Z036, Delivered to MKHL on 8 February 1944.
210.079.037: Z037. Delivered to MKHL on 31 January 1944.

210.080.038: Z038. Delivered to MKHL on 31 January 1944. W/o at Szekesfehervar on 12 April 1944.

210.081.039: Z039. Delivered to MKHL on 23 February 1944.
210.082.040: Z040. Delivered to MKHL on 28 February 1944.
210.083.041: Z041. Delivered to MKHL on 20 January 1944.
210.084.042: Z042. Delivered to MKHL on 18 February 1944.
210.087.043: Z043. Delivered to MKHL on 20 January 1944. To 5/1 NFS.
210.088.044: Z044. Delivered to MKHL on 8 February 1944.

210.091.045: Z045. Delivered to MKHL on 3 April 1944. To ABK-Z in April 1944. To 5/1 NFS. At Zeltweg, Austria, on 3 January 1945.

210.092.046: Z046. Delivered to MKHL in February 1944.
210.095.047: Z047. Delivered to MKHL on 23 February 1944.
210.096.048: Z048. Delivered to MKHL on 8 February 1944.
210.099.049: Z049. Delivered to MKHL on 30 December 1944.
210.100.050: Z050. Delivered to MKHL on 20 December 1944.
210.103.051: Z051. Delivered to MKHL on 31 January 1944.
210.104.052: Z052. Delivered to MKHL on 28 February 1944.
210.107.053: Z053. Delivered to MKHL on 29 February 1944.
210.108.054: Z054. Delivered to MKHL on 28 February 1944. To 5/1 NFS.
210.111.055: Z055. Delivered to MKHL in February 1944. To 5/1 NFS.
210.112.056: Z056. Delivered to MKHL on 4 August 1944.
210.115.057: Z057. Delivered to MKHL on 14 March 1944. To 5/1 NFS.
210.116.058: Z058. Delivered to MKHL on 28 February 1944. To 5/1 NFS.
210.119.059: Z059. Delivered to MKHL in February 1944.
210.120.060: Z060. Delivered to MKHL in February 1944.
210.123.061: Z061. Delivered to MKHL in February 1944. To 5/1 NFS.
210.124.062: Z062. Delivered to MKHL in February 1944. To 5/1 NFS.
210.127.063: Z063. Delivered to MKHL in February 1944.
210.128.064: Z064. Delivered to MKHL in February 1944.
210.131.065: Z065. Delivered to MKHL in 10 May 1944.
210.132.066: Z066. Delivered to MKHL. Damaged in belly landing at Budapest-Ferihegy, March 1944. Repaired, and returned to service by June 1944.
210.135.067: Z067. Delivered to MKHL on 9 March 1944. To 5/1 NFS.
210.136.068: Z068. Delivered to MKHL in March 1944.
210.139.069: Z069. Delivered to MKHL in March 1944.
210.140.070: Z070. Delivered to MKHL on 10 March 1944.
210.143.071: Z071. Delivered to MKHL in March 1944.
210.144.072: Z072. Delivered to MKHL in March 1944.
210.147.073: Z073. Delivered to MKHL in March 1944.
210.148.074: Z074. Delivered to MKHL in March 1944.
210.151.075: Z075. Delivered to MKHL in March 1944.
210.152.076: Z076. Delivered to MKHL on 10 May 1944.
210.155.077: Z077. Delivered to MKHL on 10 May 1944.
210.156.078: Z078. Delivered to MKHL in May 1944. W/o in June 1944.
210.159.079: Z079. Delivered to MKHL. Sustained slight damage in landing accident at Budapest-Ferihegy on 22 April 1944. Port undercarriage failed to lock in down position. The pilot, Gyula Szilaj Varga, was uninjured.
210.160.080: Z080. Delivered to MKHL on 10 May 1944.
210.163.081: Z081. Delivered to MKHL in May 1944.
210.164.082: Z082. Delivered to MKHL in May 1944.
210.167.083: Z083. Delivered to MKHL in May 1944.
210.168.084: Z084. Delivered to MKHL in May 1944.
210.171.085: Z085. Delivered to MKHL in May 1944.
210.172.086: Z086. Delivered to MKHL on 10 May 1944.

210.175.087: Z087. Delivered to MKHL on 10 May 1944.

210.176.088: Z088. Delivered to MKHL on 10 May 1944. Most likely a Me 210Da-1 variant. Flown to Italy on 8 June 1944. Landed near Fermo behind German lines. Presumed partly disassembled by the Germans, and subsequently captured by the Allies.

210.179.089: Z089. Delivered to MKHL on 10 May 1944.

210.180.090: Z090. Delivered to MKHL in May 1944.

210.183.091: Z091. Delivered to MKHL on 11 July 1944.

210.185.092: Z092. Delivered to MKHL on 4 August 1944.

210.187.093: Z093. Delivered to MKHL in May 1944.

210.188.094: Z094. Delivered to MKHL on 10 May 1944. To 102/2 FBS. Sustained 15 per cent damage in forced landing at Lesvár, 28 February 1945.

210.191.095: Z095. Delivered to MKHL on 10 May 1944. Destroyed in USAAF air raid, 8 October 1944.

210.192.096: Z096. Delivered to MKHL in May 1944.

210.195.097: Z097. Delivered to MKHL in May 1944.

210.196.098: Z098. Delivered to MKHL on 10 May 1944. Destroyed in USAAF air raid, 8 October 1944.

210.199.099: Z099. Delivered to MKHL on 10 May 1944. Destroyed in USAAF air raid, 21 August 1944.

210.200.100: Z100. Delivered to MKHL on 10 May 1944. Destroyed in USAAF air raid, 8 October 1944.

210.203.101: Z101. Delivered to MKHL on 11 July 1944.

210.204.102: Z102. Delivered to MKHL in July 1944.

210.207.103: Z103. Delivered to MKHL on 11 July 1944.

210.208.104: Z104. Delivered to MKHL on 11 July 1944. Renumbered as serial Z118. Intentionally destroyed at Lesvár on 28 March 1945.

210.211.105: Z105. Delivered to MKHL on 25 July 1944.

210.212.106: Z106. Delivered to MKHL on 11 July 1944

210.215.107: Z107. Delivered to MKHL on 5 June 1944. Issued to 102/2 FBS. Shot down by Soviet flak and crashed into vineyard W Kescemét on 30 October 1944. *Szakasvezetö* József Kovács and *Tizedes* Mihály Villám killed.

210.216.108: Z108. Delivered to MKHL in June 1944.

210.219.109: Z109. Delivered to MKHL in June 1944.

210.220.110: Z110. Delivered to MKHL on 5 June 1944.

210.223.111: Z111. Delivered to MKHL on 5 June 1944. Destroyed in USAAF air raid, 8 October 1944.

210.224.112: Z112. Delivered to MKHL on 30 June 1944.

210.227.113: Z113. Delivered to MKHL on 27 June 1944.

210.228.114: Z114. Delivered to MKHL on 30 June 1944.

210.231.115: Z115. Delivered to MKHL in July 1944.

210.232.116: Z116. Delivered to MKHL on 15 August 1944 Issued to 102/2 FBS S/d by Yak fighter and flak, crashed into house at Jászalsószentgyörgy on 13 November 1944. *Föhadnagy* Gusztáv Halmay and *Szakasvezetö* Károly Kaszás killed.

210.235.117: Z117. Delivered to MKHL on 30 June 1944.

210.236.118: Z118. Delivered to MKHL on 25 July 1944. Renumbered from Z.104.

210.239.119: Z119. Delivered to MKHL on 11 July 1944.

210.240.120: Z120. Delivered to MKHL on 11 July 1944. Destroyed in USAAF air raid, 21 August 1944.

210.243.121: Z121. Delivered to MKHL on 11 July 1944.

210.244.122: Z122. Delivered to MKHL on 11 July 1944.

210.247.123: Z123. Delivered to MKHL on 25 July 1944.

210.248.124: Z124. Delivered to MKHL on 15 August 1944.

210.251.125: Z125. Delivered to MKHL on 16 September 1944.

210.185.131: Z131. Delivered to MKHL on 4 August 1944.

210.229.135: Z135. Delivered to MKHL, 4 August 1944.

210.233.137: Z137. Delivered to MKHL on 4 August 1944. Destroyed in USAAF air raid, 21 August 1944.

210.238.140: Z140. Delivered to MKHL Belly landed at Budapest-Ferihegy on 23 October 1944 following combat sortie. *Hadnagy* Edgár Zuna and *Tizedes* András Polyák safe.

210.250.146: Z146. Delivered to MKHLon 16 September 1944.

210.157.147: Z147. Delivered to MKHL in September 1944.

210.157.148: Z148. Delivered to MKHL in September 1944.

210.157.149: Z149. Delivered to MKHL in September 1944.

210.258.150: Z150. Delivered to MKHL in September 1944.

210.261.151: Z151. Delivered to MKHL in September 1944.

210.262.152: Z152. Delivered to MKHL in September 1944.

210.263.153: Z153. Delivered to MKHL on 16 September 1944.

210.264.154: Z154. Delivered to MKHL on 16 September 1944.

210.265.155: Z155. Delivered to MKHL on 16 September 1944.

210.266.156: Z156. Delivered to MKHL on 16 September 1944.

210.267.157: Z157. Delivered to MKHL in September 1944.

210.268.158: Z158. Delivered to MKHL in September 1944.

210.269.159: Z159. Delivered to MKHL on 16 September 1944.

(210.270.160): Z160. Completed, but not formally accepted by the MKHL. Collected in December 1944, with equipment fitted by 102. FBG mechanics. Shot down by flak on 23 December. *Föhadnagy* Adolf Péterdi became a prisoner of war, with Örmester Károly Mészáras being wounded.

Hungarian-built Me 210s Delivered to the Luftwaffe

Although exact statistics are lacking, details for the first three months of 1944 show that seventy-one DAF-built aircraft had been delivered to the Luftwaffe by 31 March 1944. This was broken down as thirty-two Me 210s delivered until 31 December 1943, five in January 1944, twelve in February 1944, and twenty-two in March 1944. However, this was well below the anticipated quantity of 107 to have been delivered by 31 March 1944. The list below includes a total of 128 aircraft, divided among two W Nr batches; 210.316.001 to 210.316.026 (twenty-six) and 210.150.011 to 210.150.112 (102). Some of these Me 210s were sold to Hungary in early 1945, but it is unclear if any of them actually entered service with the MKHL.

210.316.001: Stkz RF+PA. First flight on 21 December 1942. Delivered to Luftwaffe in April 1943. To II./ZG 26 2N+ZR. W/o near Delmenhorst on 29 November 1943.

210.316.003: Stkz RF+PC. Delivered in April 1943. To I./ZG 1. S/d near Geldrup on 5 November 1943.

210.316.004: Stkz RF+PD. To Fl.Ü.G 1. Sustained 80 per cent damage in take-off accident at Hildesheim on 12 August 1944.

210.316.009: Stkz RF+PI. Delivered on 17 September 1943. Rebuilt by Blohm & Voss as dual control conversion trainer. To 3./KG 51 on 1 July 1944.

210.316.015 Stkz RF+PO. Delivered on 4 October 1943. To ZG 101. W/o on 7 March 1944.

210.316.019: Stkz RF+PS. Delivery date unknown. To *Stab* JG 300. Sustained 40 per cent damage in forced landing at Paris-Le Bourget on 12 October 1943.

210.316.022: Stkz RF+PV. Delivered on 3 November 1943. Sold to MKHL in March 1945.

210.316.024: Stkz RF+PX. Delivered on 28 October 1943. To 1 Fl.ÜG. Cr S of Radosice-Pilsen (in present-day Czech Republic) on 27 January 1944, possibly due to a technical malfunction. The crew, Uffz Wilhelm Graf and Gefr. Gerhard Palke were both killed. The aircraft was most likely on its way to a Luftwaffe unit, possibly KG 51. Fitted with BK 5 cannon. Wreck site excavated in 2009.

210.150.011: Stkz PD+VA. Delivered on 26 January 1944. To 10./KG 51 9K+CU. W/o near Ainring on 8 May 1944.

210.150.014: Stkz PD+VD. Delivered on 3 November 1943. Sustained 30 per cent damage in landing accident on 2 April 1944.

210.150.015: Stkz PD+VE. Delivered on 11 December 1943. To 2./*Ergänzung Zerstörergruppe*. W/o near Cremlingen on 7 March 1944.

210.150.017: Stkz PD+VG. Used for undetermined tests by 23 November 1943.

210.150.018: Stkz PD+VH. Delivered on 1 December 1943. To NJG 1. Destroyed in Allied bomb raid on 21 July 1944.

210.150.023: Stkz PD+VM. Delivered on 13 January 1944. To *Ergänzungstaffel* ZG 76. Still in service on 1 June 1944.

210.150.024: Stkz PD+VN. To Fl.Û.G 1 W/o near Pilsen on 27 January 1944.

210.150.025: Stkz PD+VO. To 3./KG 51. Noted at Lechfeld on 28 June 1944.

210.150.027: Stkz PD+VQ. Delivered on 7 February 1944.

210.150.028: Stkz PD+VR. Delivered on 31 January 1944. To 11./KG 51. W/o at Augsburg on 30 May 1944.

210.150.029: Stkz PD+VS. Delivered on 7 February 1944. To I./ZG 101. Sustained 90 per cent damage on 6 July 1944.

210.150.030: Stkz PD+VT. Delivered on 7 February 1944. To 13./KG 51 9K+HX. W/o on 9 April 1944.

210.150.036: Stkz PD+VZ. Delivered on 31 January 1944. To 11./KG 51 9K+AW. W/o at Munich on 17 September 1944.

210.150.037: Stkz PH+JA. Delivered on 22 February 1944. To Fl.ÜG 1. Sustained 25 per cent damage at Vienna-Aspern on 14 March 1944.

210.150.046: Stkz PH+JJ. To I./ZG 101. Sustained 10 per cent damage at Memmingen in Allied bomb raid on 21 July 1944.

210.150.047: Stkz PH+JK. Delivered on 14 February 1944. To (Z)/*Erprobungskommando* 25. Still in service on 18 May 1944.

210.150.048: Stkz PH+JL. Delivered on 28 February 1944. To I./ZG 101. Sustained 10 per cent damage at Memmingen in Allied bomb raid on 21 July 1944.

210.150.052: Stkz PH+JP. Delivered on 15 March 1944. To NJG 101. Sustained 80 per cent damage at Memmingen in Allied bomb raid on 21 July 1944.

210.150.054: Stkz PH+JR. Delivered on 15 March 1944. To ZG 101. Sustained 40 per cent damage at Memmingen in Allied bomb raid on 21 July 1944.

210.150.055: Stkz CJ+QA. To Flugzeugführerschule (FFS) B 4. Sustained 80 per cent damage near Sprottau on 3 July 1944.

210.150.056: Stkz CJ+QB. To FFS B 38. W/o near Schippenbeil on 19 June 1944.

210.150.061: Stkz CJ+QG. Delivered on 6 April 1944. Sold to Hungary in March 1945.

210.150.062: Stkz CJ+QH. To I./ZG 101 Sustained 10 per cent damage in landing accident at Memmingen on 15 June 1944. Repaired. Sold to Hungary in March 1945.

210.150.065: Stkz CJ+QK. To I./ZG 101. Sustained 10 per cent damage in landing accident at Starnberg on 30 June 1944.

210.150.066: Stkz CJ+QL. Delivered on 5 May 1944. To ZG 101. Sustained 15 per cent damage in taxiing accident on 24 May 1944.

210.150.079: Stkz CJ+QY. Delivered in June 1944. To I./ZG 101. Destroyed at Memmingen in Allied bomb raid on 21 July 1944.

210.150.081: Stkz DR+OA To I./ZG 101. Sustained 40 per cent damage at Memmingen in Allied bomb raid on 21 July 1944.

210.150.082: Stkz DR+OB To I./ZG 101 Sustained 20 per cent damage at Memmingen in Allied bomb raid on 21 July 1944. Returned to factory for repairs, but sustained further damage in another bomb raid on 14 August 1944.

210.150.085: Stkz DR+OE. To I./ZG 101. Sustained 60 per cent damage in forced landing at Memmingen on 29 June 1944.

210.150.094: Stkz DR+ON. To I./ZG 101. Sustained 10 per cent damage in landing accident at Memmingen on 22 June 1944.

210.150.097: Stkz DR+OQ. To FFS B 4. Sustained 15 per cent damage at Sprottau on 7 July 1944. Repaired. Sold to Hungary in March 1945.

Endnotes

Introduction

1. Following the reorganisation of the Messerschmitt AG in mid-1938, the Bf designation prefix was amended to Me.

Chapter 2

1. A born pilot, Ernst Udet scored sixty-two air-to-air victories during the Great War, second only among German aces to Manfred von Richthofen. Post-war, Udet embarked on a career as a stunt pilot, including a stint in Hollywood. He also lent his name to the aircraft manufacturer Udet Flugzeugbau GmbH. The company's most famous aircraft was the U 12 Flamingo two-seat training biplane. A very capable pilot, Udet was also a hellraiser, enjoying the high life of women, alcohol and drugs. Following the Nazi rise to power, Udet initially resisted joining the Nazi party. Due to the pressures of his command, Udet committed suicide on 17 November 1941.

Chapter 4

1. The best-known design of the *Aktien Gesellschaft Otto Flugzeugwerke* GmbH (AGO) was the light twin-engined Ago Ao 192. Only nine Ao 192s were built, with some being used by high-ranking officials and Waffen-SS officers. However, AGO produced numerous Fw 190s and other combat aircraft under licence during the war.

Chapter 5

1. Kosin, R.., *The German Fighter since 1915* (London: Conway Maritime Press Ltd, 1988), p. 127.
2. Previously published sources has stated that these Ar 240s were attached to 13./JG 5, operating out of Petsamo in northern Finland. This is without foundation.
3. Brown, E., *Testing for Combat* (Shrewsbury: Airlife Publishing Ltd, 1994), p. 4f.

Chapter 6

1. During his career as a test pilot, Fritz Wendel only had to bale out twice during test flights. The first occasion being the Me 210s test flight. Wendel later stated that the Me 210 was almost as bad as the Heinkel He 177 heavy bomber.
2. Kosin, R.., *The German Fighter since 1915*, p. 130. Also see Smith, J. R.., *Messerschmitt: An Aircraft Album* (Shepperton: Ian Allan, 1971), p. 95f.

Chapter 7

1. Schmoll, P., *Nest of Eagles* (Herhsam: Ian Allan Publishing, 2004), p. 39.
2. *Jet & Prop* magazine, June/August 2012 issue, p. 22. The Me 210S was a ground attack variant based on the Me 210A-1 featuring increased armour protection and reduced fuel capacity. Although the Me 210S remained a project, the armour protection for the crew, engines and radiators became standard for the Me 410.
3. Schmoll, P., *Nest of Eagles*, p. 42f.
4. *Ibid.*

Chapter 8

1. *Flypast*, April 2017, p. 75.

Chapter 9

1. This agreement resulted in a number of German aircraft, including two Bf 109s, a Fi 156 Storch, an Fw 190A, and two Ju 87As, finding their way to Japan for evaluation. Details of the Messerschmitt Me 163 rocket fighter, as well as the Messerschmitt Me 262 jet fighter also found their way to Japan, with the Mitsubishi J8M1 Shusui (virtually a copy of the Me 163) and the Nakajima Kikka (a Me 262 look-alike) being built. Although prototypes of both the J8M1 and the Kikka flew before the end of the war, none were used in combat. This agreement was not completely one-sided, with Germany showing considerable interest in the Mitsubishi Ki-46 '*Dinah*' long-range reconnaissance aircraft.
2. Csaba, B., *Az Asany Sas Nyomaban* (Budapest: Puedlo, 2008), p. 130

Chapter 12

1. Ethell, J. and Price, A.., *Target Berlin Mission 250: 6 March 1944* (London: Arms & Armour Press, 1989), p. 21f. Stehle was one of the most experienced Me 410 pilots. He had previously served with III./ZG 1 in North Africa.
2. Boiten, T. and Bowman, M., *Battles with the Luftwaffe* (London: HarperCollinsPublishers, 2001), p. 114f.
3. *Ibid*, p. 90
4. Due to a communications misunderstanding, the bomb aimer, navigator, and radio operator all baled out before Nuremberg was reached. Nevertheless, P/O Barton pressed on, dropping the bombs over the target (probably Schweinfurt instead of Nuremberg) before heading back to Britain. P/O Barton eventually made it back, only to die when his Halifax ran out of fuel. The remaining three crew members all suffered slight injuries. P/O was posthumously awarded the Victoria Cross.

Chapter 13

1. Research performed by Dr Gerhard Katschuba about his relative, Paul Katschuba, forwarded through an email dated 18 January 2018 by Neil Page to the author.
2. *Ibid.*
3. The wrecksite of Schmale and Steckler's Me 410 was excavated in 2005 by a team led by Jürgen Zapf of the Luftwaffe Museum at Berlin-Gatow. Among the items recovered were both of the engines, the BK 5 cannon, a propeller blade, and many smaller parts.
   No. 19 *FlyPast*, May 2015, p. 84ff.
4. Post-action report by Capt. Charles Pinson, 82nd FG.
5. *Ibid.*

Chapter 14

1. Kammhuber went on to organise a network of night fighter bases, searchlights, radar, and Flak installations in the Low Countries, protecting Germany from RAF night bombers. This became known as the 'Kammhuber Line'.
2. Parry, S. W., *Intruders over Britain* (Surbiton: Air Research Publications in association with Kristall Publications, 1987), p. 101f.
3. The badly bent propeller from one of the Ju 88s can be seen at the Yorkshire Aviation Museum, Elvington.

Chapter 15

1. The Luftwaffe losses can be broken down as 270 Ju 88s, 121 Do 217s, thirty-five Ju 188s, forty-six He 177s, twenty-seven Me 410s, and twenty-five Fw 190s. The RAF lost only one aircraft to enemy action, although seven more were lost to unknown causes. Another RAF aircraft was downed by 'friendly' fire. Civilian casualties amounted to 1,556 killed and 2,916 seriously injured.
2. *Flypast*, March 2017.
3. Quoted on aircrewremembrancesociety.com/luft1944/Mueller.html.
4. ghostbombers.com. The three Me 410s lost were W Nr 170009, 170031 and 170088.
5. Beale, N., *Air War in Italy 1944–45: The Axis Air Forces in Italy June 1944–May 1945* (Shrewbury: Airlife Publishing Ltd, 1996), p. 159.
6. *Ibid*, p. 163.
7. The threat against such ships was very real. During the final month of the war, one of the German ships transporting evacuees, the Wilhelm Gustloff, was sunk by a Soviet submarine, with another ship, the Cap Arcona, being sunk by RAF fighter bombers. As a result, thousands of lives were lost.
8. Thompson, W., *Northop P-61 Black Widow, In Wings of Fame*, Vol. 15 (Aerospace Publishing Ltd: London, 1999), p. 44.

Chapter 16

1. Forsyth, Robert, 'Defending the Reich. Part 1: Rockets, stovepipes and the "Crab device"', *The Aviation Historian*, Issue 17, p. 54.

Chapter 17

1. Brown, E., *Wings of the Weird and Wonderful*, Vol. 2 (Airlife Ltd, Shrewsbury, UK 1985), p. 67f.

Bibliography

Primary Source Materials

National Air & Space Museum, Washington D.C., USA
Materials on the ME 410
A19600329000DOC.1.pdf

Periodicals

The Aviation Historian, Issue 17
Flight International, 11 February 1943
Flugzeug Classic, Various issues
FlyPast, May 2015 and April 2017
Jet & Prop, June and August 2012
Katonaúság
Stenge Csaba, B., '*Vitéz Szoó Lajos és a Vaskereszt lovagkeresztje*' (Katonaúság, 1/2012); '*Egy igazi repülö sportember—Hennyey Imre*' (Katonaúság, 4/2012); '*Majoros Kornél repülö föhadnagy emlékezete*' (6/2012)
Scale Models, Various issues

Books

Aakra, K. and Brekken, A., *The Messerschmitt Me 410* (Profiles in Norway No. 7)
Beale, N., *Air War in Italy 1944–45: The Axis Air Forces in Italy June 1944–May 1945* (Shrewbury: Airlife Publishing Ltd, 1996)
Csaba, B., *Az Arany sas nyomában* (Budapest: Puedlo, 2008); Magyar repülötiszek kiképzése Németországban (Haditudósitó 5/2009)
Bernád, D. and Punka, G., *Hungarian Fighter Colours 1930–1945 Vol. 2* (Poland: STRATUS s.c. Sandomierz, 2014)
Boiten, T. and Bowman, M., *Battles with the Luftwaffe* (London: HarperCollins Publishers, 2001)
Bowman, M. W., *de Havilland Mosquito* (Marlborough: The Crowood Press Ltd, 1997)
Bridgman, L. (ed.), *Jane's All the World's Aircraft 1945–46* (London: Sampson Low, Marston & Company, Ltd, 1946)
Brown, E., *Wings of the Weird and Wonderful* 2(Shrewsbury: Airlife Publishing Ltd, 1985); *Testing for Combat* (Shrewsbury: Airlife Publishing Ltd, 1994)
Butler, P., *War Prizes* (Hinckley: Midland Counties Publications, 1998)

Ethell, J. and Price, A.., *Target Berlin Mission 250: 6 March 1944* (London: Arms & Armour Press, 1989)
Geust, C.-F., *Under the Red Star* (Shrewsbury: Airlife Publishing Ltd, 1993)
Herwig, D. and Rode, H., *Luftwaffe Secret Projects Ground Attack & Special Purpose Aircraft* (Hinckley: Midland Publishing, 2003)
Kay, A. L. and Smith, J. R., *German Aircraft of the Second World War* (London: Putnam Aeronautical Books, 2002)
Kosin, R.., *The German Fighter since 1915* (London: Conway Maritime Press Ltd, 1988)
Kováts, Lajos. A Dunai Repülögépgyár (Rt. története. Budapest, 1985)
Lang, G., *Arado Ar 240: The Luftwaffe Profile Series No. 8* (Atglen: Schiffer Publishing Ltd, 1996)
Parry, S. W., *Intruders over Britain* (Surbiton: Air Research Publications in association with Kristall Publications, 1987)
Pęczkowski, R., *Messerschmitt Me 410* (Poland: Stratus, Sandomierz 2006)
Petrick, P. and Stocker, W., *Messerschmitt Me 210/Me 410 Hornet* (Hinckley: Midland Publishing, 2007)
Punka, G., Messerschmitt Me 210/410 in Action (Carrolton: Squadron/Signal Publications, Inc., 1994)
Rosch, B., *Luftwaffe Support Units* (Hersham: Ian Allan Publishing, 2009)
Sárhidai, G., Punka, G., and Kozlik, V., *Hungarian Eagles: A Magyar Királyi Honvéd Légierö 1920–1945* (Aldershot: Hikoki Publications, 1996)
Schmoll, P., *Nest of Eagles* (Herhsam: Ian Allan Publishing, 2004)
Shores, C. and Massimello, G., *A History of the Mediterranean Air War 1940–1945 Volume Two: North African Desert February 1942–March 1943* (London: Grub Street, 2012); *A History of the Mediterranean Air War 1940–1945 Volume Three: Tunisia and the End in Africa November 1942–May 1943* (London: Grub Street, 2016)
Smith, J. R., *The Messerschmitt Me 210/410 Series: Aircraft Profile No. 161* (Profile Publications, 1967); *Messerschmitt: An Aircraft Album* (Shepperton: Ian Allan, 1971)
Stenge Csaba, B., *In memoriam Péterdi Adolf* (Magyar Repüléstörtéti Evkönyv, 2012); *Elfejtett hösök* (Budapest, Zrínyi, 2016)
Thompson, W., *P-61 Black Widow Nightfighters of World War 2* (Madrid: Delprado Publishers/ Ediciones del Prado, 2000)
Williamson, G., *Luftwaffe Handbook 1935–1945* (Stroud: Sutton Publishing Limited, 2006)

Internet

aircrewremembrancesociety.co.uk
flensted.eu.com
ww2.dk
ghostbombers.com
luftwaffe.cz
luftwaffe.no
leteckabadatelna.cz

E-books

Verliesregister 1939–1945 *Alle militaire vliegtuigverliezen in Nederland tijdens de Tweede Wereldoorlog*. Studiegroep Luchtoorlog 1939–1945, 2008.

Index